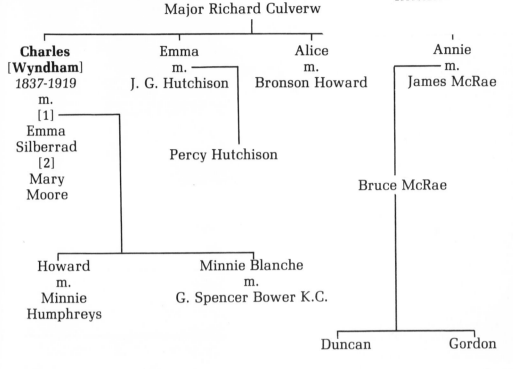

Major Richard Culverw

**Charles**      Emma         Alice         Annie
**[Wyndham]**     m.         m.         m.
*1837-1919*  J. G. Hutchison  Bronson Howard  James McRae
m.
[1]
Emma
Silberrad         Percy Hutchison
[2]
Mary
Moore               Bruce McRae

Howard       Minnie Blanche
m.           m.
Minnie   G. Spencer Bower K.C.
Humphreys

Duncan      Gordon

# ALL ON STAGE

## CHARLES WYNDHAM AND THE ALBERYS

### WENDY TREWIN

HARRAP  LONDON

To J.C.T. and his library

*First published in Great Britain* 1980
by GEORGE G. HARRAP & CO. LTD
182 High Holborn, London WC1V 7AX

© *Wendy Trewin* 1980

ISBN 0 245 53444 X

*Designed by Michael R. Carter*

Filmset by Woolaston Parker Ltd, Leicester
Printed and bound in Great Britain by
Redwood Burn Ltd, Trowbridge and Esher

# Contents

LIST OF ILLUSTRATIONS      vii
AUTHOR'S NOTE      ix
FIRST PIECE      1

1   Young Wyndham 1837–1865      6
2   Young Albery 1838–1870      13
3   'Caperbilities' 1865–1871      21
4   A Glass of Hot Rum 1870–1871      29
5   'Just Sitting About In Chairs' 1871–1872      37
6   'A Jolly Lot of Talent' 1872–1873      49
7   'From the French' 1874–1877      59
8   'Revelling 'neath the Moon' 1877–1879      71
9   'Decidedly the Fashion' 1879–1882      81
10   'Comedy! Bah!' 1882–1886      91
11   'Listen again' 1886–1889      104
12   The Only Dramatist 1889–1892      117
13   The Long Sermon 1893–1897      129
14   Wyndham of Wyndham's 1898–1901      142
15   'The Comedy Widow' 1901–1904      156
16   Red Roses for Captain Drew 1904–1908      168
17   Half a Loaf for the Public 1908–1919      181
18   'A Genius Like Wyndham' 1837–1919      193
19   'Arrangin' the Chairs' 1919–1938      199
20   The Fourth Theatre 1939–1980      215

*NOTE: WYNDHAM'S ONLY FILM*                    223
*WYNDHAM'S CRYSTAL PALACE MATINÉES*            224

*BIBLIOGRAPHY*                                 225
*INDEX*                                        231

# Illustrations

Wyndham in Federal uniform                                        22
*The Dearer than Life* Company                                    22
*Two Roses*: Irving as Digby Grant                                23
The 'Two Roses' themselves                                        23
A Criterion Playbill                                              54
Programme of *Truth!* at the Criterion                            54
Mary Moore in *The Liars*                                         55
Wyndham in *Still Waters Run Deep*                                134
Wyndham's Theatre                                                 134/135
The New Theatre, later the Albery                                 134/135
Scene from *Fourteen Days*                                        135
Mary Moore in Russia                                              150
*David Garrick* programme                                         151
Wyndham and Mary Moore in *David Garrick*                         151
Wyndham at a dinner party                                         166
All-star cast on the roof of the Albery                           166
Wyndham and Mary Moore in *She Stoops to Conquer*                 166/167
Wyndham and Mary Moore in old age                                 166/167
James Albery                                                      167
Bronson Albery                                                    167
Donald and Ian Albery                                             167
Set of *Oliver!*                                                  182
Lord Chamberlain's licence                                        183

Family tree: The Wyndhams and the Alberys                         *endpapers*

# Author's Note

First, I should like to thank members of the Albery family who have helped me to write this book: Lady (Una) Albery; Sir Donald and Lady (Nobuko) Albery; Mr Ian B. Albery; Miss Jessica Albery; and the late Mr Peter Albery. Ian Albery allowed me the freedom of the family papers; Miss Shirley Duff-Gray and other members of the staff of Wyndham Theatres Ltd, were most kind while I was looking into these. Others who helped generously with their time were Sir John Gielgud, Dame Peggy Ashcroft, Miss Gwen Ffrangcon-Davies, Mr Raymond Massey, Mr Ben Travers, Miss Sylvia Read and Mr William Fry (of Theatre Roundabout), Miss Jane Hackworth-Young, Miss Betty Hardy; and Miss Caryl Brahms and Mr Laurence Cotterell, who steered me towards the enterprise. I am grateful also to Miss Elaine Burrows of the British Film Institute, who allowed Ian Albery and myself to see the Wyndham *Garrick* film; Miss Sheila Huftel, who researched into Oscar Wilde's letters; Mrs Susan Trewin, who gave me a photograph; Miss Ellen Goodman, of the Royal Shakespeare Company, who lent me the notes of her work on the Criterion Theatre; Mr Stephen Bradshaw, who helped with photocopying; Professor Arthur Colby Sprague; Mrs Enid Foster, librarian of the British Theatre Association; my sons, Ion and Mark Trewin; and, most of all, my husband with his immeasurable patience and expertise.

I am deeply grateful to Mr Roy Minton, of Messrs Harrap, for his invariably wise observation in handling my typescript.

For permission to reproduce the photograph of Bronson Albery I am indebted to the estate of the late Howard Coster and the National Portrait Gallery; to Rex Coleman for that of Donald and Ian Albery; to Paul Weston for that of the *Oliver!* set. The Lord Chamberlain's licence is reproduced by permission of his Office.

In order not to clog the narrative, I have avoided a massive collection of notes (and, inevitably, much needless repetition). My sources are evident from the very full bibliography. Principally, I have relied on family papers, the works by Mary Moore and Wyndham Albery, conversations with members of the family, and relevant play-texts.

Naturally, I have had to select from plays at the Albery theatres during the last sixty years; such long-runners as *The Love of Four Colonels, A Severed Head, The Prime of Miss Jean Brodie* and *Once a Catholic* are safe in the stage records of their time.


*Hampstead, 1980.*                                                    W.T.

# First Piece

They stand back to back: Wyndham's Theatre looks out on Charing Cross Road ('buses pass the door'); the equally dignified Albery Theatre, once the New, is in St Martin's Lane. Yet how many of the thousands who know these theatres in today's West End of London ever give a thought to Wyndham or Albery? How many wonder who these men were? How many realize that their grandparents might have seen Wyndham on the stage? A few may have great-grandparents who saw plays by James, first of the theatrical Alberys. Among American visitors one or two may have ancestors who fought in the Civil War, and whose wounds Wyndham dressed in the haze of those forgotten years as an Army surgeon before he became an actor.

Just as the theatres named after them are close neighbours, so the men themselves came together through the plays written by James Albery and the parts played by Charles Wyndham. They were near-contemporaries: Albery was born on 4 May 1838; Wyndham on 23 March 1837. Neither had any theatrical ancestry; both, after trying other professions, were drawn easily into the theatrical net. Oddly, their closest tie was neither a play nor a part but a woman. She was Mary Moore, who married Albery; who was the mother of his three sons; and who became the leading lady and partner—and ultimately the wife—of Wyndham. Without her unwavering business sense, Wyndham's and the New might never have been built; without her the family history would have been far poorer and shorter.

At the turn of the century, and the building of these two theatres, Albery was already dead; Charles Wyndham and Mary Moore had a long splendour of sucessful Criterion management behind them. When the project was suggested the Marquess of Salisbury—who was ground landlord—said that he would have no theatre on his estate unless Charles Wyndham, the only actor he admired, built it. Later, in whichever of their three theatres they appeared, Wyndham and Moore continued to prosper until Sir Charles (he was knighted in 1902) began to lose his memory. After his death Mary Moore carried on the family business with the help of her son, Bronson Albery. He would be responsible for much that counted most on the stage of the 1920s and 1930s; for his work with the Cassons, especially on Shaw's *Saint Joan*; for the West End burgeoning of the young John Gielgud; for his advice to the Old Vic and—during the 1940s—the new Arts Council of Great Britain. A shrewd knight of the theatre, he knew, as Sybil Thorndike for one discovered, just how much an audience could take, and would demand. To the end of a long life, helped latterly by his son Donald, he ran the theatres as if they were parts of a commercial firm—which indeed they were—but also with his own instinctive taste. In spite of a few mistakes and a few failures, inevitable in this chanciest of speculations, he knew at once what would be right in a play, its treatment, and its casting. Quiet, shy, energetic, he put his own seal on everything (whether he originated it or not) that was done at the Criterion, at Wyndham's, and at the New.

Donald Albery, who succeeded his father in 1962 as the group's managing director, had added two years earlier a fourth theatre, the Piccadilly, which he bought against determined competition. He transplanted Joan Littlewood's idiosyncratic Theatre Workshop productions from Stratford-atte-Bowe; he brought the contentious *Waiting for Godot* to London after two years (and refusals by every leading actor); he presented Graham Greene's early play *The Living Room*; and when three other managements had turned it down, he launched *Oliver!*, the strongest commercial success the Alberys have had, and also the first post-war musical without overt American influence. Retiring in 1977, he received the family's third knighthood. His son Ian followed him then as head of a firm which had begun simply because two young men, born within a year of Queen Victoria's accession, could not resist the theatre. Charles Wyndham might have practised medicine to the end of his life; James Albery could have become an architect. But they did not, and that is why their names today glow still over the crowded pavements of St Martin's Lane and Charing Cross Road.

# II

What sort of theatre drew them? In the late 1850s and early 1860s both of them acted, obscurely, as amateurs. While studying medicine in London, at King's College, Charles Wyndham appeared at the tiny Cabinet, King's Cross, where aspirants would pay for their parts. Wyndham wanted to be a tragedian. Years later, he would advise all hopeful comedians to train in tragedy. His parents, against him in either comedy or tragedy, insisted instead that he should get his medical diplomas; and in trying to cure the young man of theatrical ambition his father, a Mr Culverwell, accompanied him to innumerable performances (on the argument that, surfeiting, the appetite might sicken and so die). Similarly, with the idea of brushing any false 'romance' from the theatre, he invited actors to the house to meet his stage-struck Charles. We can merely guess which actors they met, which plays they saw. It is not easy at this distance to trace influences on the man who became the sovereign light comedian of his generation.

We can see father and son walking to the theatre beneath the spluttering gas lamps, and dodging the horse-drawn wheels. This would be either from their home at 3 Great Marlborough Street, or from the hotel Mr Culverwell then owned in Arundel Street, off the Strand. (Walking to and from the theatre was a habit Charles Wyndham kept all his life.) As they took their seats they would find the air stuffy with unventilated gas and a mingled tang of oranges and ginger-beer from the pit. They would see the plays, too, as Ellen Terry put it, in 'the thick softness of gaslight with the lovely specks and motes in it, so like *natural* light'. The plays themselves would be vastly different from those of the 1870s and 1880s when Wyndham began to make his mark. The kind of comedies in which Charles would excel had barely existed in the days before T.W. (Tom) Robertson and, to a lesser degree, Albery (though he did revive a few of the plays he must have known in his youth). Burlesques of every type of drama flourished; their titles and sub-titles so long that in Squire Bancroft's words they crowded several inches of playbill, 'little better than a greasy mass of printers' ink on paper nearly two feet long'. There were many classical revivals: probably the Culverwells saw Samuel Phelps, Islington's rock of ages, in all his major Shakespearian parts, and in some others as well—Parolles, say, or Christopher Sly. They could have met the ferociously and opulently 'antiquarian' Shakespeare of Mr and Mrs Charles Kean at the Princess's in Oxford Street; they would have been as excited as the young Shaw was by the stage fights of Barry Sullivan as Hamlet and Macbeth. Charles might have fallen in love (even Macready did) with beautiful Helen Faucit on one of her now rare appearances. Certainly he could have pitied Ben Webster as the starving poet in *Masks and Faces* at the Haymarket, or laughed at J. B. Buckstone in the same theatre, or at 'comic bustling and natural' Charles Mathews as Mr Affable Hawk, or Sheridan's Mr Puff, or as Dazzle in *London Assurance*, a part not obviously golden, that one day Wyndham himself would burnish.

Among older actresses he might have watched (or helped to entertain) Mrs Stirling, who had played Shakespearian heroines with Macready, or Isabel Glyn, the day's portentous tragedy queen. If the Culverwells had crossed the Thames they could have found Edith Heraud equally regal in an obscure Sarah Siddons part at the Surrey. Among players of the future were J. L. Toole, the scholarly Hermann Vezin, Marie Wilton (later to be Lady Bancroft), and possibly Kate Terry, talented enough but—because she retired on her marriage—with no future as an actress. (At her farewell in Manchester Charles Wyndham played the first and almost the last of his Shakespearian parts: Mercutio, Claudio, Laertes.) By 1860 the doctor was also a married man. He could not lightly discard a profession in which he seemed already to have failed; but he did the next and most convenient thing—he went as an amateur to the Royalty Theatre in Dean Street, Soho, and there met Kate's younger sister, Ellen. Towards the end of the year—at this point the theatre had changed its name to the Soho—he acted the seducer in Tom Taylor's *Still Waters Run Deep*, put on for the Saturday Half Holiday Movement, and received a cool notice to the effect that his was a creditable amateur performance, 'but marred by a sameness of manner and voice'. (Throughout his life people argued about his voice.) Badly noticed or not, he kept on. Young Dr Culverwell would simply disappear. His father's cure had not worked.

# III

James Albery, a South Londoner, had gone into an architect's office where his thoughts drifted from drawing-board to exercise-book. His son Wyndham, editing the Albery plays in 1939, speculated on the influence of the florid Surrey Theatre in Blackfriars Road. Living in neighbouring Southwark, James could have found, during the management of William Creswick and Richard Shepherd, most things between classical tragedy and roaring melodrama: Creswick in Shakespeare, Lytton's *Richelieu*, with 'the curse of Rome', or the *Virginius* ('Roman tunics, but a modern English heart') of Sheridan Knowles; Miss Marriott on one of the ninety nights when she broke every heart in *The Flower Girl; or The Convict Marquis*; and the drolleries of Widdicomb, during eleven years the Surrey's beloved low comedian. For a young man eager to write plays the Surrey was high heaven when (said the dramatist Westland Marston) Creswick became Shakespeare's apostle 'to transpontine London . . . as Phelps was to north London'. Albery would have learned something about the technique of adaptation; work, not glibly undertaken, in which he became conspicuous (William Archer felt as warmly about Albery's manipulative skill as about his original plays). At this time Creswick acted at the Surrey in a sequence of dramatized novels: *David Copperfield*, for one, *Adam Bede*, and Wilkie Collins's *The Woman in White* of which a contemporary critic wrote

> We have seen many adaptations but this is the worst. Had it not been for the blue fire, shootings, etc., the piece would have been a decided failure.

We would suggest to the management to call this drama a farce, and the audience will laugh at it and enjoy it accordingly. Nothing in the whole piece is more comic than to see the fine acting of Mr Creswick wasted on such an unseemly part. The irresistibly funny way in which Mr Holloway did a tragic scene also deserves mention.

An aspiring dramatist might at least have learned what to avoid.

In 1860 Albery, himself aspiring, 'kept the audience in one continued state of hilarity' during his own sketch, *A Victim of Intemperance*—it was an alarmingly prophetic title—at the Southwark Literary Institution; a public entertainment by the local elocution class. (When the youthfully arrogant Albery appeared in other people's plays and sketches he was apt to rewrite his parts.) He belonged also to the Ingoldsby Club, which in 1864 gave at the Walworth Literary Institute a brief farce called *Alexander the Great*, by Albery and the insignificant J. J. Dilley. Here (with no need for rewriting) he chose to act the landlady. The farce did not vanish at Walworth; we shall hear more of it presently, under another name.

We perceive that, though our two men of the theatre began their careers simultaneously, Wyndham's at first was the more discouraging; nowadays he would be called a late starter. His first two attempts to become a professional actor ended in rapid dismissal; but when he reached the top he did stay there. Albery never repeated his early successes; his last years were blurred by failure and ill-health. Whatever their relative graphs, the two men have remained together in the stage history of London, and today their names stand equally high above the turmoil of the West End.

# CHAPTER ONE
# Young Wyndham
# 1837–1865

Charles Wyndham's real name was Culverwell; the family seems to have derived from Somerset, but at the time of Charles's birth its home was in Liverpool. The Culverwells moved south when Charles was still a boy, and whenever he spoke of the past he ignored his birthplace. For our record, it was 19 Tithebarn Street, then made up chiefly of shops and offices. As his father at that point in a protean career was a watchmaker, the family is likely to have lived over the shop; and in this, and in this only, Charles's early background resembled James Albery's. On 18 July 1837, as the second son—the elder having died in infancy—he was baptised at St Peter's, Church Street, Liverpool, a building demolished in 1922. He had three sisters, Annie, Emma and Alice, all of whom through marriage were to have theatrical connections. Later the Culverwells moved to 45 Tithebarn Street, where Charles's father was now in business as a victualler.

There has been some confusion about Mr Culverwell, who is often described as a doctor: a confusion which began partly because his brother, Robert James Culverwell, was an eminent physician and author of many books; medicine was in the family. Culverwell senior may have been frustrated because he had no professional qualification; certainly he resolved that his son must be a doctor. From his curious first name, Major, people might have assigned him to the Army; he must have done practically everything else. Major Richard Culverwell was a London pioneer of Turkish baths. He was a hotelier. He was (more or less) tinker, tailor, watchmaker, victualler. Whatever he did he prospered, for he was able to send his son to schools in England and abroad. The first of these, when Charles was ten, was at Sandgate, near Folkestone in Kent; and Mary Moore recalls that he showed her the hotel in which his parents

6

stayed when they visited him. After this he went to a school in Germany, and there he made his public début—not as an actor, but as a preacher. He and another boy, an ardent Methodist, started their own church, with the laudable idea of reforming their fellow-students. It went more or less calmly until a clergyman's son (presuming on heredity) claimed that the pulpit was his. Charles resisted the suggestion; the boy told him to go to hell:

> The very place that I had been trying to save him from! The pillars of my church shook with agony at the exclamation. They tottered till at last my poor church died a calm and peaceful death, leaving no trace behind.

This was something Charles loved to repeat, and to dramatize (as he did during a speech in 1890 to the Twentieth Century Club in Chicago).

Paris next, though it is doubtful whether his parents sent him there as a relief from too religious an atmosphere. More likely they wanted him to learn French as well as German. (One day German would serve him during an astonishing theatrical adventure.) Anyway, he saw something of the Parisian theatre, the Comédie Française in particular; and he would recall a schoolboy scrape—getting locked out, wandering about the city until six o'clock next morning, chancing his only sou on 'gingerbread roulette', and winning the largest piece, which sustained him until he got into the house. As he was climbing the stairs he met the headmaster, who scolded him for getting up too early. Charles had a precocious talent for slipping out of trouble.

Later, as a student at the University of St Andrew's, he was allowed to act in a private theatre at Sir Hugh Playfair's house. Founder of St Andrew's as a fashionable resort, Sir Hugh was a golfer and amateur actor (Arthur and Nigel Playfair were related to him). We do not know the parts Charles Culverwell played, but obviously at home he would have talked about the excitements of acting. His father, set on a medical career for the boy, responded in character. A child whose hand was passed through a candle-flame would learn to fear the fire. Very well, then. Promptly Mr Culverwell installed a private theatre in his own house at 3 Great Marlborough Street in the West End of London. This was a time when Culverwell senior was in his most versatile mood: his enterprises during the 1850s and 1860s included baths at 19 St Martin's-le-Grand, and on the corner of Argyll and Regent Streets, the site of yet another private theatre. He advertised these baths as 'medical'; he was also involved with Dr Kahn's curious anatomical museums, another sign of a besetting interest. Dr Kahn was no more a doctor than Culverwell; the prefix was simply a *nom-de-guerre*, and his museums at 14 Coventry Street, 17 Harley Street, and 3 Tichborne Street were no more than popular side-shows. Mr Culverwell also owned the Clarendon Hotel at 17–18 Arundel Street, off the eastern end of the Strand. Several other hotels existed round here—one in Norfolk Street belonged to Major's brother, Samuel Henry—and one (a competitor, the Arundel) advertised itself as 'patronised largely by professional men, officers of both Services, and Americans and their families, for whom is especially provided a fine "WATER COOLER"'.

Though worried by Charles's inexplicable desire to be an actor, his father did have friends in the theatre (surprising if he had not). Ellen Terry said quite firmly in her memoirs that he backed a season of two short plays in which she and her sister Kate as children appeared at the Colosseum, Regent's Park. Even so, as Charles explained to a Chicago audience forty years on:

> For a son to tell his father that he wanted to become an actor was next door to saying he wanted to become a burglar. My father reasoned with me, until at last he suggested a compromise. 'Get your diplomas; get a means of livelihood at your fingers' ends, and then you may do whatever you like.'

We can be sure that Charles, studying at King's College, found distractions. Not only was he 'forced'—his own word—into a constant round of theatregoing with his father, he was also acting when he could in the Cabinet at King's Cross. Already in 1860 it was an 'old-established' amateur house where actors paid for their pleasure (Henry Kemble, grandson of Charles Kemble, once bought the First Gravedigger for 6s. 6d.). Dickens, in 'Amateur Theatres' (Sketches by Boz), mocked such theatres as the Cabinet and their carefully graded price-lists: two pounds for the Duke of Gloucester, a pound for Richmond, twelve shillings for Catesby, and so on: 'Such are the sums extracted from the shop till, or overcharged in the office expenditure, by the donkeys who are prevailed upon to pay for permission to exhibit their lamentable ignorance and boobyism on the stage of a private theatre.'

For Dickens, though he loved acting, these proceedings were as absurd as hilarious: 'The actors who are to be discovered are hastily arranged, and the actors who are not to be discovered place themselves in their anxiety to peep at the house, just where the audience can see them . . . the bell rings—the tragedy(!) opens—and our description closes.' We know that Charles Culverwell, in his amateur days, wanted to play tragedy. Whether he did (and what the price was), no one can say. Time has shredded the casting; we do know that it was at the Cabinet that he met William Blakeley, a fellow of infinite jest, who would act with him one day at the Criterion, as Hardcastle to his Young Marlow, and may have remembered their Cabinet meetings. Theoretically, private jokes on the stage are intolerable—for one actor to make another laugh is known as 'corpsing'—but they have to happen sometimes to relieve the tedium of a long run. It would have been strange if on those Criterion nights

Wyndham and Blakeley had failed to recall that they had once spent sums they could ill afford, to act together in the highest seriousness. To escape from his London diversions, Charles Culverwell went across to Dublin, where he studied at the Peter Street Anatomical School and met another and more romantic diversion: he fell in love with a widow of nineteen. 'Imagine the treble attraction of youth, beauty, and a widow's cap!' Of course, he responded as any stage-struck youth would respond to her 'halo of romance'—she had been widowed on the afternoon of her wedding-day. For the first time and the last he hurtled into poetry (unquotable); then romance withered. As he had work to do and examinations to pass, he forgot the widow, and she married her brother-in-law.

## II

At length, in 1860, having gained his diplomas, Charles got married himself and set up as a general practitioner. His wife was Emma Silberrad (a grand-daughter of Baron Silberrad of Hesse-Darmstadt), whom he had known and loved for some time before he met the widow. Small and fair, she had little knowledge of the theatre. She had some money—not much, but more than he had. His practice, though, was still-born: 'Not a patient darkened my door. In vain I wore stiff white neckties; in vain I prayed for a bald head and a slight rotundity of body—things which I now look forward to with dread every morning.' (When he said this he was fifty-three, and looked remarkably young. His hair remained crisp to the end of his life.)

Though no patients consulted him, he was not idle. On 30 November 1860 he acted in a charity performance of *Still Waters Run Deep* at the Royalty Theatre, renamed the Soho—the little house in Dean Street had several names during the 1850s and 1860s. Charles, we gather, was unsuitably cast as Captain Hawksley, who attempts to seduce Mrs Mildmay, and is prevented by her aunt, once his lover. Like much else in the mid-century, the play had been adapted (by the prolific Tom Taylor) from the French, and altered to suit Victorian prudery. In the original, Captain Hawksley's lover was Mrs Mildmay's mother—not her aunt—which apparently made all the difference. For Charles Wyndham (he had resolved now to move from Culverwell for stage purposes) a rake and villain would be quite untypical. He would act this one again, and, more happily, Mr Mildmay, the complaisant husband in whom still waters ran deep. (He appears to have chosen his new name at random—whether with regard to other theatrical Wyndhams or, for that matter, to Charles Wyndham, second Earl of Egremont, 1710–1763, it is now impossible to say.)

It was during February 1862 that he appeared as a professional actor at last, in an unknown dramatist's play called, desperately, *Christopher of*

*Carnation Cottage* and done at the Royalty, which by now had reverted to its old name. Wyndham appeared as Christopher; neither play nor part would be lasting. This was during the régime of the exotically named Madame Albina de Rhona, a little dancer from Paris who fascinated thirteen-year-old Ellen Terry (she had never met a Frenchwoman before). In her first part at the Royalty Ellen had to scream when a snake coiled itself round her neck. After tears at rehearsal, she got both the scream and the snake right and the audience applauded this more than anything else. The piece, *Attar Gull*, from a story by Eugène Sue, had soon to be replaced; indeed, runs were disastrously short, and Ellen learnt five new parts between 21 November and Christmas. Wyndham, at the Royalty for six months, appeared himself in six other plays, all of them ephemeral except *The Lady of Lyons*, in which he was Beauséant who says to Claude Melnotte: 'Thou wilt be sent to the common gaol as a swindler.' While they were both relatively unknown in the theatre he and Ellen would meet again.

Another stranger in Madame de Rhona's company was W. H. Kendal—later Madge Kendal's husband—who intended to be an artist like his father. The manager, noticing his talent, gave him the run of the house; he stayed long enough to decide on a new career, played several parts, and acted for the first time with Ellen Terry in the comedietta called *A Nice Quiet Day*. Another promising young man, David James, would later make his name in burlesque and act with Wyndham at the Criterion. Madame may have been misguided in her choice of plays, but usually she could find something to celebrate with supper parties in the green-room. Unable one evening to resist looking through the keyhole, Ellen saw an admirer drinking champagne out of Madame's slipper (an insanitary habit); her mother, who had been searching for her, soundly boxed her ears. Before long she would have to leave for wider experience in the stock company at Bristol, and presently too Madame's creditors were asked to get in touch with a firm of solicitors. (Mineral water now instead of champagne.)

Since he had qualified, Culverwell/Wyndham had learnt a lot about failure. First, his practice had failed. Then it was the theatre, where one unmemorable play pressed upon another. His banking account 'like the church of my earlier days', he said, 'died a calm and peaceful death, leaving no trace behind.' It was essential to make money—so why not use his professional skills? When his father suggested he might go to America he agreed. The Civil War had begun, but in war there might be opportunities. He went.

# III

Soon after the abolitionist Abraham Lincoln had become President in 1861 eleven Southern states seceded from the Union, and war broke out along the whole of the new frontier from Virginia to Missouri. In Britain, Lancashire cotton-mills began to close as raw material from the Southern plantations failed to arrive; funds were raised to help the starving mill-hands; angrily, people took sides. Charles was young enough to welcome adventure, and human enough to want success. So, in 1862, having left some money behind for his wife, he arrived in New York with 45 dollars (then about nine pounds). Many times he would talk of his arrival and his pursuit of an Army appointment, a marvellous after-dinner story for any actor, and especially a comedian: more dramatization, of course. Though he had determined to enter the Federal Army as a surgeon, there would first be a theatrical experience. From a New York gallery—he must not make too deep a hole in his 45 dollars—he saw the buoyantly authoritative Lester Wallack as Charles Surface in *The School for Scandal*. He was excitedly impressed; at the same theatre, Wallack's, Charles himself would one day take up this part in which he was said to be unexampled.

Going now for a medical examination, he was accepted as a sergeant—hardly what he had planned. There might, he thought, be more chance of a medical post if he went to Washington, so he left (now with 35 dollars) and vainly buttonholed a variety of generals. For two days he sat in the public room of Willard's Hotel with an illustrated book on surgery well displayed on his knee. (Twenty-five dollars left.) The irony was that, though he had been offered a letter of introduction to General Nathaniel Banks, he had refused to wait for it to come from Paris, believing that in the land of opportunity it would be needless. At last an elderly man, who was also in the room, supplied him with a letter to Banks. He was P. T. Barnum; Charles could not escape from show-business. Banks in turn gave him a letter to the surgeon-general Hammond; and he was in. Through life he would be reticent about his experiences, but Mary Moore concluded that 'from the things I heard him say . . . he had a very rough time.' Once, in 1899, during the Boer War—in the course of which he raised £1,700 for the Soldiers' and Sailors' Fund—he referred modestly to 'some stray records of a period when not with bayonet and rifle, but with bandages, probes and chloroform, I served with the Federal forces during the longest and most bitter conflict of modern days.'

Wyndham was in the 19th New York Infantry during the second Bull Run slaughter when the Federals lost 14,000 men, and the smaller Confederate Army, under Robert E. Lee, 9,000. He was attached to the force organized for the invasion of Texas,

> that land of milk and honey and horse, all most desirable luxuries to soldiers, never too generously sustained, and who ultimately in this case were reduced to stone-like biscuits. They were stamped "B.C.", and so hard that the soldiers irreverently declared that they were thus marked because they must have been baked before the days of Pontius Pilate.

He had been told that when entering a captured city it was the thing to wear a new uniform. He had one, but never wore it. During the campaign they were ordered to retreat and to leave their goods behind them. As they retreated, with the enemy's guns pursuing them, the ambulance men shouted, 'Make way! Make way!' The road was narrow and rutty, and the wounded were tossed about on springless vehicles. During that uncomfortable night's journey Wyndham began to wonder if the prisoners and deserters whom they had so gladly captured during their advance had been let loose on them purposely to lead them into that fool's paradise.

In after-years he always preferred to describe his winter escapes from the theatre of war to the theatre of entertainment. He had circulated among American managers a few press notices from his amateur days—resourcefully, he wrote some himself—and one manager took him on for a season in Washington. This man soon decided that Wyndham would never make an actor, and told him so, whereupon he took the hint, resigned and returned to the Army. Ordered to New Orleans, he served with Banks, who captured Port Hudson on the Mississippi, and led the Red River campaign (which General Sherman called 'one damned blunder from beginning to end' and which ended Banks's career). That winter Wyndham got away again—to New York now, and an engagement with Mrs John Wood at the Olympic Theatre. The play was *Brother and Sister*, in a double bill with *Married Daughters*. In his New York début he had to announce that he was 'drunk with enthusiasm'. When he got to 'drunk' the words vanished. 'Ma' Wood, an English comedienne who had been acting in America for ten years, would soon return to London and in the course of things appear (at £100 a week) in Wyndham's Criterion. Henry James said of her: 'She moves the springs of laughter with a powerful hand.' For the moment, with her powerful hand, she removed an incompetent actor from her cast. What Charles's father, who came to New York during his stay, thought of all this is luckily unrecorded. A photograph taken during his visit shows him surrounded by three of his children: Charles, bearded and in Army uniform; and two daughters in billowing crinolines.

Soon after that humiliating affair at Mrs Wood's Olympic, Charles sailed for England, resolved to succeed in the theatre. As he would say on the stage on innumerable occasions as Jack Rover, 'I'll try a *London* audience!' Dr Charles Culverwell was not heard of again; but everyone after 14 April 1865 had heard of a former fellow-actor of his in the Washington company, John Wilkes Booth. That day Booth had shot and killed Abraham Lincoln in a box at Ford's Opera House, Washington, during a performance of *Our American Cousin*.

CHAPTER TWO
# Young Albery
# 1838–1870

Southwark was London's earliest theatreland, in Shakespeare's world the home of the Rose, the Swan and the Globe. If Swan Street, just off Trinity Square, was named after the second of the Bankside theatres, it was a birthplace fit for a dramatist—for James Albery. Born on 4 May 1838, he was the eldest of six children of a ropemaker with a shop and warehouse in the clamour of Blackfriars Road. The young Alberys, four girls and two boys, James and Walter, grew up near the murky river, among the alleys, innyards and early Victorian slums of the Dickensian Southwark of *Little Dorrit* (the Marshalsea Prison was there until 1842), and near the medieval church of St Saviour, not yet a cathedral. Of all the buildings round about, James must have been happiest in the Surrey Theatre (once the Royal Circus), temple of transpontine melodrama glorified by an affectionate rhymer:

> I gape in Covent Garden's walls,
>   I doze in Drury Lane;
> I strive in the Lyceum stalls
>   To keep awake in vain.
> There's naught in the dramatic way
>   That I can quite abide
> Except the pieces that they play
>   Upon the Surrey side.

Albery's first playgoing coincided with the Richard Shepherd-William Creswick partnership, so he could admire one man's generous comedy and the bold Shakespearian acting of the other, besides many visiting players who were often among the most efficient of their time, and who never disdained the Surrey and its noisy audiences.

As a youth James Albery entered an architect's office in Fenchurch Street over the river. He remained in it without noticeable enthusiasm until his father's death in 1859 compelled him to leave before he was twenty-one, and take over the family business. Described on his letter-heads as a twine-spinner, he lived above the shop with his mother and one unmarried sister. His brother became a commercial traveller (in rope or otherwise). His own passion for playwriting began to show itself very soon, certainly in his early twenties. Local literary institutes liked a little home-grown drama. When he gave *A Victim of Intemperance* at Southwark during 1860 *The Players* journal encouraged it as 'one of the best little humorous sketches that we have heard for a long time; it was delivered to perfection'.

At home, when the vagaries of twine-spinning allowed, he went on writing. It so happened that his first full-length comedy, completed in 1862, did not reach the stage for another eight years, and then in a new version and with two different titles, a time-lag that has confused historians. Because his plays echoed Tom Robertson's subtlety and naturalism, and because they were produced later than *Caste* and the others, Albery was labelled as Robertson's 'successor' or 'disciple'. This, we can see, was never strictly true. Indeed, when Albery began, he could have no idea that some other dramatist was writing plays comparable with his own. Probably he went later to the old Prince of Wales's in Tottenham Street to see the Bancrofts and John Hare in Robertson comedies, and this may have influenced him. At first there could have been no such influence.

# II

Most of his life he lived in that bizarre, semi-Bohemian half-world of the professional mid-Victorian dramatist; a man about the Strand and its grouped theatres, for ever writing, adapting, revising, readapting, retitling, never without a script, tragical, comical, historical, or all three; a chameleon at the call of every manager, player, audience. It was a life just outside the fashionable pale. Not very far back, the proud and sensitive actor Macready would rage at snobbish condescension, resent the insolence of men who shook hands by offering a single finger. It would be some time yet before Queen Victoria, no stranger to it, officially acknowledged the theatre with a knighthood for Henry Irving. Life, as Albery and unluckier men knew it, was a constant twilit or gas-lit battle, a sequence of transient play-titles, private (or sometimes public) quarrels, angry letters, temperamental tantrums, nights of sudden recognition— Albery had his at *Two Roses*—and nights of failure when a dramatist

14

could say simply, with Sam Weller, 'It's over and can't be helped, and that's one consolation, as they always say in Turkey ven they cuts the wrong man's head off.' Every dramatist had to have nine lives and unlimited resource. There must have been periods when James Albery, man of humour and feeling that he was, wondered why he had left the relative security of a Southwark twine-spinner's for this confusion of make-believe in a small, insulated and chaotic world.

On finishing a five-act comedy, *The Starchbacks*, he first sent it from the twine-spinner's to Mrs Charles Young, an actress who would marry Hermann Vezin, for some years among Albery's most valuable theatrical friends. He must often have gone down the road to see Vezin as Hamlet or Othello, Shylock or (fashionable then) King John at the Surrey. Possibly he even went round after a performance: dressing-rooms would have been romantic. Jane Young had been praised for her sensitive way with the heroines when she played Shakespeare with Samuel Phelps at Sadler's Wells in north London. She had appeared too at the Haymarket, which was why she passed on the young man's script to W. H. Chippendale, a leading actor there. Chippendale's headlong letter to her (2 June 1862) must have encouraged Albery:

> I can assure you its perusal gave me much pleasure—it is seldom so many good things are given in one piece. I need not tell you it requires condensation—5 acts—though classical—like many other classical matters are gone out—3 is the fashionable number—and we must succumb to the tyranny of the day.
>   It would have given me great satisfaction to have handed it to Mr Buckstone, but he has enough already by him—with the sequel to Dundreary—to fill up the next two years and a half—besides a revival of popular pieces.
>   The writer, however, need not despair—for there is that in his comedy—if I am not greatly mistaken—will one day make him a man of dramatic mark.

More excitingly, the rugged Samuel Phelps himself, who had read *The Starchbacks*, invited Albery to call at his home next Sunday morning: 'I should like ten minutes' conversation with you.' As he had proved in those dedicated years at the Wells, Phelps, least showy of actors, put the theatre first; he must have decided that this young man was worth encouraging. We can be sure (even if nothing came of it) that the meeting did take place as arranged, in the decorum of 8 Canonbury Square, Islington, where Phelps lived so conveniently near his work. We can be just as sure that Albery noticed the veteran's modesty: most domestic of actors, it was like him to suggest meeting at his house instead of in a more public place.

Albery's ten minutes or so with Phelps were in the summer of 1863; on 23 September he heard from Vezin, who had also read the play. Others had, but it was never produced in its original form. As *Two Thorns* it was

15

the first of Albery's plays to assure the young and perceptive William Archer that 'here at last was the work of a dramatist with some power of construction and mastery of dialogue', but that would be in a hidden future. For the moment this alert, good-looking young man with the prominent eyes (his wife believed that he looked aggressive) was not easily put off. True, he had less reason for discouragement than Wyndham, who had been told flatly that he would never make an actor. None of Albery's correspondents told him he would never write a good play. Rather the opposite.

Vezin's letter is interesting for several reasons. It mentions for the first time Albery's link with the many-titled, often-adapted cloak-without-sword drama known best as *David Garrick*, in which to cure an infatuated maiden Garrick pretends to be a drunkard. (Various such devices have been ascribed to sundry harassed actors: John Philip Kemble, encumbered with an amorous and well-born lady, solved the problem by marrying another.) The ancestry of the Garrick piece is intricate. It derives from the publication in 1836 of a novelette called *Garrick Médecin*. Adapted for the stage as *Le Docteur Robin*, this was done in Paris as a vaudeville during 1842.

Seven years later Vezin saw a German version which he himself translated

> For a benefit occasion [he told Albery] or to strengthen a weak first piece ... It *goes* well, and there is scope for *good* acting in it. If you think of any slight improvement let me know of it. It isn't worth much trouble or thought. ... There are however, more effective bits in *Doctor Robin* than those you mention, as I hope to show you some day. I thank you for your compliment on my Romeo as much as I can thank anyone for what I don't deserve.

Albery, it seems, had told Vezin that *Doctor Robin* was worthless, and that playing a famous actor would be awkward. Though Vezin agreed, he added that if an audience made comparisons it would be its own fault. The letter tells us something about both men: Albery's arrogance, Vezin's honest approach to acting. The other translation from the German was *Reinhard and Leonora* which Vezin now wanted Albery to 'hurry into ship-shape'. Obviously, he thought more of it than of *Doctor Robin*, but it was not heard of for nearly ten years, when two versions by Albery (under two different titles) would cause an unfortunate rift. Dramatists of the day were eager to make things as difficult as possible. For the present, anyway, Albery and Vezin remained good friends. In Southwark Albery was getting earnest experience as an amateur. With J. J. Dilley, a man apparently as stage-struck as he was, but otherwise obscure, he wrote *Alexander the Great*, a short farce in which a servant has to impersonate a statue. As we have seen, at the Walworth Literary Institute in 1864

Albery chose to play Mrs Piper, the landlady: Victorians took pleasure in what we now call farcical drag.

Next year, for a week at Greenwich Vezin put on the Garrick play which had been renamed clumsily *How to Act: A Lesson Taught By Garrick*. Albery by this time had remodelled the plot, rewritten the dialogue (his special talent), and introduced a new character. W. G. Wills, later at the Lyceum and a dramatist of all work, had tinkered with the script, but Vezin regarded Albery's share as more important, and went out of his way to describe him as sole author. In fact, Vezin was so anxious for Albery to be recognized that after the production he wrote to *The Sunday Times* (16 February 1865):

Sir,
    Some notices have appeared in the "Sunday Times," "Herald," "Standard," and other papers, speaking in high terms of a piece called *How to Act: A Lesson Taught by Garrick*, which I produced on the 6th instant at the New Theatre, Greenwich. So well deserved indeed is the praise, that I wish I could take the credit of being its author, as the above papers have asserted. The facts are simply these: Four years ago I translated from the German a piece called *Doctor Robin* (itself founded upon the French original) and played it successfully in the provinces; but there was so much false sentiment in it, so much that was unnatural and un-English, that I determined to have it altered. Mr James Albery, the real author, has so entirely re-modelled the plot, re-written the dialogue, and recreated the characters that it might be called original, as it certainly is quite new. To him, therefore, belongs the merit of having written this brilliant little piece, an achievement very much beyond the literary powers of your humble servant.

                                                                    HERMANN VEZIN

He could hardly have been more magnanimous.

Twelve months afterwards, at the Lyceum, Vezin reappeared in the piece—now with still another title, *Doctor Davy*. It succeeded, and he revived it often in London and the provinces. He was not the only David Garrick of the 1860s; E. A. Sothern had appeared in Robertson's play of that name at the Haymarket in 1864, and it was this that presently would become Charles Wyndham and Mary Moore's surest standby down the years. Other leading actors—one was Donald Wolfit in the 1940s—have yielded, in one version or another, to what Théophile Gautier called 'the everlasting story of Garrick, Talma, or Kean curing some foolish girl of a passion for them as actors by exhibiting themselves in private life under the most repulsive conditions'. Why Wyndham failed to use Albery's version is not clear, unless it was a matter of copyright.

Naturally, the Garrick plays were compared. This, whatever Dogberry's view, has always been one of the joys of criticism. The *Sunday Times* could 'safely predict that not a few will be found to insist that Mr Vezin's is the better of them. In some minute respects it is certainly the more pleasing, and is sufficiently distinct to be estimated strictly on its

17

merits.' Audiences were used to similar 'doubles'; nearly every theatre in those days lived on pirated adaptations from abroad.

# III

No doubt Albery was pleased to be featured on the bills if not in the notices; but he had already soared off on something more ambitious: *The Jesuits*, a five-act costume drama written partly in blank verse. The dialogue is scattered with such oaths as 'God's bud' and 'Gad's precious,' and such exclamations as 'Hey! Smoke the Puritans!' and 'Tis a damn'd impudent jade.' As only two and a half acts of this kind of thing survive, the plot remains a mystery. It sounds now like the more obvious satire, though Albery meant it to be taken seriously. No one who read it was tempted to put it on, and we cannot ask why.

Loyally, in spite of the impudent jades, Vezin continued to sponsor his friend. He even sent *The Jesuits* to Joseph Knight ('Good Night' to his colleagues), then critic of the *Athenaeum*. Knight was

> singularly impressed. . . . No future is too bright for a man who at his years can write as he does. But while I admit the remarkable brilliance of his dialogue and his skill in the elucidation of character, I am far from believing that *The Jesuit* [*sic*] as it now stands would be a success. In fact to be thoroughly candid with you [he wrote to Vezin] I am sure it would be a failure. It is very long, much, very much, too long, and far too scantily provided with excitement and bustle.

Knight expanded into a discourse on the nature of tragedy:

> Admirable as are the dialogues, there is far more dialogue than an audience will stand . . . as a display of genius *The Jesuit* is a splendid production; as a work of art it has very serious defects. As an acting play it is nowhere.

Strangely, in the context, he talked about Sheridan, and ended a long letter disarmingly: 'Pray don't let your friend be cross with me for my frankness.' James Albery may have been cross or saddened; not discouraged. Going on to work that would be more actable, he was on the very edge of personal success. As for *The Jesuits*, his own son Bronson—who knew better than anyone how much an audience would stand—would surely have responded to the script as Joseph Knight did. Vezin, most intellectual of Victorian actors, and here a trifle avuncular, probably saw some literary merit in Albery's verbose drama; he went on believing in the young man's promise. During the years after *Doctor Davy* they discussed many projects, among them the retouching of Vezin's dialogue for *Anna Lisa* (still more from the German), and a version of Dickens's *Cricket on the Hearth*.

On the brink, then, but there would have to be one more abortive effort before Albery emerged as a dramatist in his own right. He and the inevitable Joseph J. Dilley (of *Alexander the Great*) worked on a nautical drama, *The Mate of the Mountjoy*, which they entered for a competition inaugurated by T. P. (Tippy) Cooke, famous for his vigour in the nautical melodrama of *Black Ey'd Susan*, and also remembered by H. S. Leigh in the *Carols of Cockayne*:

> Can I forget those hearts of oak,
> Those model British tars,
> Who crack'd a skull or crack'd a joke
> Like true transpontine stars?
> Who hornpip'd *à la* T. P. Cooke,
> And sang—at least they tried—
> Until the pit and gallery shook
> Upon the Surrey side?

We can understand Cooke's solemn belief that plays 'on a Nautical or National subject would earn . . . large sums in royalties'. The large sums were to go to a Royal Dramatic College, a scheme to provide homes for aged and infirm members of the profession, and, eventually, a school. As its Master, a respected veteran, Ben Webster, laid the foundation-stone in 1860; the Queen promised her patronage; Charles Kean, Charles Dickens, William Makepeace Thackeray and Webster himself were trustees; and Webster offered a gift 'without any attempt at ostentation . . . large masses of stone I have in Wales—approved, good stone—sufficient to face the whole of the twenty tenements . . .' A site (to the pleasure of every topical jester) was granted by the London Necropolis Company, but Ben reassured his critics—quite a number of them— that the College, and its masses of good stone, would be four and a half miles from the cemetery, at Maybury, Woking.

Funds had to be raised by a variety of methods,—one being a charity performance in 1861, when Cooke played his original part in scenes from *Luke the Labourer; or The Sailor's Return*—elsewhere in the same programme the ghost of Mrs Bracegirdle emerged obligingly from Hell and addressed the audience in indefatigable verse. Cooke died in 1864. His will contained this optimistic passage:

> Judging from the profits of some of the pieces in which I have myself been engaged, as *The Pilot, The Red Rover, The Flying Dutchman, My Poll and My Partner Joe,* and *Black Ey'd Susan,* some of which had a run of two hundred and fifty successive nights, and even calculating on moderate success without taking into account the chance of an "immense hit" on a nautical or popular subject, or favourite actor, or a fortunate cast, the pecuniary results to the funds of the College I should hope would be considerable, irrespective of what may arise from the copyright from provincial acting and other sources.

19

The first prizewinner, *True to the Core: A Story of the Armada*, by D. A. R. Slous, did fulfil Tippy's hopes. Originally at the Surrey Theatre, it earned £500 in royalties for College funds. Albery and Dilley's play, which won the prize of about £120 in 1868, unluckily failed to excite any manager. It was not performed. As for the College (though the school was never built), it served its purpose temporarily, but not for long; in 1880 lack of support enforced its sale. Like the College, the script of *The Mate of the Mountjoy* disappeared. Even so, Albery would soon achieve what he really wanted. A play of his own was staged in the West End, and won more acclamation than he ever had for any original work.

He has been bracketed with T. W. Robertson. But we have seen that, because none of his plays has endured with Robertson's *Caste*, criticism has relegated him to a 'disciple'. That is unfair. As so often happens, both men were writing at the same time plays urgently needed in a theatre of outworn tradition. One day Pinero would explain: 'for modern poetic drama the audience were still asked to listen to the jog-trot rhetoric of James Sheridan Knowles, and to the clap-trap of Edward Bulwer-Lytton'. That was why Albery's first efforts were praised so lavishly, and why experienced men of the theatre, hunting for comparison, looked back to the eighteenth century, to *The Rivals* and *The School for Scandal*. They agreed that the plots could be weak (they always were); but the dialogue 'without anything like imitation, recalls the brilliancy of Sheridan'. Here the speaker was Westland Marston, himself a useful dramatist, to whom Vezin had sent *The Starchbacks*. Albery was about to establish his name. The curtain was ready to rise, the first words to be spoken: 'Our Mr Jenkins will have the pleasure of waiting on Mr Digby Grant . . .' and the actor who spoke them would make his own name as well.

# CHAPTER THREE
# 'Caperbilities'
# 1865–1871

Home again, Charles Wyndham made several provincial appearances. Though these proved less discouraging than in America, they could have made him wonder whether after all he might not do better as a doctor. When he played Shaun the Post, indomitable hero of Dion Boucicault's *Arrah-na-Pogue* (a part the author, enjoying his own heroics, originated) he was told in effect that his Irish accent was bad enough to cause another Fenian Rising. Certainly it asked a good deal of an inexperienced player, without any evident Irish blood, to roll his tongue around such language as this:

> This is my weddin' morning'; sure my breast is so big wid my heart this minit, that I feel like a fowl wid her first egg. Egorra, and this same love brings a man out in a fine perspiration, long life to it. And there's Arrah's cabin; the oysther-shell that's got the pearl of my heart in it. Arrah, suilis! Arrah, mo millia storeen! If you are slapin' don't answer me; but if you are up, open the dure softly.

His rendering of Boucicault's version of *The Wearing of the Green* brought out the most extreme Irish nationalism.

More heartening, he had a kind reception at the Theatre Royal, Manchester (July 1865) for his own play, *Her Ladyship's Guardian*. Adapted from a novel, *Lady Lee's Widowhood*, it was played with a farce, *His Last Legs*, in a double bill so popular that it went with almost the same company for a brief season to the Queen's, Dublin. One evening, to the dismay of both company and audience, a limelight exploded. Two of the actors rushed into the street, still in costume, and the audience threatened to stampede. Eventually, calm (and the actors) returned and

21

the performance continued: this sort of thing was an occupational risk then for both players and spectators.

Presently Wyndham's days as a provincial actor were over. In May 1866 he went back to the Royalty Theatre, whose manageress, 'Patty' Oliver, familiar in burlesque, chose her plays less disastrously than Madame de Rhona had done. When she revived an unsophisticated melodrama, *All that Glitters is not Gold*, she cast Wyndham as Sir Arthur Lascelles, obviously a wicked baronet. All baronets in melodrama tended to be bad; Wyndham leered at a number of them. The play was sometimes called *The Factory Girl*, a salute to a heroine who, in a noble effort to open the eyes of Lady Valeria to the wiles of Sir Arthur, is herself compromised. At the turn of the plot the factory girl observes of Lady Valeria, 'She stands upon the brink of ruin! Shall I not snatch her from destruction? Yes, yes! I will save her, whose mother preserved mine!' (*Looks at Sir Arthur and drops her bouquet as a sign*). These lines were first uttered in 1851. We do not know how seriously the players could take them: probably very seriously indeed, for theatrical fashions soon fade. At least, the recurring 'Take a card' did become a catch-phrase in a period of catch-phrases.

During ten months at the Royalty Wyndham added helpfully to his scope. Thus in Tom Taylor's *Still Waters Run Deep* he played a new part—John Mildmay, the husband, which he would repeat on both sides of the Atlantic. There is a picture of him standing on a ladder with a paintbrush in one hand. Impracticably, he is wearing a dinner jacket and stiff white shirt. When Mildmay tells his wife:

> Trust me, henceforth, to make you what a wife should be. I should prefer to win you by a lover's tenderness, but if I cannot do that, I know how to make a husband's rights respected. . . .

her reply is submissive—no trace of the New Woman here, or (yet to come) of Henry Arthur Jones's Rebellious Susan whom Mary Moore would create.

When Miss Oliver put on something called *Meg's Diversion*, with the author, H. T. Craven, in the cast Wyndham produced (or, as we should say, stage-managed): still more experience. Then, in *Black Ey'd Susan*, F. C. Burnand's burlesque of Douglas Jerrold's nautical melodrama—shades of Tippy Cooke—'Patty' Oliver played Susan, very much her kind of part; and Wyndham, as Hatchett the smuggler, stopped the show with an energetic dance that he made up himself. Years later (28 May 1898), after someone had described Wyndham as a 'super' in the revival, Burnand wrote facetiously to the *Daily Telegraph*:

> Sir
>
> Should Mr Charles Wyndham desire, as from his letter to the *Daily Telegraph*, May 24, a certificate from "the author" as to his singing,

'Not with bayonet and rifle but with bandages, probes and chloroform.' Charles Wyndham, aged twenty-seven, as an Army surgeon during the American Civil War

As the heavily bearded prodigal son, Wyndham (back row *l.*) stands behind J. L. Toole (seated *l.*) as his father, while Henry Irving (front row *r.*) glowers beside Lionel Brough as the gin-soaking uncle: *Dearer Than Life* (Queen's, 1868)

'A little cheque' proffered by Henry Irving in
*Two Roses*. He originated Digby Grant, Esq., at
the Vaudeville in 1870, and revived the play
at the Lyceum in 1881

'One scarcely feels the burden of having to support such dear children,' remarks
Digby Grant, Esq.  Maude Millett and Annie Hughes in the 1887 revival of *Two Roses*
at the Criterion

dancing, and acting, when taking the part of Hatchett in *Black Ey'd Susan* (burlesque) I shall be most happy to offer it to him as "testimonial to character" in his next piece. "More than a Super." "Very much more." Why, as Hatchett, the bold smuggler, Mr Charles Wyndham's singing, acting and dancing, especially the last two, were the admiration of hundreds of audiences for many hundreds of nights.

To Mr Charles Wyndham's terpsichorean energy, to his "caperbilities," as we should have said in the good old punning days, after the marvellous performance of the dancing Dervish of a Danvers as the Dame, who attained popularity "by leaps and bounds," and after Patty Oliver's captivating "trill", were due the six or seven nightly encores of the dance that contributed so largely to the unprecedented success of *Black Ey'd Susan*; or *The Little Bill*, written by—

Yours faithfully,

F. C. BURNAND.

(Edwin Danvers played Dame Hatley in Burnand's burlesque in 1866.) Wyndham left before the long run was over. After an unpropitious start he had begun to learn what success felt like, and (from the nightly encores for his dance) how it sounded.

# II

In 1867 he joined Miss Louisa Herbert's company, then firmly established at the St James's. Remotely situated, in a theatrical sense, the St James's had not always been lucky. A handsome theatre, with its two tiers of pillars facing King Street, it had been thoroughly versatile. Distinguished visitors had acted there—Ristori and Rachel, for example—and London had a first glimpse of the everlasting David Garrick theme in De Melesville's *Sullivan, comédien de Drury Lane*, in which Queen Victoria and Prince Albert saw a French company during 1854. 'The beautiful Miss Herbert', as she was shown, had sat for Rossetti; she was a Pre-Raphaelite type (though whether her neck was the required 'ten kisses long' is not recorded). At this point she was about to put on, optimistically, an adaptation of Ouida's novel *Idalia*. Wyndham and Irving shared a dressing-room. This was not their first meeting, which had been outside a manager's office waiting for the chance of an engagement at two or three pounds a week. Wyndham would remember it because he had struck his arm through a window: 'I don't know whether you are aware of it, but to stick your elbow through a manager's window-pane while you are trying to worry an engagement out of him is considered a breach of etiquette.' Neither he nor Irving had the money to pay; but the manager said agreeably that it was of no consequence. Probably he was right.

When they were at the St James's Irving had just completed a strenuous decade in the provinces. He did not yet own a dress suit, so Wyndham lent him his to wear at a party given by Mrs Sartoris (formerly Adelaide Kemble, Fanny's sister and John Philip's niece). Irving confided next day that one man he envied desperately: someone who 'entered the room with quiet assurance, greeted Mrs Sartoris as though he were conferring a favour upon her, and took a seat with a dignity that one might have expected in a duke.' Wyndham asked Irving who he was, and got the surprising reply: 'Oh, nobody; a noodle, as it turned out.'

In *Idalia* Irving played the villainous Italian count. Wyndham was the hero. During the first scene Irving had to attack Wyndham and leave him, apparently dead, on a rocky incline. A waterfall effect had overflowed; the stage was slippery; and Irving and another actor both slid to the ground. Hearing a shout, the heroine (Miss Herbert) rushed on: 'Ah!' she cried perceptively: 'A body on the bridge! 'Tis he!' Then she too slid to the ground, covering Wyndham with her dress. By the time the scene was over the house had dissolved in laughter. More troubles enlivened the next scene. Massive rocks were knocked over by falling bodies. The audience loved every minute. 'Need I tell you', Wyndham said later, 'that, in the last act, the actors had become, through sheer helplessness, as demoralised as the audience—that I assured my love, in a voice smothered with laughter, that nothing would shake my firmness in belief in her—that she chuckled out she believed me—and that Irving came on to die in a white shirt, a blood-red spot on his breast, and his face all grins, dying the most facetious death ever died?'

Wyndham left the St James's to take part in Kate Terry's farewell season at the Prince's Theatre, Manchester. Ellen's talented elder sister was about to marry the wealthy Arthur Lewis. She had said a London farewell as Juliet at the Adelphi on 2 September 1867. 'It is seldom that a theatrical chronicler has to describe a scene like that', *The Times* reported:

> The curtain rose for the farce; still the thunder roared. One of the actors, quite inaudible in the clamour, began the performance, but the roar grew louder and louder, till at last Mr Phillips came on in the dress of Friar Lawrence, and, with the stolidity so well assumed that it seemed perfectly natural, asked, in the stereotyped phrase of the theatres, the pleasure of the audience: "Kate Terry!" was the reply from a chorus of a thousand stentorian voices; and then the fair favourite of the night appeared once more, pale, and dressed to leave the theatre....

In Manchester Wyndham had almost the only Shakespearian parts of his career, Mercutio, Claudio and Laertes—they would have suited him. Mary Moore always regretted he never played Benedick—'he would have been the finest of his generation'. (For that matter, she would have been perfectly cast as Beatrice.) He was in other 'farewells', including the last play, *Plot and Passion*, in which Kate Terry was Marie de Fontanges. On the night of 5 October Arthur Lewis clasped round her wrist a gold bracelet bearing the inscription: 'To Kate Terry on her retirement from the stage, from him for whom she leaves it.' Wyndham acted with Ellen in a supporting piece.

A fortnight later Kate married Mr Lewis and settled to domesticity; and on 24 October Wyndham opened in London at the new Queen's in Long Acre. This large theatre, built on the site of a concert hall, brightened a dreary corner of Covent Garden. It was an ambitious project; the décor had Greek influences; Telbin had designed the drop-curtain, representing a temple; and the footlights were so tactfully arranged that they emitted neither heat, smell nor vapour. The lessee, Henry Labouchere, journalist and politician, was about to marry Henrietta Hodson, leading lady of Alfred Wigan's company. For 'Labby', ardent radical and founder of the periodical *Truth*, the Queen's would be an expensive wedding present; but on this October evening, when the curtain rose on a one-act trifle unluckily entitled *He's a Lunatic*, no one would have thought of failure and brokers' men. *The Double Marriage* followed, a romantic drama, adapted by Charles Reade from his own novel, in which Wyndham, a dashing figure in a French colonel's uniform, had to arrive just in time to prevent the hero's marriage. Ellen Terry, childlike in white muslin, walked downstage, towards those vapourless footlights, with the heroine's baby in her arms, nobly claiming it as her own. On the first night, Ellen—who had returned reluctantly to the theatre after the failure of her marriage to the painter G. F. Watts—had a cold. When Wyndham asked, 'Whose child is this?' she replied, 'It's bine.'

That was enough for audience and company. 'They seem to be hissing', murmured Labouchere to the author. 'What of that?' Reade replied. 'If you want to please such a public as this, you shouldn't come to me for a play.' His play never recovered, and throughout the run, Ellen Terry confessed, 'the very thought of it used to send us into fits of laughter. We hung on to chairs, helpless, limp, and incapable.' Mrs Wigan, the manager's wife, was furious. If they laughed again on the stage, she warned them, she would go in front and hiss, and she did. 'The very next time we laughed', said Ellen, 'a loud hiss rose from the stage-box. I was simply paralysed with terror.'

After the play's failure Alfred Wigan fell back on *Still Waters Run Deep*, in which he had made his name as Mildmay as far back as 1855. In the Queen's revival Wyndham reverted to Captain Hawksley, the part he had first acted as an amateur; now he made a genuine hit. On Boxing Night Irving, a newcomer, appeared (for the first time with Ellen Terry) in Garrick's emasculated version of *The Taming of the Shrew*. Neither made any impression on the other, or, for that matter, as Katherine and Petruchio. Irving told Ellen years later that he found her hoydenish, and she found him stiff with self-consciousness. The salary list at the Queen's for the week ending 27 December 1867 so struck Mary Moore in years ahead that she had a copy of it framed. Probably when she was in management, and actors came to see her, she would have shown them how little they would have earned then, and stressed how much in comparison she was offering them now. When (not too gravely) she offered Ellen Terry an engagement at the same terms she had had 'in the pride of her youth and beauty' Ellen (not too gravely) declined. The document shows why:

QUEEN'S THEATRE
PAY LIST
*For the week ending Friday, Dec.27.1867*

| GENTLEMEN | £. s. d. | LADIES | £. s. d. |
|---|---|---|---|
| Messrs. Ryder | 7.10. 0. | Miss Terry | 5. 0. 0. |
| Irving | 2.13. 4. | Addison | 2. 0. 0. |
| Wyndham | 3. 0. 0. | Savile | 2. 0. 0. |
| Clayton | 2.10. 0. | Heath | 1. 0. 0. |
| Charles | 2.10. 0. | Hodson | 3. 0. 0. |
| Brough | 2.10. 0. | Markham | 1. 5. 0. |
| Stephens | 2. 0. 0. | Batty | 1. 0. 0. |
| Terrott | 2. 0. 0. | Turner | 1. 0. 0. |
| Sanger | 1.10. 0. | Hullah | 10. 0. |
| Seyton | 1.10. 0. | Jordan | 10. 0. |
| Peel | 1. 0. 0. | Everard | 1. 0. 0. |
| Crellin | 15. 0. | Masse | 13. 4. |
| Woodfield | 15. 0. | | |
| Vincent | 12. 6. | | |
| Wigan | 8. 6. 8. | | |
| Toole | 10.16. 8. | | |
| | £49.19. 2. | | £18.18. 4. |

| SERVANTS | £. s. d. |
|---|---|
| Men dressers | ........... |
| Women dressers | ........... |
| Check takers | 3. 0. 0. |
| Cleaners | ........... |
| Hall-keeper | 1. 8. 0. |
| Attendant | ........... |
| Messenger | 1.15. 0. |
| Fireman | ........... |
| Watchman | 1. 5. 0. |
| | £ 7. 8. 0. |

| BAND | £. s. d. |
|---|---|
| Mr. Wallerstein and Band | 15. 0. 0. |

Wyndham earned slightly more than Irving because he doubled acting with stage management. J. L. Toole, with star salary, had recently come to the Queen's for a pair of farces which were given with *Catherine and Petruchio*, and made the evening for most people. Toole, who had begun at the Walworth Institute (the place where James Albery tried out his own first farce), could mix pathos with humour, as he proved in the next Queen's play, *Dearer Than Life* by the prolific H. J. Byron. He was the honest father ruined by his prodigal son (the hero, Wyndham), whom a flashy friend, Bob Gassett, had misled. Irving's Gassett was splendidly reviewed. In a celebrated photograph the cast is gathered round a table, with Toole, as the still prosperous father, smoking a churchwarden; Lionel Brough, as an alcoholic uncle, brandishing a gin bottle; Wyndham's handsome face completely hidden in the bushiest of beards; and Irving, as the raffish Gassett, wearing a formidable moustache. Later in the play the family is forced to live in an attic, the churchwarden abandoned and the gin bottle empty, until the son, having made his fortune in the colonies, returns at the twelfth hour. (More and more of these men from the colonies would arrive in the London theatre; Wyndham himself played several of them.)

*Dearer Than Life*, the first Queen's success, came off at length to make way for *Oliver Twist*: Irving as Bill Sikes; his first love, Nellie Moore, as Nancy; Toole as the Artful Dodger; and Henrietta Hodson as Oliver. (Convention somersaulted: in the Elizabethan theatre boys played the women; in the Victorian theatre women played boys.) Wyndham appeared in a sequence of one-act plays and burlesques; and in H. J. Byron's melodramatic *A Lancashire Lass* he was again the hero, with Irving as a villain who 'stroked his heavy moustachios with blood-stained fingers'. Though Dickens (in spite of his predilection for melodrama) found the play 'rather too much of a good thing', he told his family 'there was a young fellow . . . who sits at a table with Sam Emery and is bullied by him; the young fellow's name is Henry Irving, and if he some day doesn't come out as a great actor I know nothing of the art'. He was a good judge. In *A Lancashire Lass* Nellie Moore had her last part; her death soon afterwards was a tragedy for Irving; if she had lived he might not have made his unfortunate marriage.

The two 'young fellows', building their reputations, were now on the rim of great things. When Irving played the melancholy Faulkland in *The Rivals* Wyndham was Sir Lucius O'Trigger (had his Irish improved since Shaun the Post? Possibly). At Irving's benefit—which earned him £57, as he told his fiancée proudly—Wigan revived an old success, *Plot and Passion*; for a change Irving played the hero, and Toole a police spy, Wyndham—as at Kate Terry's farewell—De Neuville. In the curtain-raiser, *Trying It On*, he was (rather differently) Walsingham Potts, a name that seems to say everything, and a part to which he frequently returned. Before long Irving and Toole had left the Queen's to go on tour, evolving elaborate practical jokes, and enjoying a friendship that would endure; but Wyndham stayed on, his good looks and tall figure condemning him to the colourless hero in plays where the villain had always the best of it. Still, he was getting so much experience that he felt confident enough to venture into management himself. This, at the Princess's, was in May

27

1868; he continued to act at the Queen's just up the road, and his new responsibilities cannot have bothered him, for the plays were soon withdrawn.

After a brief appearance at the Olympic Theatre in the summer of 1869, he left for New York, arriving at an exciting period of Broadway development. Augustin Daly had opened his first theatre; standards rose and remained. There was then, as uninterruptedly since, constant cross-fertilization between the stages of London and New York. If two liners had met in mid-ocean their combined passenger lists could have provided casts for a wide repertoire. At Wallack's, second theatre of that name founded by a family originally from England, Wyndham played Charles in *The School for Scandal*; it was the theatre in which seven years before he had sat in the gallery to see Lester Wallack, and this revival was a copy of the production he had seen. Prompt-book entries at Wallack's were followed to the letter and stage business was unchanging. Unmatched in the part for many years, Wyndham looked superb in eighteenth-century costume: 'He might have stepped from a canvas of Reynolds or Romney or Gainsborough.' Certainly his first Charles must have pleased the management: it kept him on in *Caste*, as the husband (again) in *Still Waters Run Deep*, and in other plays as the light comedian. By then he began to feel secure enough to try management for a second time, and more profitably than at the Princess's.

# CHAPTER FOUR

# A Glass of Hot Rum
# 1870–1871

The scene on a spring day was the Edinburgh tavern in the Strand; the interior, I trust, was suitably dark for a clandestine occasion. Henry Irving, up and coming, not yet fully established, had been invited to meet James Albery there. The story has been told in various versions: in one, Irving received precise instructions from Albery: 'I shall be sitting in the second compartment with a large glass of hot rum before me. The glass will have a sugar crusher in it.' Irving must have liked the touch; in this version, when he arrived at the second compartment he said, 'Mr Albery, I think—to judge by the refreshment which I see before me!' At the time Irving was acting in an unsuccessful melodrama with which the new Vaudeville Theatre had opened on 16 April 1870. Albery had been impressed by Irving's performance in *Uncle Dick's Darling*. and had written a part for him: Digby Grant, Esq., in a play called *Two Roses*. As yet the part was only roughly sketched—would Irving help to add the finishing touches? As he foresaw trouble with others in the company, Albery asked for the meeting to be kept secret. Unnecessary, Irving felt, but he agreed to hear Albery read the script and decided at once that he would play Digby Grant if it were offered to him. (Whether he suggested any finishing touches, who knows?) We do know that Albery's cloak-and-dagger approach did not put the actor off—it was entirely remote from his play—and the two remained good friends. Albery's eldest son would be christened Irving.

Albery loved Dickens, and this is reflected in his plays; it has been suggested that he based Digby Grant on William Dorrit, Father of the Marshalsea. This would give Irving just the chance he needed at this point in his career. He had married, as it proved unhappily, a wife with no experience of the whirligig of theatrical fortune, and she was expecting her first baby. A long run and good prospects ahead gave stability—at least for a time—to his home life.

When that conspiratorial talk took place the Vaudeville managers had already accepted Albery's *Two Roses*. Before then they had taken an option on his *Coquettes* for which he had received £25—possibly to compensate for their decision not to do it—and a commission to write another play: hence *Two Roses*. 'They' were a triumvirate: David James, H. J. Montague and Thomas Thorne, three actors known collectively as the Jew, the Gent and the Gentile. David James had appeared with Wyndham during Madame de Rhona's time at the Royalty; Harry Montague was a personage who on entering a room, said Clement Scott, 'gave the impression that for months or weeks past he had been dying to see the men and women with whom he so gracefully and earnestly shook hands.' (He died young, in America, where he had been as popular as in England.) Thomas Thorne, from a theatrical family, had been for some years at the Surrey. Both Montague and Thorne were in the cast of *Two Roses* which opened on 4 June. In Digby Grant (says the historian George Rowell) Albery created a character 'as shrewdly observed and perhaps more forcefully drawn than any Robertson himself provided'.

This comparison between Albery and T. W. Robertson, later familiar in histories of nineteenth-century drama, seemed inevitable in the notices of *Two Roses*. Thus the *Daily Telegraph* critic, E. L. Blanchard, said boldly that 'whether Mr Albery would ever have written *Two Roses* if Mr T. W. Robertson had not cleared the way for him by showing that modern life required a modern form of theatrical illustration, may be a question for the curious to discover'. But, let me repeat, Albery cannot be called Robertson's disciple; he was writing his early comedies before Robertson had 'arrived'. It often happens in the theatre, as elsewhere, that two authors unbeknown to each other are creating a change in style, a revolution in form; each as he writes believes that he is alone. So it was with Robertson and Albery. Both had originally responded to a need for naturalism in the drama without any idea that another colleague was at work.

Both wrote best for small theatres: Robertson for the Bancrofts at the Prince of Wales's behind Tottenham Court Road and Charlotte Street, and Albery for the compact new Vaudeville in the Strand (the first theatre in this story which still remains alive and well). Their effects needed more subtlety than the early Victorian stage had known; Robertson in particular stage-managed his plays with the attention to detail that Pinero especially appreciated, as he shows in the affectionate portrait of Tom Wrench in *Trelawny of the 'Wells'*:

I tell you, I don't have doors stuck here, there and everywhere; no more windows in all sorts of impossible places! . . . Windows on the one side, doors on the other—just where they should be architecturally. And locks on the doors, *real locks* to work; and handles to turn.

Albery's plots were weaker than Robertson's; but he did write delicate naturalistic dialogue, his humour was unstrained and his characters were recognizable. Digby Grant's Dickensian quality is evident in the first moments of the play. He is a broken-down gentleman full of guile and false pride. When the simple landlady of the local inn demands payment of her bill he charms her into lending him money.

GRANT   Ah! Mrs Cupps, how do you do.

MRS C   [*stiffly*]   I'm very well, I thank you.

GRANT   And the "Hen and Toothpick" prospers?

MRS C   Oh! yes.

GRANT   [*blandly*]   That's well.

MRS C   I've called for my little bill, Mr Grant.

GRANT   [*taking bill-file*]   I'm glad to hear it. I was afraid you'd called for the money. [*Takes bill off the file and hands it politely*].

MRS C   Mr Grant, this is not right.

GRANT   Very likely not, I haven't cast it up. I never do. The tradespeople *mean* to rob me, I *mean* to pay them—we both fail; but the good intention is with me, thank heaven.

MRS C   Well! *I've* not robbed you; and you'll find this is a debt you can't help paying.

GRANT   Mrs Cupps, that's new. I've always found 'em debts I can't help owing.

MRS C   And yet you pay away money without occasion; last night you gave my potman sixpence to fetch you a cab, but I must go without.

GRANT   Mrs Cupps, you do not understand the feelings of a gentleman. I cannot be under an obligation to a potman—absurd! Your case is different. There's your account; I acknowledge the debt, I do not dispute it, or attempt to deduct over-charges, or take off a discount for cash like a common cad. If you bring it me next year, I shall still acknowledge it; I can do no more. I am a gentleman. I can do no less.

MRS C   I don't care for all your fine talk. I'll have my money, or I'll know the reason why.

GRANT   What can be fairer? You shall know the reason why. I haven't got it.

MRS C   Well! You must find it somewhere.

GRANT   There again, nothing can be truer; I must find it if I get it. The thing is, where?

MRS C   Don't you know anyone you wouldn't mind borrowing it of?

GRANT   Plenty, but they would mind lending.

MRS C   Surely you've some old friends.

GRANT   Yes, but they're so old I've worn them out.

MRS C   Well! haven't you any acquaintances?

GRANT   I used to have, but I've turned 'em all into friends.

MRS C   Well! I must have my money, so it don't signify.[*sits*].

31

GRANT   If it don't signify, why not wait?

MRS C   [*rising indignantly*]   I haven't common patience. Good morning [*going*].

GRANT   Mrs Cupps, stay. [*rises*] You shall be paid. I'll do it.

MRS C   Dear me! What? [*returning*].

GRANT   This little room—lowly indeed, for I do not hold the position I did—is still the abode of honour and innocence, of me, a broken gentleman, and my fair daughters—two roses, as my very worthy, though plebeian friend, John Wyatt, calls them,—two roses—white and red. This floor shall never be polluted by the tread of a broker. I will do it.

MRS C   Dear me! Do what?

GRANT   I will sacrifice myself.

MRS C   Not kill yourself, Mr Grant?

GRANT   No, I will only slay my pride. A lady who has wealth has almost asked me to share it; I will marry her for the sake of my daughters—and you shall be paid.

MRS C   I—I could wait a little while, Mr Grant.

GRANT   No, you shall not wait. She is not a fair woman; she has not your comely figure nor pleasant smile, Mrs Cupps.

MRS C   Oh! Mr Grant.

GRANT   She has not your gentle voice.

MRS C   Do you think my voice gentle?

GRANT   She will not be such a mother to my girls—as—as—you would make, but I have pressing need. She will, I know, lend me twenty pounds at once—and—you shall be paid.

MRS C   Oh! It seems a great pity you should sacrifice yourself, Mr Grant. It's very noble, but—

GRANT   I will do my duty.

MRS C   I—I—could lend you twenty pounds, Mr Grant, if—

GRANT   [*takes her hand*]   Mrs Cupps, these lips have touched a royal hand. [*kisses her hand*] I—I—cannot express what I feel at this proof of your—high esteem;—I would not have you see my emotion. Leave me—and—bring the money.

MRS C   I will, Mr Grant; good-bye.

GRANT   Good-bye; I shall never be able to repay you for your kindness. Allow me. [*opens door and bows her out; closes door*]. That's a damn'd silly woman.

What is this but another version of the scene in which Falstaff (*Henry IV Part II*) extracts a loan from the angry Hostess, who has just had him arrested for debt?

No wonder Irving, as Digby Grant, established himself; as he said: 'The critiques on *Two Roses* are the best I've had.' Unlike Irving, Albery did not progress; but for the moment that night looked like the start of great things for him as well. As one critic put it: 'Never was there such a first night's triumph for a playwright's first piece.' Advertised as 'written expressly for this theatre', the comedy had notices that must have made Albery confident of his future anywhere. (It must have also saddened him that his mother, who died in March, never knew of his success.) *The Times* (John Oxenford) called Albery a most promising writer, with one reservation: 'Disregard for plot is with him carried to a degree not to be found in the master of the "school." Mr Robertson's theatrical chessboard is not the field for complex combinations, but you always know the particular square on which the piece is placed.' Blanchard, in the *Telegraph*, was just as sure that Albery

> should henceforth take a prominent position among writers for the stage. Both Robertson and Albery are sympathetic in their scorn of the old conventionalities, and in their quick apprehension of the demands of the age for a more vivid reflection of the realities around them. In the comedy produced here on Saturday evening, with a success . . . best attested by the unflagging attention secured, we have evidence of remarkable freshness of thought.

Blanchard was perturbed—not uncommon with him—that Albery, pointedly and superfluously, should have specified that the second act took place on a Sunday. As Wyndham Albery says, the critic did not realise—and after all, critics are fallible—that Sunday was the only day in the week when a journalist, a piano-tuner and a commercial traveller could be at home.

All that happens in *Two Roses* is Digby Grant's realization, first that he has inherited a fortune, and then that this is a mistake. The money goes to his daughter's sweetheart, a journalist (played by H. J. Montague). 'Our Mr Jenkins', a commercial traveller who bestows samples on the impoverished Grant household, has nothing to do with the plot. If he were cut the main body of the play would survive; but he is a personage almost as actable as Grant, and Albery was more interested in characters than plot.

Irving's notices were as cheering as Albery's. Oxenford, in *The Times*, had no doubt: 'As a delineator of character our new dramatist does himself great credit. The pompous humbug of Digby Grant, Esq., is capitally sustained throughout, and Mr Albery has his reward in the admirable acting of that most conscientious artist, Mr H. Irving.' We can imagine from the text how Irving dealt with his encounter with Furnival, the solicitor:

FURNIVAL   [*bowing*]   Mr Grant?

GRANT   Yes.

FURNIVAL   Dear me! There is my card. Perhaps you expected me. May I look round?

33

GRANT    Certainly. [*Furnival looks through a double eye-glass at samplers on the wall*] "Furnival, Solicitors." [*aside*] What mess am I in now?

FURNIVAL    [*referring to samplers*]    Excuse me, you bought these at your sale.

GRANT    Sir, I remember with pleasure that when they were put up no one would bid for them.

FURNIVAL    Dear me! [*To say this he turns from samplers, but keeps his eye-glass, through which he has looked, unmoved*].

GRANT    Except a Jew broker, who got bonneted. That chair my wife sold a ring off her finger to buy in. No one would bid against her, such was their great respect for *me*. You know something of my affairs.

FURNIVAL    Thoroughly; I've been engaged on them for some time. Allow me to sit?

GRANT    Certainly.

> *They sit opposite each other on either side of table and during the scene, while examining papers, each uses a double eye-glass, but, when looking up from the papers, both keep the eye-glasses unmoved, and look over them at one another.*

FURNIVAL    [*takes out papers and hands one*]    That is right, I think. You are Digby Grant, and distantly related to De Chaperon.

GRANT    Sir, it is the comfort of my life.

FURNIVAL    Dear me! you seem a strong man; good nerve;—anything in that bottle?

GRANT    Sherry.

FURNIVAL    Good?

GRANT    Very.

FURNIVAL    Take a glass [*Grant does so*] Well now!—perhaps you'd better take another. [*Grant does so*] Now you can bear it. That is all correct.

GRANT    Perfectly.

FURNIVAL    I congratulate you. You are worth ten thousand a-year.

GRANT    [*jumps up*] I? [*rises, throws off smoking cap, and goes to window overcome*].

Later Irving must have revelled in the business of allowing cheques to slip from his fingers to those of his long-suffering debtors 'with all the touches of a finished artist'.

Naturally, the reception delighted the Vaudeville triumvirate. During a run of 294 performances—a long life then—the author received £3 a performance. This was reasonable enough in 1870, but Joseph Knight, who had once commented generously on *The Jesuits*, Albery's unplayed and unplayable poetic drama, sent his advice:

> When a theatre is small, a company tolerable, a manager safe, and the play is comedy, insist on "sharing terms." Thus only is money to be made by the writer, with whom I need not tell you, rather than with managers, my sympathies are.

34

Albery did not achieve 'sharing terms', perhaps because this was his first original full-length play. Knight, as impressed as his colleagues, broke a rule in writing to a dramatist: 'Your play is a fine work and I warmly congratulate you on its production and on the career now open to you.' He had offered to arbitrate at the time of 'the difficulty' (possibly the management's rejection of *Coquettes*), but this offer was refused.

Montague, early in the run, had told Albery that business was good—'thank God *and yourself*'. While he was out of the cast recovering from an operation Lin Rayne played the journalist. Irving wrote to tell Albery that Montague would 'return to us (thank God!) about the hundredth night. Lin Rayne is better—but at best, the Rain is but Slush. The returns on last Saturday were the *largest* we've, or they've ever had.' Irving's eldest son was born on 5 August, and he reported in a gossipy letter to Albery: 'All at home are very well, thank you. I'm the *all* by the bye—for mother and child are at Southend. Come back and we can have long chats. Hope to see you tomorrow. Shall prepare Sweet Epps for your coming.' This preparation, much advertised in theatre programmes, was cocoa.

Albery's wit in conversation was becoming known; Montague was 'utterly abashed' by his repartee. Convivial, Bohemian by inclination, he was beginning a life that would help to destroy him. During 1870 he left the twine-spinner's in Southwark, though for another eight years he retained an interest in his family business; he and his unmarried sister went to live at 1 Clarendon Villas, Putney. Not too seriously, Pinero claimed that out of the *Two Roses* royalties Albery had invested large sums in a rope-walk which came to grief, 'I believe from mismanagement, not from any lull in the infliction of capital punishment.'

If—and it is likely—success went to Albery's head, we can hardly blame him. Public response apart, actors and managers congratulated him. E. A. Sothern, creator of Lord Dundreary in *Our American Cousin*, and of David Garrick (Robertson's version), went to the first night, of which 'there seems to be but one opinion'. He apologized for not catching Albery's name when Robertson introduced them—'I had no idea who you were. Kindly accept this apology in the same candid spirit in which it is written.' Sothern was fated to apologize. In another letter he feared a script sent to him by Albery had been lost 'in one of my trunks'. He was anxious to have a powerful, interesting domestic drama with a rattling, droll underplot: 'I've a great fancy for playing an intensely pathetic part *but* require constant light and shade.' Wilson Barrett, already imperial in melodrama, expressed his unqualified admiration for *Two Roses*, and asked if Albery had disposed of the provincial rights of *Coquettes*. Or was there a play with a part that would suit his wife, Caroline Heath? Albery, it seemed, had nothing suitable to offer.

Presently, when *Two Roses* opened on Broadway, at Wallack's Theatre, the *New York Times* critic also talked of Robertson. Still, the character of Digby Grant proved that Albery was 'capable of much better things than go to make up the staple of his drama. . . . Mr Charles Fisher's striking picture . . . would alone save the piece.' After New York *Two Roses* travelled to Boston, Philadelphia, Chicago and San Francisco; and *Coquettes* succeeded it at Wallack's: a series of American performances for which Albery received £243 19s. 1d. in royalties.

Meanwhile at the Prince of Wales's Theatre in Liverpool, a first English production of *Coquettes* opened on 29 October. Written before *Two Roses*, and later renamed *Two Thorns*, the comedy has at its centre a Member of Parliament deeply in love with his second wife, formerly an actress and an incurable flirt. She causes him much pain, especially when her admirer, mistaking him for the butler, confides the story of their love affair, with references to a 'mouldy old husband'. Edgar Bruce, who played the admirer, went in August 1871 to America and joined Charles Wyndham's touring company there—one tangible link between Wyndham and Albery, who (as we shall see) would be linked more closely during the next twenty years, and beyond.

# CHAPTER FIVE

# 'Just Sitting About In Chairs'
# 1871–1872

Wyndham, settling now into the role of light comedian in post-Civil War America, planned to start a company of his own in partnership with Louisa Moore. From a theatrical family, and sister of Irving's first sweetheart, Nelly (they were unrelated to Mary Moore), she had acted in a Robertson comedy with the Bancrofts, and she was already in America with her mother when her sister died so tragically in 1869. Opening in Washington, she and Wyndham did *Caste*, in which Wyndham probably played 'the long swell' Captain Hawtree—in New York he had been George D'Alroy. As Hawtree we imagine him making the most of

> Mr Eccles, don't you think that, with your talent for liquor, if you had an allowance of about two pounds a week, and went to Jersey, where spirits are cheap, that you could drink yourself to death in a year?

The pair appeared too in a comedy adapted from the French that had almost as many titles as revivals: *Un Fils de Famille, The Lancers, The Gentleman's Son, The Discarded Son.* Wyndham played a dashing lancer; Louisa Moore an heiress who, for the plot's sake, masquerades as the barmaid of a country inn. (It sounds like *She Stoops to Conquer.*) Some years later the Kendals put on a new version, called this time *The Queen's Shilling*, with John Hare as an irascible colonel (in the Victorian theatre baronets were bad, colonels were irascible).

Though there had been peace for five years, Wyndham's second visit to America was not without danger. In 1871, when he and his Comedy Company had played to small Chicago houses at the vast Crosby's Opera House the manager, sure that business would improve, asked them to stay for another week. Wyndham, booked to go to St Louis, was hesitating when he received a telegram from the St Louis manager. Because of floods, another company had been unable to reach them, and so wanted to play there during the following week. Could Wyndham maybe come for two weeks after that? The house at Crosby's on Saturday night was no better; but in its Sunday edition *The Chicago Times*—which had not mentioned the company before because it had had a row with the theatre—published two columns of praise. It seemed that on Saturday evening the manager had met the editor by chance and they resolved their differences; the Wyndham Comedy Company did stay on for another week, houses built up as a result of the publicity, and by the end the theatre was full, and Wyndham flooded with offers from every Chicago theatre. He chose the smallest, Dearborn Street, where he played for three months to capacity.

Wyndham arranged to go back in the autumn for another three months, now at his original Chicago home, Crosby's, which had been redecorated. The opening date was to be 9 October. On 8 October fire broke out and raged across Chicago for three days, destroying the city and driving 100,000 people out into the prairies. Only a fortnight after this the Wyndham company played in a large room in the German Club. A new theatre went up in an incredibly short time, but because by then he had been engaged for another town two hundred miles away Wyndham had to divide his company and commute between the two theatres, acting on alternate nights in each. For a while this worked, until people began to ask where the real Charles Wyndham was, and he had to merge the companies again and resume the tour. On reaching Savannah in the deep South they found that the local newspaper announced: Last nights of the Wyndham Comedy Company by general request. (The phrasing is ambiguous.) The request, it seemed, was for one particular play. Some States demanded strong drama; and in a town in Ohio the audience asked indignantly for its money back: 'Do you call *that* acting? You just sit about in chairs in the same kind of clothes as you go out in.'

It was during this eventful American tour that Wyndham met the dramatist Bronson Howard, and bought his play *Saratoga*, which had just ended a long run at Daly's Theatre in New York. Several years later Howard became Wyndham's brother-in-law; Mary Moore got her first engagement with Wyndham through Mrs Howard's intervention.

# II

While Charles was in America James Albery was being swiftly recognized as one of the best of the younger dramatists. Soon after *Two Roses* had begun its long life at the Vaudeville, the management added the one-act farce *Chiselling* (we met it before as *Alexander the Great*); David James, the third of the triumvirate, had a part in this. Albery could hardly keep up with requests for plays: a dramatist's dream too seldom realized.

Irving took a benefit on 26 March 1871, at the 291st performance of *Two Roses*. At curtain-fall he reappeared in evening dress (his own, presumably, by this time) and recited Hood's *The Dream of Eugene Aram* with so much effect that H. L. Bateman tried at once to engage him for the Lyceum. Bateman has gone into stage history for three things: first, his curious names—Hezekiah Linthicum; then his daughters, whom he put on the stage, not always successfully; and, most important, for having established Irving at the Lyceum. Born in Baltimore, he had, or assumed, a Southern manner which caused him to be nicknamed 'Colonel'. He took the Lyceum as a shop-window for his daughters; and at length they arranged for Irving to join him during the autumn when the tour of *Two Roses* had ended. Albery contributed to Irving's benefit his own rendering of a specially written sketch in which he was a secretary recalling a scientific society's inventions—one an air pump which exhausted the lecturer and created a vacuum only in the minds of the audience. And so forth: amusing enough, but it had in all senses to be Irving's night.

Albery, even so, was something of a celebrity himself. Mrs John Wood, steadily popular in farce, who had dismissed Wyndham in New York, was now managing the St James's. There she put on *Two Thorns* (once *Coquettes*), with Mrs Hermann Vezin as a former actress whose marriage to an M.P. has satisfied her social ambition, but whose drunken father is a tiresome incubus. Ellen Terry used to tell a story of Mrs Alfred Wigan (*née* Pincott), who desired above all things to move in high society. One evening a bleary-eyed old man in a shabby growler drew up at the stage door and asked for Leonora Pincott. On being told that there was no one of that name, he said, 'Well, I think she's married and changed her name, but she's 'ere right enough. Tell 'er I won't keep 'er a minute. I'm 'er bloody old father.'

We have to wonder whether Jane Vezin remembered the first version of *Two Thorns*—then called *The Starchbacks* and unfashionably in five acts—which an unknown James Albery had sent to her. At the St James's William Farren was the husband understandably disturbed by his wife's flirtation with 'Mr Jones' (a peer's son incognito). *Two Thorns* contains a certain amount of 'just sitting about in chairs'. Although it was performed, as *Coquettes*, in New York and Philadelphia, there is no record of it going farther west and rousing an Ohio audience to wrath. Much of the comedy depends upon class-consciousness, as is evident in this conversation between Minton, the husband, and Sir Kidd, his partner:

SERVANT  Lord de Lay is within, sir.
Sir KIDD  I'll be with him directly. Come along, Arthur.

[*Exit* Servant]

39

MINTON   No; I just want to change my dress, and then I want to see my
   wife; besides, I'm not in the humour to talk to that solemn old pedant.
Sir KIDD   An old pedant! Twenty thousand a-year and a peer of the realm,
   and call him a pedant! If you don't respect his estates, you might his title.
MINTON   So I do.
Sir KIDD   You?
MINTON   Yes. I respect his title because it once belonged to a great man. I
   respect it as Hamlet did the skull of Yorick, though the original tenant
   was gone, and it was filled with such vile earth and smelt so.

   [*Minton turns and goes to garden seat*]
   [*Re-enter* Servant]

Sir KIDD   [confused]   Smelt so—pooh, pooh! Lord de Lay don't smell.
SERVANT   Not that I'm aware of, sir; but he can't wait no longer.
Sir KIDD   Why! the man's mad!
SERVANT   Who, sir?
Sir KIDD   Hamlet—no, Yorick.
SERVANT   Sir?
Sir KIDD   [*recovering himself*]   What are you staring at?
   Bless my soul! I forgot his lordship. Get out of my way.

The new title, used to avoid confusion with *The School for Coquettes*,
and to link the play with the long-running *Two Roses*, had little to do with
the plot. To cover this Albery added a couplet to an epilogue spoken by
the heroine:

   The weak man's fears her stronger brother scorns,
   And gathers roses where he saw but thorns.

Tom Robertson had just died prematurely. He was only forty-three, and
Albery, so often compared with him, could now lead the day's dramatists.
Comparisons were not always in Robertson's favour. Years later, William
Archer would say of the two men that Robertson was apollinaris to
Albery's champagne. *Two Thorns* ran for seven weeks at the St James's
—not an entirely satisfactory engagement. The trouble was that after the
play had opened 'Ma' Wood found it so protracted that a burlesque in
which she appeared herself (she was immensely popular in this sort of
thing) came on too late in the evening. When she tried a compromise by
putting the burlesque on first, and the play at the end of the bill, this did
not work either, so on 21 April *Two Thorns* was withdrawn. Years
afterwards, when Pinero looked at Albery's plays with another
dramatist's eye, he discerned their abiding weakness: 'Apart from *Two
Roses* and *Apple Blossoms*, in his other original plays there was the
sparkling, promising first act; and then came the slackening of grip and
the signs of infirmity of purpose. Yet ... none failed to reveal a keen

insight into life, and often a vein of genuine poetry.' John Oxenford of *The Times* liked much in *Two Thorns*, especially in its first two acts, but he did feel obliged to add, 'We shall not dwell at length on the fourth act which is as remarkable for constructive laxity and vagueness of purpose as the second is remarkable for constructive skill.' Though Blanchard (*Daily Telegraph*] praised the crisply written dialogue, he held that 'the threads of the story should be more neatly fastened or more ingeniously knotted and intertwisted'. Albery 'should remember that much more will be expected from the author of *Two Roses*'.

Two nights after the St James's première Hermann Vezin revived *Doctor Davy* at the Court. Sadly, a friendship of almost ten years was about to end; but for the moment Albery and Vezin were on good terms. Since he had first worked on the play out of friendship, Albery waived his royalties.

# III

*Two Roses* ended at the Vaudeville on 12 May; and next night Irving, Montague, George Honey, W. H. Stephens and Amy Fawsitt went to Bristol to begin a tour there. Meanwhile the Vaudeville management staged an extravaganza by H. J. Byron, and on 27 May added Albery's two-act comedy *Tweedie's Rights* as a first piece. David James could hardly go wrong as an eccentric stonemason who fears in drunken delirium that he has deprived his nephew of a fair share of his inheritance. Yet more drink, and the man believes that a statue has come to life. (Albery, we recall, put a 'living' statue into his first play, *Alexander the Great*.) *Tweedie's Rights* depends for its laughs on occupational 'shop': thus the stonemason talks of worms, and graves, and epitaphs; a groom chatters in racecourse slang, and a comic widow accompanies her order for her husband's tombstone with a stream of memories of the dear departed. When Blanchard in *The Daily Telegraph* said, 'The jokes which will set one half of the audience in a roar, set the teeth of the other half on edge' we get the point. His doubt was obvious from his final paragraph: 'The audience was unusually enthusiastic and when Mr Albery was called before the curtain he could not have had a better reception if he had fulfilled his early promise.' Oxenford, in *The Times*, was better pleased: 'Notwithstanding the faults which a careful revision will remove, we are by no means sure that *Tweedie's Rights* is not an advance on *Two Roses*.'

At the Theatre Royal, Dublin, just then, Digby Grant (so Irving wrote to his wife) was 'sweeping every part in the piece before it'. One evening a red-haired youth of sixteen, seeing the actor for the first time, compared him unfavourably with his idol, Barry Sullivan, a comparison with uncommonly little basis. Bernard Shaw would write of this much later: 'It so happened that I saw[Irving] first as Digby Grant in *Two Roses*, a play which seemed new and promising in a dramatically benighted age which produced no considerable playwrights except Robertson.' Robertson yet again.

Albery would have a great year in 1871. Early that spring he had running at the same time two full-length original comedies, a farce of which he was part-author, and an adaptation. Not surprisingly, actor-managers clamoured for plays. He seems to have promised one to E. A. Sothern; certainly he failed to deliver it. Sothern wrote

> All right. The end of Feby be it. But as you said you cd. "write better when pressed" I thought I'd just press you! If I have the piece say by the 20 or 21 Feby it would take a week copyg MS. and parts and then I cd play it in one or 2 small towns—before coming to London with it. What are you doing this afternoon? Will you do an early 5.30 dinner?

Edgar Pemberton, biographer, was at Sothern's house in Kensington one day when Albery was there (it might have been at that 5.30 dinner). As they came away Albery assured Pemberton that he was brimming over with ideas and eager to be at his desk; 'there was no difficulty in the world'. That sounded suspiciously like bravado, and Pemberton's later note was reasonable: 'Somehow that play was never written, and if written never produced with the same success.' In fact Sothern never appeared in an Albery play, though *Married* may have been written for him.

During the *Two Roses* tour Harry Montague, who had thought of leaving the Vaudeville to set up on his own, wrote from Newcastle to ask if Albery could write a comedy, or comedy drama, for him in

> six weeks from the present time. . . .
> If "Yes" I will give you my notion of a *cast*. It wd. be *small* but very *strong*. As to my giving up my share at the V.T. I do not mind sacrificing the immediate present, which with yr new comedy I feel sure will be good, because I have to look to and *must* look to the future, and my opinion is that I shall be doing myself more good by disassociating myself from my partners—straightforward and honest as they are—than by remaining as at present. It will be an experiment, I know, but I venture to think it will be a successful one—if—particularly if—I have yr co-operation. Write me.
>
> Fraternally and sincerely yours.

It was all very well for Albery to say he could 'write better when pressed', but this, surely, was asking too much? And in six weeks at that! Montague did leave the triumvirate, took the Globe Theatre at the east end of the Strand, and did Albery's *Forgiven*. For the moment, though, Albery was attached to the Vaudeville; and Montague, as well as Thorne and James, signed a contract for *Tweedie's Rights* (author's fee £2 a performance). This was merely a stop-gap because *Apple Blossoms* was not yet ready;

*Tweedie* ran until 19 August 1871, and *Apple Blossoms*, which opened on 9 September, ran until 5 January 1872.

The setting is a Cornish inn. Albery laid on what he assumed to be the local dialect so thickly that it curdled. 'Cornish' can be disastrous in the theatre, and here the very first lines are on the splinter-edge of parody:

[*Enter the Crier who rings his bell*]

KITTIE    Watching for un again, Jennie?

JENNIE    How you steal on one! un Kittie.

CRIER     To Mark Tremmen, up to Martin's Bottom—fishmonger: John dorry, mackerel, bream, sooles, dried herrins. [*rings bell—two distinct strokes*] Tonight, up to the Town Hall:—The Gurt Baggs en es wonderful emper-so-nations. [*rings bell as before*] Larst, [*puts on glasses, and reads from paper*) "Larst, a full grawd ignisfat—oous, with double-action hingun, turned ventricles, and spotted diaphragm, whoever will return the same to the Gurt Baggs will receive two hundred pawnd reward."

          [*Crier takes off glasses and exits in a businesslike manner, and is heard faintly afterwards in the distance*].

JENNIE    Then he'll be here soon.

KITTIE    He! *who*, Jennie?

JENNIE    Who? Why! the "gurt" Baggs.

KITTIE    Do ee expect him to come by saa, Jennie?

JENNIE    Why! of course; you can't drive a yacht up the street.

KITTIE    But does Mr Baggs come in a yacht?

JENNIE    No; why! of course Mr Baggs comes in—Oh! what a tease you are! un Kittie.

KITTIE    Tease! Jennie. Ef I had my hand on the pump, but held my jug to the beer-tap, should I call anyone a tease who said it worn't water I wanted to draw?

JENNIE    What do you mean, un Kittie?

KITTIE    Why! you're thinking of Mr Tom, Jennie. There's a little boat he tows behind es yacht is called Jennie; and it's well named; for wherever he goes Jennie follows un.

The hero, who is called not too plausibly Tom Penryn, quarrels with his choleric father over a love affair with the landlord's niece; but the old man (whom she has nursed through a long illness) wants to adopt her. Situations are improbable; the 'gurt' Baggs, travelling phrenologist advertised by the Town Crier, stops the show in the wrong way at every appearance. He is one of those characters better off-stage than on. When the landlord goes to London he meets Baggs, and this is more genuine fun, though the Cornish remains highly dubious:

JENNIE    What did you see in London, Bob?

BOB       Well! I don't know where to begin. I saw sich a sight o' things. But

43

the first thing I notices was that everybody sticks them gashly labels, like Mr Baggs do do awnly they are much beggerer, and they're all ovver the walls and pailins, and among um I see waun, a gurt picture of Mr Baggs, and under et, et said, "Where are you goin?" Then et said "I'm goin to see the gurt Baggs at the Gipsy Hall, Pickledilly."

KITTIE    Why! isn't he dead?

BOB    Naw; he warn't this morning.

JENNIE    Ah! his tricks again.

KITTIE    Did you see un, then?

BOB    Iss, I did; and I axed un to tell me a good inn to stop at, and he said Furnival's Inn was the cheapest and best, and axed me to meet un for a game of cricket in Lincoln's Inn Fields in the morning. But it was all es gammuts, agen; the Inn wasn't a inn, and the fields was a gurt square.

KITTIE    Ah! you ought to have taken me with you.

BOB    So I ought. But a worse very kind, and a said he knew the man that kipt the British Museum and the Natural Gallery, and he'd get me in for nawthin!

TEMPLE    [the lawyer]    Baggs took you in nicely.

BOB    Aw! That ee did,—very nicely; for we went to the Museum, and a jist nodded to the man, and a let us in without payin' nawthin', and we saw everything theere es all ovver the world. Then we went to the Natural Gallery.

TEMPLE    [laughing]    And did he just nod his head again?

JENNIE    And you had to pay nawthin'?

BOB    No, nawthin'; and they took our stecks. A told me that was 'cos the Prince of Wales had lost es steck, and they were lookin' to everyone's to find et. And there I saw a lot of pictures that semmin' to me waunted paintin' up a bit, and waun or two I dedn't like at all.

TEMPLE    Which were they?

BOB    Well! one wors the Judgment of Paris, and— [looks at the women and stops]

TEMPLE    [laughing]    Well?

BOB    Well! it wasn't proper; there was no saa, norra any bathing machines, and they ought to be dressed a bit; and I ses, ef that es their judgment I doan't thenk much of it.

JENNIE    It's a treat to hear you again.

BOB    And then a said he'd take me to a theatre to see a lady and lions; and a ded, and I see the lady; and aw! my dear [to Jennie], she was a sight.

KITTIE    What had she got on?

BOB    Aw! it wasn't on. [Temple laughs] It's true, Mr Temple, her dress was all dragglin' on the ground, and she'd gote nawthin' on her poor shoulder; [to Temple], and I thoft, do you know, that praps she'd been to Paris and gote some of their judgment.

KITTIE    Ded ee see the lions, Bob?

BOB    Naw. I ses to Mr Baggs, "Where's the lions?" and a ses ef ee doan't caall for un they woan't come; so I called out for un, and what do you think Mr Baggs ded?

KITTIE I don't know.

BOB Why, a pretended a dedn't knaw me, and says "Turn un out"; and a gashly policeman came and took me away, and Mr Baggs—he helped un, and when we gote outside I thoft he'd a ben ill with loffin, and he took me and gave me a pint of beer.

On the Vaudeville first night an exceptionally warm house called for the author after each act. *Two Roses* was still so recent a triumph that expectation (as an older dramatist had put it) sat in the air. The night's applause was hardly sustained next day. Notices were mixed, though *The Times* said that Albery never wrote better dialogue. Baggs, all agreed, was a mistake: 'The sooner he is banished to the music-hall the better' (*Daily Telegraph*). *Apple Blossoms* lacked above all else a Digby Grant (and an Irving), but it did run for a hundred nights.

William Archer, just down from the university and living in Edinburgh, saw a touring company in four Albery comedies. Looking back on this experience of playgoing in 'a little provincial theatre, very smoky and dirty and full of the smell of stale gas', he remembered with affection 'the delicate idyll' *Apple Blossoms*, though (he had to admit) 'it tells a simple story so slight that it almost falls to pieces on analysis'. Archer transferred the setting to Devon, a fault for which no Cornishman would forgive him, but after all he was a Scot: he could not know that the dialect on paper—perhaps the company wisely diluted it—was as agonizing as Shaw's Cockney in *Captain Brassbound's Conversion*, where Felix Drinkwater talks like this:

Their mawnds kennot rawse to Christiennity lawk hahrs ken, gavner; thets ah it is. Weoll, ez haw was sayin, if a hescort is wornted, there's maw friend and commawnder Kepn Brarsbahnd of the schooner Thenksgivin, an is crew . . .

# IV

No sooner was *Apple Blossoms* launched than the next Albery loomed. Bateman wrote from the Lyceum on 27 September

Go ahead—let me have your scene plot at once—but bring it with you—and explain as to length of time, etc. I wish to do it with *Fanchette*. We can commence 15 minutes earlier—so that the comedy could have an hour and a quarter to twenty minutes, but all this we can talk over when we meet.

Go ahead! Life for Albery now was a continuous going-ahead. No wonder inspiration weakened in his last acts. But the most significant sentence in

Bateman's letter speaks of a meeting at the Junior Garrick Club. Albery was distinctly clubbable; more 'sitting about in chairs' (but not on the stage), less concentration. As Pinero summed him up:

> His early success was his undoing; self-indulgence led to the gradual loss of such will-power as he possessed and the attractions of Bohemia did the rest.

For the moment, all was more or less well; but the shooting-star would come gradually to earth.

The scene plot Bateman needed was a *Pickwick Papers* version known first as *Pickwick*, later as *Jingle*. One of a good many stage versions, it had to be selective—unavoidable in the circumstances, but worrying to many Dickensians. 'Very bad indeed', Blanchard recorded in his diary; 'Mr Albery takes one of the most sacred works of fiction we possess . . . and he sets about mangling it.' Dickens, almost beatified then, had died only just over a year before *Pickwick* opened (on 23 October) at the Lyceum. Albery was treading on holy ground when he 'tore the book to ribands'.

For one thing, he took only the first part, beginning this with Dingley Dell and Jingle's elopement with Aunt Rachel. He ended with Pickwick's arrest and the accompanying revelation that Jingle has designs on the daughter of Mr Nupkins, the Ipswich magistrate. No room for Mrs Bardell, the trial, the cricket match, or the Eatanswill election. Albery even invented one episode in which Jingle hands Pickwick's watch to the waiter at the Great White Horse at Ipswich, and allows Pickwick to overhear an affecting conversation:

WAITER    Did you ring, sir?

JINGLE    Yes, I rang. [Pickwick *turns and starts*] Someone left a valuable watch; don't know who may come in and take it,—great temptation,—people should be more thoughtful;—careless—very.

> [*Exit* Waiter *with watch*]

PICKWICK    [*aside*]    Well! at least, he's honest.

JINGLE    [*to* Trotter]    And now, Job, have you seen her? [Trotter *looks in wonder*] You have! I see by your expression—you have. How is she, Job?

TROTTER    [*doubtfully*]    Better.

JINGLE    My poor mother! [*Pickwick, who is going, stops*] She little thought when she dandled me on her knee—a bright little child—misfortunes and a damned, wicked world would make a rascal of me—scoundrel—very.

TROTTER    [*going*]    Don't give way.

JINGLE    Can't help; better feeling—[*slaps heart*]—here—boyish—but can't help it—foolish—very. [*wipes his eyes*]

TROTTER    Don't give way. [*with an ugly grin*]

46

JINGLE   But has she all she wants? Hardly a penny left—but I do what I can.

TROTTER   [*enjoying it*]   No, she's very poor.

JINGLE   Not destitute—say she's not destitute!

TROTTER   Nearly. Sickness has prevented her working at her needle. [*aside*] The old boy's beginning to feel it.

JINGLE   Oh! Job, that ever she should work at her needle—she who was born a lady! [*weeps*; Pickwick *takes out handkerchief and wipes his eyes*]

TROTTER   [*going*]   He's touched. She owes—

JINGLE   [*aside*]   Twenty-five—

TROTTER   Twenty-five pounds; and, unless it is paid, they will sell up her little home.

JINGLE   Oh! Job, this is a fearful blow. [*aside*] What's he doing?

  [*Pickwick takes out pocket-book, counts out five five-pound notes, writes "From a Friend," on a slip of paper, and lays it on the table near Jingle.*]

As this shows, Jingle was clearly the leading man. Irving, who stole the notices as usual, kept the scene in every later version.

At the Lyceum just previously, *Fanchette*, which Mrs Bateman had adapted from the French of George Sand, had failed partly because Irving, miscast as the peasant lover, was still identified too closely with Digby Grant. (True, there were touches of Grant in his Jingle, but this was more reasonable.) Irving suggested keeping *Pickwick* on with *The Bells*, a melodrama he had longed to do ever since its adapter, Leopold Lewis, had shown him the English text. The 'Colonel' had nothing else ready; houses were thin, money scarce, but still he hesitated. Though he had admired Irving in *Eugene Aram*, he thought of him as a comedian, not a haunted Alsatian burgomaster. In the end Bateman had no choice. On Saturday 25 November, when *The Bells* reached the Lyceum programme the obligatory farce was called *My Turn Next*, for Irving a prophetic title. His turn was coming, and he took it. For a quarter of an hour all that happened on the stage prepared the way. The assembled company prattled with the innkeeper's wife; the storm outside reminded villagers of the night, fifteen years before, when the Polish Jew was murdered. A crash of broken crockery as the wind blew open a kitchen window gave Irving his cue; the Burgomaster entered—or, rather, made his entrance—on the crash. 'It is I!' he shouted, and began to unbutton his gaiters. When he spoke of what he had seen at a fair a neighbour took up the story. Could not a mesmerist send a man to sleep and make him reveal what was on his conscience? At the word 'conscience' Mathias paused. In a celebrated passage (from *Henry Irving*, 1930) Gordon Craig recalled the moment:

  Irving was buckling his second shoe, seated and leaning over it with his two long hands stretched down over the buckles. We suddenly saw these fingers stop their work; the crown of the head suddenly seemed to glitter and become frozen—and then, at the pace of the slowest and most terrified snail, the two hands, still motionless and dead, were seen to be coming up the side of the leg ... the whole torso of the man, also seeming frozen, was gradually and by an almost imperceptible movement seen to be drawing up and back, as it would straighten a little, and to lean a little against the back of the chair on which he was seated.

'Exactly!' Mathias whispered. The house was poor, but it was held as few audiences had been in the London theatre of that day. When the last curtain fell it was shocked first into silence and then into wild applause. Irving's turn had come—at the age of thirty-three. For Albery, another man of thirty-three, the triumph was propitious. After the interval Irving's Jingle in *Pickwick* brought him, tragedian-turned-comedian, such cheering—on a historic night—as he had never known. The Bateman family fortunes were saved; for the actor a domestic drama was about to flare. As he and his wife Florence drove home, she was utterly unable to understand what the night had meant. 'Are you going to make a fool of yourself like this all your life?' she exclaimed. Irving said nothing. Merely telling the driver to stop, he alighted, and he neither saw her nor spoke to her again.

For Albery it could hardly have been a more exciting year. Two of his plays ran on into 1872, and he had commissions for the Vaudeville and for Montague at the Globe. The same year brought the theatre close to Mary Moore and her family. That Christmas Day the Royal Victoria Hall at the corner of the New Cut and Waterloo Road was reopened as, temporarily, the New Victoria Palace, reconstructed and refurbished ('noble, lofty, and well-ventilated'). Mary's father, Charles Moore, had promoted this, and she became one of a Surreyside audience that knew exactly what it wanted, and got it:

> ... those wicked lords.
> Their voices and their calves.
> The things they did upon those boards
> And never did by halves!

In the plays Mary saw as a little girl at the Vic people did not just sit about in chairs; these were thunderous melodramas—*The Bleeding Nun* and *The Hidden Hand*—and they sent her home to the most lurid dreaming. It was all good experience for an actress-to-be. The New Victoria was her father's first theatrical adventure. He had been a political agent; but once he had reached Waterloo Road he could hardly complain if his children became stage-struck – notably Mary (born in London, 1862), though as far as we know, she never aspired to the ecstasies of the bleeding nun.

# CHAPTER SIX
# 'A Jolly Lot of Talent'
# 1872–1873

Albery's share in Irving's extraordinary success continued. *Jingle*, shortened to fit its strange partnership with *The Bells*, ran until 25 March 1872, though in January Charles Warner replaced Irving (if at that time anyone could). Meanwhile handsome Harry Montague had opened in Albery's *Forgiven* out at the Globe. A romantic comedy, its kind hearts more than coronets, the plot is overladen with love letters that get into the wrong hands: the hero is an artist—the currently fashionable hint of Bohemia—who falls in love with Lady Maud for her title, and the gardener's daughter Rose for her sweetness. Like Tom Penryn, he has a Cornish town, Redruth, for a surname; the opening dialogue sounds like a continuation of *Apple Blossoms*, so much so that the *Daily Telegraph* placed *Forgiven* in Cornwall, though the setting is more likely to be Devon: Redruth goes sketching 'close by, at Ilfracombe'. The gardener Cudlipp's dialect is certainly 'thickee'.

CUDLIPP  Yes, 'tes a surprising forward year, considering it's only the middle of June. There's a sprig of lovage I gathered aneest thickee wall that's just ready to blue, and orver in Arish's garden I saw some rosemary in flower.

COUNTRYMAN  Well! old Hyssop was complaining.

CUDLIPP  Oh! when every waun else have a be happy, he's a carking; don't matter what he's got in his own crock, he thinks his neighbour's got better; some men, if you send 'em a sack o' sov'rins u'd grumble ef you didn't pay the carriage of it; he thinks his taters ought to dig theirselves up and put theirselves into baskets; I think things are very vorward.

The plot rests on Lady Maud's unlikely change of heart; to atone for breaking the marriage between Redruth and Rose she disguises herself as her own sister and educates Rose to become a suitable wife for the artist. There is a regrettably arch woman novelist:

MRS CREMER    Look what they say in the *Northern Times* and the *County Mail*. Today I called on Mrs Branscomb, and there was Mr Feeder, who's considered such an excellent critic. I tried not to be noticed, but he found me out, and said, loud enough for everyone to hear, "Mrs Cremer, there is only one thing equals your genius, and that is your modesty." Of course, everyone hearing my name turned round, "Oh! is that Mrs Cremer, the authoress of that beautiful book?" You may guess how poor, modest me felt.

There are signs of hurried writing in the repetition of catchphrases: the swell's 'don't you know,' and the Member of Parliament's insistence that, when he was introduced as Mr Chatham Pole, M.P. should be added. No wonder *The Times* felt that 'by some fatal law the development had to spread itself over four acts and those acts had to be filled up with personages who retarded instead of assisting the process'. Much of the comedy, Town versus Country, echoes Touchstone's conversation with Corin:

CUDLIPP    I'm a gardener to Nickletavy. It's a dirty business, but Adam was somewhat in thicka way; 'stilling gin is much more respectable, but vlowers and such like don't so often kill people as t'other do.

He keeps medicinal herbs in his hat—another catchphrase of a sort:

CUDLIPP    Got a cold, sir? [*takes off hat*] There's a bit of wood betony. You powder that and mix it with honey; it'll cure you. If you've any vear of drepsy, a vine thing; and thickee's a root of briony. *That*'ll draw spots out of your vace.

One can only sympathize with the recipient who just does not want to carry weeds about. All the same, as the *Telegraph* recorded after the first night, the gardener 'alone fairly weathered the storm ... he was frequently, warmly, and deservedly cheered'. When a new farce entered the bill at the Globe the *Telegraph* was even less enthusiastic. Montague—unwisely, perhaps—appealed to the public to ignore the notices, and to this the critic objected strongly:

If ever there was a manager who appealed directly to the better and more intellectual class of playgoers, that manager was Mr Montague. Nettled, however, at the fact that *Forgiven* did not, in the opinion of the warmest enthusiasts for genuine stage-work, turn out to be an artistic comedy, or acceptable to the class of audience the Globe Theatre should attract, the manager appeals for protection to the public, and evidently resents the criticism to which the play has given rise.

Montague claimed in reply that all he had done was to tell the public that

> notwithstanding, but in consequence of, the adverse opinion of some of the professional critics, the play had drawn capital houses, and had been received by the paying public with delight.

It was Albery's play that most struck William Archer when he saw it among several done by a touring company. The scenery was meagre and the acting generally mediocre. Writing some years later, he remembered that the concluding scene of one act—

> I think the third—seemed to me the most brilliant and poetic piece of dialogue I had heard in modern comedy. I state my impression of the moment for what it is worth, as I have not since had an opportunity of testing its correctness. The play is still in manuscript, and I have never again seen it on the stage. My recollection, however, has been confirmed on several occasions when I have heard *Forgiven* spoken of as being, with all its faults, the best of Mr Albery's original comedies. This phrase, "with all its faults" is one which must unfortunately be applied to most of Mr Albery's efforts. Few writers are more faulty, but none redeem their faults by such striking beauties. Mr Albery has narrowly missed being *facile princeps* among modern English playwrights. He has escaped that distinction by lack of constructive power, lack of taste, lack of earnestness. As it is, he stands unrivalled in the sphere of dialogue. His fanciful wit and witty fancy might under better direction and more favourable circumstances have contributed works of genuine merit not only to the stage, but to dramatic literature.

# II

For most people the chief fault (in both *Forgiven* and other plays close to it in time) was the absence of anyone as theatrically strong as Digby Grant, Esq. 'With all its faults', *Forgiven* ran for eleven weeks. It also seriously breached Albery's close friendship with Hermann Vezin. At some time during those eleven weeks Vezin must have sat in the Globe Theatre, watching the performance with rising horror as he spotted the resemblances to *Reinhard and Leonora*. This was the play he had translated from the German, and as far back as 1863 had asked Albery to get 'into shipshape'. Some years later Albery had wanted to make a free adaptation, with the main idea of *Reinhard and Leonora* as its basis, but otherwise differing so much that Vezin might still make use of the original piece. He proposed to allow Vezin half of what he made from the play, up to £100. This was in 1870, and Albery called his version— dogmatically, we might think—*The Right One*. Reasonably, two years later, Vezin must have found it hard to contain his anger as he listened to *Forgiven*. Certainly he went home and wrote the first of a long series of letters: .

"Reinhard" (Redruth) an artist finds that a country girl "Korle" (Rose) loves him and marries her. Reinhard (Redruth) comes to town and meets with a swell love of olden times, the Countess Ida (Lady Maud). There is a scene between the women. Reinhard (Redruth) is ashamed of his wife and is lured into swell society again, consequent domestic misery, split up and reconciliation. If you meant what you wrote to me *Forgiven* is a drama out of the profits of which you meant to pay me a share. If you did not mean what you wrote, of course there's an end of the matter.

Worse still, *Forgiven* was a title Vezin had himself considered. Now he suggested asking 'one or more gentlemen whom we both respect and believe in' to arbitrate. Albery refused. Letters whirled back and forth. Albery insisted that his play was *'not the piece'* Vezin spoke about. Whereupon Vezin asked pointedly if *Forgiven* would ever have been written if Albery had not known *Reinhard and Leonora*; and who, in the circumstances, would accept another version? Albery then sent a list of eleven points that 'it might be well to consider', the last being the key:

Whether *R. and L.* is damaged in the least. (It is not; scene by scene it is totally different).

When Albery returned from an Egyptian holiday the argument was still acrid. Friends of Vezin who had read his script, and seen the play, entirely agreed with him. Albery insisted that Vezin had not the slightest right to *R. and L.* His offer of half the proceeds, up to £100, had been 'an act of generosity that applied to a piece then hurriedly produced'. In the same letter, written from Putney on 22 July 1872, he said that he would probably call on Vezin—'not about *R. and L.* but about a little help I want from you.' This roused Vezin to his sharpest retort, a letter (22 July 1872) from a man who probably feared his own temper:

Dear Albery,
Your letter of today's date just to hand. I hope you will receive this letter in time to prevent you calling here, as I should not like to see you. Our friendship is at an end.

Yours truly,
HERMANN VEZIN

Next day Albery replied gently to this melodramatic gesture:

Dear Vezin,
I received your letter with deep sorrow. You say our friendship ends. Yours may; mine will bear more yet.

For all his 'deep sorrow', he could not behave like Vezin, whose sense of injustice and readiness for argument made him continue in lucid, well-constructed letters. *Reinhard and Leonora* was not the only play in dispute. When Albery asked for an uncut version of *Doctor Davy* which he proposed to enter at Stationers' Hall, and to make over to Vezin for ten or twenty years, Vezin replied indignantly that he thought *Doctor Davy* was his anyway. This extended the quarrel. Vezin was quick to observe that when Albery wrote a portion of *Doctor Davy* he was

> an utterly unknown man. To have your name attached to a successful piece was of the highest importance to you. I know of clever authors who have waited years for an opportunity. You yourself, from the time when I read your first comedy of *The Starchbacks*, had to wait eight years before the production of *Two Roses*, and this, altho' during those years I left no stone unturned to bring you into notice. Your comedy was read, at my request, by some of the most eminent authors, critics, actors, and managers in London, and if your opportunity at last presented itself by accident and not thro' my immediate means, that does not detract from the disinterested trouble I took to achieve such a result. The most important service I rendered you was the production of *Doctor Davy* with your name as the author, and if I gained some advantage by acting Garrick (the strongest point in which, the story of the child, being word for word my translation), you must remember that you gained a much greater advantage, since it lifted you from obscurity into the light.

Finally, when Vezin was about to appear in August at the Court Theatre he confessed to being heartily sick of the whole business and begged Albery not to write again. Anyone interested, he said, could read the complete correspondence, which he had had printed, and he enclosed two copies.

At this distance who can say whether Vezin's accusations were just? Neither man could move the other. The letters' chief value today is not to prove who was right, but to show something of the character of each man in a controversy very much of its period. Albery might not have been an intellectual match for Vezin; but he did have a sense of humour (very proper in a writer of comedies) that his adversary could not share. When he showed part of the correspondence to two of his friends they laughed—and we know how he would have enjoyed that. Vezin would have become even more affronted. He might indeed have found material for another letter.

# III

After *Forgiven* had closed Montague took it, with *Two Roses*, on tour. Carlotta Addison, who played the gardener's daughter in town, wrote to her Dear Author to tell him that on the previous Saturday in Edinburgh they had acted *Forgiven* to 'a wonderfully intelligent audience'. They were a *big hit*. Edinburgh, she said, also liked *Two Roses*, which they had done eight times, but she was writing now in Newcastle, where the pieces were far beyond the audience's intellect. Montague wrote cheerfully from Dublin during September to say that, though business was good,

I'm knocked on the head by Barry Sullivan, the greatest favourite ever known in Ireland, and *an Irishman*. If you knew what that meant you wd. say our bus. was immense.

Will send you the papers—*Two Roses* tomorrow night. Will wire you how it goes.

Goodbye, old boy

(Tolerantly, the Irish forgave Sullivan for having been born in Birmingham.)

Albery was regarded now as a leading dramatist. It was natural, then, that W. S. Gilbert, already powerful in the theatre and as explosive as talented, should ask him to join others in agreeing on a minimum rehearsal period. When Gilbert's *On Guard* failed he complained acidly that it had been 'pitchforked on to the stage in ten rehearsals'. Miss Litton, the Court Theatre manager, began to sue him for libel, an action later dropped. 'If you can assist me', Gilbert now wrote to Albery, 'you will be doing me a great favour.' Within less than a year Gilbert was just as ready to pick a quarrel with Albery, and, typically, to apologize on the same day when he saw that he had been wrong. He thought, when his *Wicked World* opened at the Haymarket, that Albery had attacked it in the *Figaro* after getting an advance copy of the book

on the plea of sympathy with a fellow-craftsman in the same field of literature . . . I can't believe . . . you could possibly have applied it to the purpose of bringing its author into public contempt. I only wait your denial to silence the malicious propagators of a report which is likely to do you so much injury.

That same evening, having read the offending article more carefully, Gilbert decided that it could never have been Albery's. So, in a second letter, as urgent as the first, he told Albery that no denial was needed 'as the thing speaks for itself. It is weak, foolish and vulgar—epithets which your work never has and never can deserve. Please accept my apology in the spirit in which it is offered.'

Albery did. Already he had worked briefly with Arthur Sullivan, who would have his own problems with Gilbert. The composer had written music for 'Hide aching pride with gladness', a lyric that Montague had sung, no doubt affectingly, in *Forgiven*. Moreover, Albery was going also to work with Frederic Clay, a Bohemian after his own heart, who had brought Gilbert and Sullivan together. Clay was gregarious, prolific and carefree. At least three of his songs ought to have made his fortune; instead, he sold them for £5 each. They were 'The Sands of Dee' (Mary calling the cattle home), 'She Wandered Down the Mountain-side', and the apparently eternal 'I'll Sing Thee Songs of Araby'. When he agreed to compose incidental music for Albery's 'romantic legend' *Oriana* he had already written the score for three of Gilbert's operettas.

*Oriana*, which Montague presented at the Globe on 7 March 1873,

Charles Wyndham's début at the Criterion on Boxing Night, 1875. He appeared in the three items of the bill; his energy and comic talent continued to fill the theatre for 25 years

Suffering from the reproaches of a formidable mother-in-law, a timid husband is forced to tell a white lie which his prim wife cannot forgive: *Truth!* by Bronson Howard. A typical Criterion programme of the 1870s

'I only want to play Juliet sometimes.' Mary Moore as Lady Jessica Nepean in *The Liars* (Criterion, 1897)

takes place 'near the Happy Isles in days gone by'. A neglected Queen seeks a magic ring which will restore the King's love; the ring passes through several hands, including the King's own (it makes him, like Narcissus, fall in love with himself) before it reaches the Queen. At last they are reconciled; and a crippled fairy whose magic powers have brought this about bids

> Spirits still; I fear some harm;
> Send, oh send a potent charm,
> That whate'er befal the King,
> She may never lose the ring.

Spirits promptly reward the good fairy with wings; she can cast away her crutch. On the first night—and ought this to surprise us?—the audience grew restive. 'The later portion', E. L. Blanchard recorded grandiloquently in the *Telegraph*, 'was not heard without some discordant signs of impatience.' Not unexpectedly critics reported an uncommon variety of sources: Gilbert, *A Midsummer Night's Dream*, an old German legend, *Le Roi Carotte*, *The Tempest*; even, in the utterances of Oxeye, the demagogue who leads a revolution, the doctrines of Jack Cade. This political satire disturbed the house. When at the end Montague announced *Oriana* 'for nightly repetition' several 'dissentient voices were audible; but the appearance of Mr James Albery and Mr Frederic Clay together before the footlights provided, nevertheless, the signal for a greeting of friendly plaudits.' (*Telegraph*).

*The Times*, impressed by 'a work unique of its kind', benevolently concluded:

> Its affinity with the two fairy plays of Shakespeare is clearly the result, not of deliberate copying, but of an inspiration derived from the love of the old poet and his poetry.

Even so, 'romantic legend' and inspiration lasted only three weeks. Frederic Clay, who thought of it hyperbolically as one of the 'most beautiful and poetic creations of the English language,' believed it needed a larger theatre and cast ('great masses of people on the stage, richly costumed'). Had it run three years instead of three weeks he would not have thought one whit better of it. He assured Albery, 'You have such a jolly lot of talent (I would call it genius if I were writing to any one else but yourself!) that you are sure to take a series of revenges on the public for their apathy in the matter of *Oriana*.' The two men certainly got on; Clay looked forward to working with Albery again, but they never did. Probably they met at the Savage Club—it would have been a likely and congenial place.

This was Albery's 'fairy' year; in September his spectacular extrava-

ganza *The Will of Wise King Kino* arrived at the Princess's. By then the
vogue for burlesque had faded; 'extravaganza' refined the *genre*. The
Kino score was a medley of such composers as Offenbach and Gounod.
Ballets intervened. The satire, though obvious, was not crude. In the
Kingdom of Clencantia, people, it seemed, had numbers instead of
surnames; the lower the number the higher the status:

> The hundreds with the millions will not mix
> And in our sphere, if one is forty-six
> His great desire is to be forty-five.

The State Clock, perpetually wrong, symbolized Clencantian misrule.
Something was undeniably rotten in a country where everyone must be
judged by outward appearances:

> Veneer! Veneer! There's not a creature
> Is wholly as he would appear!
> The smiling kindness on each feature
> Is only very thin veneer.

(Gilbert would say much the same thing in Bunthorne's recitative during
the first act of *Patience* (1881): This air severe/Is but a mere/Veneer!)
  Done in the same bill as Byron's sepulchral *Manfred*—possibly a few of
the Princess's public had expected something by H. J. Byron—the fairy
extravaganza, though generously received on the first night, died after five
weeks, and was never exhumed.

# IV

Albery and Wyndham had not worked together in the theatre. Wyndham
was now safe as a light comedian; and he had learnt a good deal from the
adventure of touring the United States in a mixed repertory. His
Wyndham Comedy Company used several of Robertson's comedies;
some other pieces, long forgotten; and one at least that has endured:
*Saratoga*, which the Royal Shakespeare Company revived in London at
Christmas 1978. On returning home, Wyndham went to an old haunt, the
St James's, in a Sardou adaptation; then he toured for a time in Wilkie
Collins's *Man and Wife*, in which just previously the Bancrofts had played
minor parts at the Prince of Wales's in Tottenham Street. Only minor
parts, maybe, because they were preoccupied with a theatrical innovation,
electric lighting for the storm. Presently, when the play was travelling,
Wyndham as the hero, and Ada Dyas opposite him, acted, said Squire
Bancroft, politely if not originally, 'with great *éclat*'.
  Back at the Royalty, under Henrietta Hodson, Wyndham played in John

Tobin's verse-drama *The Honey Moon* (1805), as Rolando, a sailor-misogynist who marries his love and excuses himself on the perplexing ground that she is not a woman but an angel. The plot drew on *The Taming of the Shrew*, *Philaster* and *Rule a Wife and Have a Wife*, with a touch of Grimm's *King Grizzlebeard* as well. Interestingly, Wyndham would revive this, with Ellen Terry as the heroine, for one of his Crystal Palace matinées, still in the future. He had begun to store plays for later use: first, *Saratoga* (which one day he would do as *Brighton*), and now Tobin's curiosity. Next, at the Royalty, he had a part in *The Realm of Joy* by F. Latour Tomline (alias W. S. Gilbert), who inserted oblique references to the Examiner of Plays' objection to his previous *The Happy Land*.

We do not know exactly where Wyndham and Albery first met. They must have spoken—if not for the first time—at the year's end when Albery's *Married* came on at the Royalty, opened to a hissing barrage on 1 December, and came off before Christmas. More farcical than anything he had tried, it was about two bored girls who for a joke get married to each other. One has impersonated her own brother; he is at once reported drowned, and the 'bride' has to assume widow's weeds. Needless to say, the brother lives; Wyndham, according to Blanchard, gave 'a bright, genial and merry performance', which probably helped.

Almost simultaneously, Albery's five-act comedy *Fortune* opened with a flourish Augustin Daly's second Fifth Avenue Theatre in New York (the first was burnt down in 1873). Preceded by an address in verse by Oliver Wendell Holmes, *Fortune* failed utterly; one reason was its excessive length supplemented by the first-night extras (special music; the address). The *New York Times* complained:

> We wish we were able to say that the entertainment was worthy the theatre and the spectators. We are forced to admit that it was not. At least one half the assemblage quitted the place after midnight—about an hour before the performance ended—without the faintest idea of the purpose of Mr Albery's play.

The simple enough plot does not call for five long acts. Like Digby Grant (but he is not so amusing), a Major Hawley is short of money. When his young housekeeper inherits a fortune he tries to prevent her marriage to his son by hinting that she has been his own mistress. The play came off after four nights; a few performances were slipped into the programme later in the season. It was never produced in England, although Albery may have written the part of Lady Keating, shrewd and sarcastic, with Mrs John Wood in mind, and John Hare told him that he thought, with some alterations, it might succeed.

> I was sorry to hear that it has not been successful in America; that I am not surprised at; in the first place the piece is too delicate, I should think,

57

for them, and I presume it was "pitchforked' onto the stage. Such a play requires every nicety in handling. All I can say is that had I a theatre I should produce it tomorrow.

Nothing much lasted at the Royalty, but Wyndham must have had one shining experience; after *Married* Miss Hodson let him play Jack Rover in *Wild Oats* by the blind late-eighteenth-century dramatist O'Keeffe, casting herself as Dame Amaranth, the young Quakeress. Having seen Phelps as Rover, Wyndham had always wanted to play the part, and indeed to put on the play himself. He had £30, and so had a friend, but as the Strand Theatre manager wanted £60 a week and three months in advance, the project collapsed. Perhaps he suggested the play to Miss Hodson; certainly Rover, the 'strolling gentleman' who talks in an almost unbroken anthology of quotations from classical drama, was so far his most rewarding part in London; in the future it would be financially rewarding as well. As Rover says of Amaranth: 'That face is the prologue for a play of a thousand acts.' For Wyndham the speech was prophetic.

# CHAPTER SEVEN
# 'From the French'
# 1874–1877

It was about this time that Albery moved from the outer fringe of Putney, where he had been living with his sister Amelia, to the core of his own world at 10 Southampton Street, Strand. His life was becoming (and perilously) more social than domestic; Pinero, who of all men knew how much concentration and energy a dramatist needed to keep going, surmised years later that Albery's life-about-town would have had its effect. For all that, he was still uncommonly prolific in several modes, and though he had had no real winner since *Forgiven*, long-memoried managements still asked for his plays.

Soon after this a very young actress, Mary Moore, aged twelve, had her first experience of failure: the collapse of the Victoria Theatre Company with which her father was involved in Waterloo Road. Probably the shock caused her to think carefully about money for the rest of her life. To do what she could, her elder sister went on the stage. As principal girl in a pantomime, she took Mary for company to Hull. In shabby lodgings on the edge of the map time passed slowly; knowing nothing about the understudy system, Mary learnt every female part and hoped she might be called for in an emergency; but nothing happened.

After his Royalty engagement Wyndham had another chance to play Charles Surface, slipping into the period as fluently as he always did. Then, on 25 May 1874, at the Court Theatre (the first bbuilding, on the south flank of Sloane Square where W. H. Smith's is now) he opened as the *flâneur* Bob Sackett, in *Brighton* (otherwise Frank Marshall's anglicized version of *Saratoga*) which he had toured in America after its record at the Fifth Avenue Theatre, New York. Sackett was obviously a light comedian's dream. 'The more and more I see her, the more and more I love her', he declares of every pretty girl he meets, and pretty girls form much of the population of Saratoga Springs, a fashionable resort in the north of New York State. Sackett's philosophy is Tom Moore's:

When we are far from the lips we love,
We have but to make love to the lips that are near.

At Saratoga he must pursue—and avoid—four girls in particular: two maidens, one widow, and the young wife of an old man. In the last act they descend on him in one fell swoop (a phrase that few Macduffs ever get right). It is an invasion that summons all the ingenuity and panache of both actor and dramatist. The play's London triumph was double-edged: it became notorious, always excellent box-office. Several people found it unbearably vulgar—among them William Archer, whose Scots blood predictably boiled at 'home-made Anglo-Saxon indelicacy'. Though he dismissed *Brighton* in one packed summary as 'a saturnalia of watering-place flirtation', Archer applauded Bronson Howard's comic invention, at least, up to a point:

> It is not the character of Bob Sackett with his amorous eccentricities that jars upon one . . . It is a creation of frank farce, ludicrously impossible, and therefore almost inoffensive. The worst point in the play is the conduct of the numerous so-called ladies who crowd the stage. Ordinary modesty, not to say delicacy of feeling, is apparently a thing unknown and undreamt of among them. "Give me a middle-aged man," says one of them. "Well, I'm sure so-and-so is middle-aged," replies another. "I mean a man of the middle-ages" is the reply, "one of the men that always went about in armour, drank in his armour, went to bed in his armour—" "A nice husband for cold weather," remarks Miss Effie Remington, the heroine of the play, in so far as it has a heroine—and the audience roars. I feel that an apology is due for even quoting such passages as this.

After which the now unpredictable Archer would acknowledge, as graciously as astonishingly, that Howard's *The Old Love and the New* had been one of the 'strongest and healthiest' plays on the English stage for a long time.

Howard, formerly a journalist, had got the idea for *Saratoga*, his first play, from a set of articles on *The Girls of the Period* by Mrs Lynn Linton. When Daly put it on in New York after numerous managements had declined the play was regarded as 'advanced'; Laura Keene, a redoubtable comedienne acting then in Philadelphia, said that it was 'too fast'; and a Boston theatre manager refused to allow these girls on his unsoiled New England stage. Pleased with the English version, Howard admired Wyndham's approach to Bob Sackett, 'never a flirt' but always intensely in earnest when expressing his love.

> always really sincere when thinking of each particular woman he is interested in. He is seriously and honestly in love with one woman at a

time— and the one he happens to be thinking of—and never has the slightest intention of trifling with her. This, probably, is the greatest charm, as it is the greatest novelty of Wyndham's Bob Sackett.

Wyndham understood the importance of being earnest in any farcical imbroglio. Just as earnestly, he understood the value of hard work. Not content with acting every night in *Brighton*, he began a sequence of matinées at the Crystal Palace, starting in September with *Wild Oats* and his old part, that dictionary of quotations, Rover. During the next three years, though (one would have thought) totally engaged in the West End, he produced nearly a hundred plays at the Palace. Situated immediately beneath the glass roof in the centre transept, the theatre had a high proscenium and a lofty interior that called for plays to be declaimed: usually Wyndham's choices recognized this. In 1873 J. Steele Mackaye, an American actor, had appeared there as Hamlet in a version abridged by Tom Taylor. Frank Archer, the King, remembered that, for a Hamlet 'deficient in voice, power, and physique, the Crystal Palace with its huge auditorium, and at that time defective acoustic properties, was very trying'. After six matinées, and a not especially helpful provincial tour, Mackaye returned to America and devoted himself to playwriting, theatre management and planning, and a cluster of stage enterprises.

Wyndham coaxed some exceptional artists to join him at the Crystal Palace. There Ellen Terry came down as the wife so gently tamed in a veteran comedy, *The Honey Moon*. When William Creswick (Shakespearian from the Surrey) played Shylock, with the flinty Genevieve Ward as Portia, and Wyndham himself as Bassanio, a boy and girl from Forest Hill with their German governess were in the house. Theatregoing was frowned upon in their Quaker family, so they came in secret, the girl's first experience of Shakespeare and one she never forgot: in later life she devoted herself to the theatre. Her name was Annie Elizabeth Fredericka Horniman, and she would found the Gaiety, Manchester, and with it the English repertory movement. Possibly after all her parents could have forgiven their governess for taking the children out. The Crystal Palace, said that experienced theatre-man J. Bannister Howard, was looked upon 'as a kind of semi-religious institution, probably because of its association with the good Prince Consort'. (Some years later, the versatile Bannister Howard managed another theatre built in the grounds and Wyndham acted there for him.) The Crystal Palace also impressed another little girl born in the neighbourhood: Elsie Fogerty, to be renowned one day as a speech-trainer. At the Palace she directed her first Greek play.

Just why Wyndham should have given so much time to these matinées is not clear; maybe, like many actors in a long run, he wearied of life in a single play. But his vigour was enormous. When he produced Genevieve Ward in the *Antigone* of Sophocles an actor blundering through the silent part of a soldier had to be changed. No trouble in the world. Wyndham himself stepped in: 'I'll be a classic myself!' he said amiably. Genevieve Ward wrote of him with unsuspected gentleness:

> Charles Wyndham, the best of managers for one reason, perhaps, because he was also the best of artists; he thought only of the piece as a whole, even to the point of absolute self-sacrifice. On one occasion, in *Antigone*, he came on as a supernumerary to fill a void.

The Palace directors insisted, as business-men would, upon a pantomime, but Wyndham retorted that he knew nothing about it. Knowing nothing themselves, they could not see why a man who had staged so many plays—remember that Greek stuff—could not do a pantomime for Christmas. Simple, surely? Then, when a young man came to him and suggested himself as producer the Board sternly refused: suspicious of an unknown, it continued to demand that Wyndham should be in charge. To placate the directors Wyndham sat on the stage throughout rehearsals. This well-meant solution merely annoyed the newcomer; he was doubly annoyed when the pantomime notices gave Wyndham the credit. Wyndham warned him that contradiction would do no good; much better if it was announced that because of this year's success he would be re-engaged for the following year. He was Augustus Harris, who as Drury Lane producer of the most expensive pantomimes in English theatre history would be known one day as Druriolanus. Not that anyone who saw him later as one of Wyndham's Criterion actors—the balloon boy at Cremorne in *Pink Dominos*—could have prophesied this.

# II

In April 1874 the perpetually resourceful low comedian J. L. Toole appeared as a simple-hearted, starving barrister in *Wig and Gown* at the Globe. Albery had written the Dickensian part especially for him; to get the best from Toole it had to be both comic and sympathetic, and this was how the part of Hammond Coote was devised. When the play opens Coote is chronically out of work; he and his wife spend the first act attempting to disguise their poverty. Just as her scissors are poised, ready to cut up his gown as a jacket for one of their children, a brief arrives. He is engaged fraudulently on the undertaking that he will lose his client's case; and he looks like doing so until suddenly—coincidences jostle—he recalls a vital clue from his own childhood. From that moment he no longer bungles his cross-examination:

COOTE [*crying as he rises*]  And did the poor fellow recognise his mother's grave?
SIEL [*the villain*] He did.

62

COOTE   Poor fellow! Where was she buried?

SIEL   In a small churchyard on the right going to Kensington.

COOTE   Is there a footpath through it?

SIEL   There is.

COOTE   Ah! I know it.

JUDGE   You seem affected.

COOTE   My mother was buried there; where did she die?

SIEL   In a little street at the back.

COOTE   Anywhere near to Cole, the baker's?

SIEL   She lodged in his house.

COOTE   What kind of lady was she?

SIEL   A very good-looking woman, with a vast quantity of brown hair, blue eyes and a very soft voice.

COOTE   [*in great haste takes out papers, etc., from pocket of coat*]   Now! Don't you be flurried. Did she sell her piano before she died?

SIEL   She did to pay her debts.

COOTE   And she fretted a good deal about it?

SIEL   She did.

> [Coote *gradually begins to gain confidence and* Siel *to lose it, while all present begin to pay more attention.*]

COOTE   Is there any monument to her grave?

SIEL   No.

COOTE   Is it close under the wall near the porch?

SIEL   It is.

COOTE   Now! the little boy? You kept him till he went to sea?

SIEL   Yes.

COOTE   You'll swear to that?

SIEL   I do.

COOTE   What proof have you?

SIEL   Proof?

COOTE   Yes, did he tell you he was going to run away, or did he write to tell you he was gone?

SIEL   [*hesitating*]   He—he informed me of his movements when he came back.

COOTE   Oh! and you were very kind to him always?

SIEL   I was.

COOTE   You've heard of a place called Red Lion Street in Holborn?

SIEL   I think I have.

COOTE   And perhaps of Mrs Brownson who lived there?

SIEL   I—I—did know a woman of that name.

COOTE   Did you take the boy there?

SIEL   Yes—he—he—

COOTE  Now! be careful.

SIEL  He lodged there.

COOTE  Because he would keep wandering to the churchyard?

SIEL  He was very fond of going there.

COOTE  And you beat him for it?

SIEL  Beat him! I was as kind—

COOTE  Now! come! come!—With a yellow cane with a gold dog's head on the top and a green tassel?

SIEL  [*overcome*] I—I—forget.

COOTE  And locked him in a little room without a stove, at the top of the house, with a pigeon-trap outside the skylight?

SIEL  I—I—I am very unwell.

COOTE  One moment more. [*hands letter*] Look at that writing. Is that the dead lady's hand?

SIEL  I—I—think it is.

COOTE  Don't go off for a minute. [*hands picture*] Just look at that portrait. Is that her portrait?

SIEL  It is—I—[*fainting*]

COOTE  Then you're a perjured old villain, and that man's another. It was I you beat. It was I who went to the churchyard. It was I you locked in the little room. [*takes off wig and gown*] Here! swear me, somebody; put me on my oath. I'm the lost boy.

> [Siel *faints in the box; everyone is surprised; even the* Judge *rises.*]
> CURTAIN

Here, for such a box-office actor as Toole, applause must have sounded like the storm on the heath. But because he was booked for America, *Wig and Gown* lasted only six weeks after grudging notices. Primarily a 'vehicle' for Toole, it satisfied his London public; at Wallack's Theatre in New York it failed, as so many imports have done. Toole's humour was ineradicably English.

The Vaudeville management had to wait over two years for Albery's *Pride*, which it had commissioned. Ultimately this was done on 22 April 1874 in a triple bill and with a cast of familiar names, James and Thorne among them. In J. Cadman Cadbutton (a preposterous christening) Albery created another rascally middle-aged man. Unlike Digby Grant, this one was rich; like Grant, he was also a snob. Hence his attempt to stop his daughter's attachment to his secretary; and his delight in dragged-in references to his brother-in-law, 'the baronet', a dependant unspeakably bullied, and impoverished by unwise gambling. Once more *The Times* said Albery had achieved pre-eminently a play of character, and 'one of the most remarkable modern comedies' since T. W. Robertson. Clement Scott, in the *Daily Telegraph*, was less enthusiastic (his usual reaction to Albery). *Pride*, which lasted for seven weeks at the Vaudeville, swelled the repertoire of three provincial tours.

The plot. as we know, was Albery's chief weakness. His next West End play, *The Spendthrift*, an eighteenth-century comedy, had what *The Times* called 'almost a superabundance of plot'. (There it did resemble its Restoration forbears.) The spendthrift himself, having exhausted his inheritance, is the kind of hero to appear unexpectedly at crucial moments; with each appearance the plot moves forward. Just the man, indeed, for Henry Neville, the romantic actor who (with Albery) staged this 'comedy of adventure' at the Olympic in Wych Street during May 1875. Historians note that the young Johnston Forbes-Robertson played a small part, and little else matters now. Reviews were tepid, though E. L. Blanchard recorded in his diary: 'This is a clever, odd, amusing piece that has been rather severely dealt with.' It ran for four weeks; New York production plans faded.

Thenceforward, probably discouraged by their brief lives, Albery wrote fewer original plays. He had never matched *Two Roses*. In any event, club evenings were consuming his energy. He belonged to the Arundel, the Junior Garrick, and, most recently, the Savage, whose members appreciated his verbal quickness. It was at the Savage that he received a letter from the prolific Henry J. Byron, whose comedy *An American Lady*—with himself and Mrs John Wood—had opened the Criterion Theatre in what was known then as Regent Circus. Byron, as the joint manager, offered Albery 'a nightly fee, eh?' for a comedy which he wanted to have ready when the current play, or the next one, came off: 'I'm afraid this seems a little foggy, but I can't leave myself in the lurch.' Not unexpectedly, nothing emerged from the fog which for a while enveloped the theatre. Played as a Criterion after-piece, W. S. Gilbert's *Topsyturveydom*, in which furniture stood on the ceiling and a chandelier sprouted from the floor, left 'an absolute blank' in Gilbert's mind when someone asked him, years later, for his recollections. After this a season of *opéra-bouffe* had opened happily enough with *Les Prés Saint Gervais*, but its successors failed, and Alexander Henderson, Criterion manager for its proprietors, Spiers and Pond the caterers, searched round for a three-act farce.

# III

He had not far to look. Charles Wyndham had reappeared as Bob Sackett at the Haymarket. Now, while on tour with *Brighton* at (reasonably) Brighton, he received three telegrams. One was from Tom Smale, formerly business manager for Thorne at the Vaudeville, asking if Wyndham would go into management with him. A second, from an agent, asked if he would accept the management of a London theatre. And a third, from Alexander Henderson, inquired simply: 'Can you open at the Criterion next Monday?' By then Spiers and Pond were so anxious to secure *Brighton*, a play that would clearly go on and on, that they offered Wyndham the theatre rent-free if he could open at once. So it was immediately arranged. On Boxing Day 1875 he appeared at the Criterion in all three sections of a triple bill—*Brighton*, preceded by a 'musical absurdity', *The Debutante*, and followed by the grand duo from *The Huguenots*: Stalls, 7*s*. 6*d*.; Dress Circle, 5*s*.; Boxes (bonnets allowed) 4*s*.; Pit, 2*s*. This was a key moment; the charming little underground theatre would be 'his' for the rest of his career; in 1879 he became its lessee, and until the turn of the century it was his only permanent theatrical home. The lofty Crystal Palace must have seemed as far as the South Pole from the elegant little subterranean box of the Criterion auditorium.

Really, the Criterion was not meant to be a theatre at all. It evolved almost accidentally at the heart of what we call now a complex. In 1870 the caterers Spiers and Pond decided to develop the site on the sloping ground between Jermyn Street and the present Piccadilly Circus; and after a competition for the right design that of the architect Thomas Verity was the first choice from fifteen entries. No other large building in the neighbourhood resembled Verity's façade. He used Portland stone in a part of the West End where brick and stucco predominated. The exterior—not much altered after a hundred years—shows French Renaissance influence; and by agreeable coincidence, the little theatre soon became the home of a number of plays 'from the French'. Verity had no idea that he was designing a theatre; all that had appeared in the specifications was 'Minor Hall for lectures, concerts and similar purposes, will be in the basement.' His imposing façade, beneath its mansard roof, hid much else besides the minor hall which rose to a theatre.

Understandably, when Spiers and Pond applied for a licence some doubt supervened: the Metropolitan Board of Works had to vote twice—at the first count, votes for and against were equal—before it decided to acquiesce. Though the Board's architect conceded that the building was handsome, he did hope that he would not see many more structures 'with a ballroom at the top, dining-rooms in the middle, and a theatre at the basement, which had to depend on air pumped into it by machinery'. It says much for Wyndham's drawing powers that he could entice people to risk asphyxiation. (Today the building of underground theatres is no longer allowed.)

The Criterion foyer looks larger than it is—all done with mirrors, decorated tiles and painted ceiling panels. To reach the auditorium you first descend a steep staircase lined with tiles manufactured by Simpson and Company and bearing composers' names: reading these helps to shorten the downward journey. Not that everyone thought Simpson's art tiles were pleasing. The *Building News* of 14 November 1873, having objected to the 'general appearance of crockery-ware' at the Victoria and Albert Museum—with which Verity had been associated—allowed grudgingly that the Criterion tiles were more to its taste. All the same, it added portentously and polysyllabically:

> No soul will be better for the post-prandial contemplation of his surroundings, while anyone who has studied nature, or its representation by artists who deserve the name, may possibly suffer indigestion from the continual dislocation of anatomy, or rather constant disregard of it in the figures which are supposed to adorn the apartments and their approaches. . . . Some labels attached to certain figures lead one to suppose that mythological personages were intended to have been represented by them, but the slightest glance will betray the fact that nothing but conventional emblems stand for their attributes, since the shapeless forms and distorted limbs and expressionless features, belie alike the presumable semblance to humanity and Godlike reputation.

The author of this involved diatribe held also that it was 'a great mistake, from the sanitary point of view, to place the theatre so much below the street-level'. Verity, who would have an important architectural career, said in a mild reply:

> The ceiling of the principal staircase is not tiles or "crockery," but is painted on plaster in the usual way. I certainly should have preferred the former, but I do not know of any economical way of surmounting the difficulties of fixing them on the soffit of an arch.

*Building News* and others had objected to the term 'art tiles'. Verity disowned responsibility for it: 'This name, as a kind of trade distinction, was I believe, applied to them by the makers.'

Today, having been amused by the tiles, or depressed by them; having threaded various bars and been surprised by your reflection in many mirrors; you reach the gentle intimacy of the auditorium. There you sit in one of the 660 seats, either in the stalls, dress circle or upper circle. From most of these you believe that if a pin were dropped on-stage you would hear it; if a hair moved you would see it. Whatever the play, the Criterion does remain in effect a drawing-room. In the eighteen-seventies, when its first coat of paint still shone, and its 'crockery' sparkled, no one could have been more at home (or made you feel so) than Charles Wyndham. Sparely built, tall, good-looking, with crisp brown hair, he was now nearly forty, though for years he would seem younger than this. His timing, his general technique, was incomparable; his choice of play seldom failed him, or his theatre: he was not the kind of actor-manager to indulge himself without thinking of his box-office.

# IV

When, unwillingly, *Brighton* ended, Wyndham went to Germany and played it in German (more Crystal Palace vigour); from Paris he returned with a script which those legal figments John Doe and Richard Roe (otherwise Clement Scott and Arthur Matthison), adapted as *The Great Divorce Case*. At that time, though plays could be freely adapted, Wyndham insisted on paying the French authors (MM. Hennequin and Delacour), who responded gratefully by giving him 'for a song' the English rights of their newest success. Thinking that the plot was too much like *The Great Divorce Case*, he hesitated. But before this, on 15 April 1876, he became manager of the Criterion, beginning with his new play 'from the French' (a phrase almost automatically present on Criterion bills). He acted a husband terrified of his mother-in-law; with a friend similarly afflicted he goes out on the town. To put their families off the scent each man writes a letter to the other, suggesting a quiet dinner to discuss 'the great divorce case'. The result, inevitably, is French farce. After a useful run Wyndham replaced it with *Hot Water*, another farce 'from the French' in which a single example of comic business stopped the show. During a court scene a witness, bidden to bare her hand while swearing to tell the truth, the whole truth etc., undid innumerable tiny buttons on a glove that reached almost to her shoulder, and then slowly unpeeled it to the undisguised excitement of everyone in court—the judge included.

Wyndham had asked Albery to adapt *Pink Dominos*, the other Hennequin–Delacour farce: a verbal arrangement (we gather) which was unlucky, as it led to a dispute over terms and a sheaf of acrimonious letters to the press. Earlier, Albery had been corresponding with John Hare over a possible production which never surfaced, *Fearns* or (as it was renamed, *Genevieve*). Unlike most of his original plays, it was intensely dramatic, and ended with the hero's death by drowning. Albery must have worked on *Fearns* during 1876; in December *The Man in Possession*, his play for Toole, began at the Gaiety where Toole had long been loved. At the première, after his absence in the provinces, the audience was eager to see him. *The Times*, in a distinctly cold notice, was less welcoming:

> A London audience is generally—and at this theatre particularly—of
> excellent temper and patience. It is loth to disbelieve that, where it has
> once been pleased, it will not be pleased again ... To speak plainly,
> Albery's first act is about as dull and spiritless a performance as one could
> wish to see ... As the play proceeds, however, it certainly improves. No
> stretch of the imagination can raise it to the merits of a good play; but a
> few ingenious, we think, original ideas peep out as the story is unravelled,
> and, indeed, the story itself is, in its leading feature, by no means an
> unhappy conception.

The story concerns a broker's man, Edward Titscrap (name again). Put in possession of a house where a woman is dying, he adopts the baby daughter and brings her up as a lady, even going to the length of buying portraits of Queen Elizabeth, Richelieu, George IV and William of

Orange, and pretending that they are her ancestors (a tale she is simple enough to believe). When his brother, a reformed convict, turns up from Australia (where else?) the girl is surprised that her uncle (William of Orange, no less) is clean-shaven, without armour. She threatens to leave her fond adoptive father, and at once Albery provides the pathos inescapable from any part for Toole. 'The probabilities are not to be considered too curiously', said the *Daily Telegraph*, using a critic's escape route. Joseph Knight, in the *Athenaeum*, was friendlier: 'Titscrap's clumsy guardianship and his rough efforts at consolation, belong to the highest walks of humour.' Some years later he picked out Titscrap in Albery's 'scarcely remembered but clever drama' as 'one of the most notable illustrations of the pathetic side of Toole's acting'. Reviews generally were bad enough for the Gaiety's manager, John Hollingshead, to tell Albery that they were 'quite as disheartening to me as to you. . . . It seems that humour and fancy are to be written down—and nothing but stage carpentry and buffoonery written up. I hope the piece will run in spite of this opposition.' In the end *The Man in Possession* lasted for six weeks in London, and went on tour with Toole.

# V

Constantly tours of the Albery comedies atoned for diminishing runs in London, New York and Boston. Moreover, *Two Roses* reached Australia, New Zealand and Canada. At home Wyndham did Albery's *Pickwick* in the gulf of the Crystal Palace. Then, early in 1877, *Pink Dominos* started its 555 Criterion performances, a figure at that time beaten only by the massive Vaudeville score of *Our Boys*. And this was the play that Wyndham, as we have seen, had bought cheaply from its French authors. As usual when adapting 'from the French', Albery anglicized settings and characters. He also craftily twisted the last act, and a programme note requested the audience to remain seated 'as interest in the comedy is retained up to the final tableau'.

Like many a *succès de scandale*, the fuss about *Pink Dominos* seems unbelievable now. What caused it? Simply the idea that two young wives should go masked to the ballroom at Cremorne in Chelsea, to test their husbands' fidelity. A popular summer resort for Londoners, Cremorne opened in 1845, grew seedier and seedier, and actually closed down in the year *Pink Dominos* opened. But audiences responded instinctively to the name: married men who made assignations with 'other' women at Cremorne were up to no good. Albery's choice of scene was precise, an example—one of many—of his gift for adapting 'from the French' to something recognizably English. Albery used to tell a story of a Margate barber who liked the theatre: 'Seen this 'ere new piece of Albery's?' Albery said he had. 'Well, he's making a pretty fool of himself.

Introducing Cremorne on the stage and making out it's from the French. I calls it a swindle; if it's French it's a swindle to say so if it ain't; everybody knows Cremorne's English and a nice awful affair, too, to get a introducing of it to our wives and families. I should like to kick that Halbery!' 'You'd better shave him,' said Albery, 'it will pay you better.'

As one of the husbands Wyndham reinforced a reputation that hardly needed it. A quicksilver comedian, infinitely delicate—almost imponderable—playgoers adored him. Laughter filled the little house; if it had not been built below a ballroom and dining-rooms the roof might have risen. Naturally, some people dissented, but when word got round that something rather shocking was going on at the Criterion, demand for tickets trebled. One critic in particular did object—Blanchard of the *Telegraph*. Everyone anxious to keep the British drama pure must have noticed regretfully, he said, that a Piccadilly theatre was emulating the Palais Royal:

> Old fashioned folk visiting this theatre might take the play as truly revealing the hideous condition of profligacy into which modern society has fallen, and it may be, therefore, worth while to guard them against any such misapprehension. Without asserting that English morals have reached the highest standard at the present day, and that the relationship of the sexes knows no divergence from the paths of purity and honour, it is yet right to assume that conjugal infidelity has not yet become recognised as a trait in the national character, and that husband and wife are not, in this country at least, passing their existence in trying to deceive, dishonour, and detect each other.

A moody beginning. Though he did observe some dramatic talent among the profligacy, the actors and actresses were unworthily employed: 'the louder the laughter, the more saddening it becomes'. This was, of course, a splendid selling notice; the public poured in. (Many readers took the writer to be Clement Scott.) Blanchard's blood-pressure must have soared alarmingly whenever he went through Piccadilly Circus and saw that the play was still on, and the tiny foyer crowded. At least he had the comfort—as his diary records—of knowing that his proprietor, Mr J. M. Levy, 'approved of my notice'. William Archer, who had blushed at the way the girls behaved in *Brighton*, could not decide whether *Pink Dominos* should be performed or not. Determined to make sure, he saw it several times, and would go again: 'It is certainly the cleverest play of its kind the English stage has ever seen . . . but I would no more take ladies to see it than I would choose the *Decameron* for family reading.' One very young lady who went to see it was neither shocked nor amused. To the embarrassment of a friend who had taken her to a matinée, she wept at the end of the first act because of the way Charles Greythorne (Wyndham) was deceiving his wife. A good playgoer; she was Miss Mary Moore.

# CHAPTER EIGHT
# 'Revelling 'neath the Moon'
# 1877–1879

Mary Moore, aged fifteen, got her first theatre engagement in the summer of 1877. Life for her family had been hard during the past three years. Having lost money in the Victoria venture, her father left home to live with the 'other woman'; her mother had only a small income; and the family was split up—two elder brothers sent abroad, one to America and one to Australia. When her sister Haidée got a pantomime engagement in Dublin it was arranged that her mother—suffering not unnaturally from strain—should go as well: born in Ireland, she still had friends there. While she and Haidée were away Mary, then thirteen, had to collect the rents, her mother's only source of income, from slum houses in Hoxton: at her age an alarming experience, and probably one of the things that helped to turn her into the alert business-woman she became. At school, after several changes and chances (for she and her sister Fanny had to be taken away whenever her mother could no longer afford the fees) Mary was adopted temporarily by a German couple who wanted her to accompany their daughter to school at Warwick Hall in Maida Vale. It was all good experience, for she learnt a little German, which would be of inestimable value to her later. While she was at this superior establishment she met a girl called Eliza Davis, who lived in Maida Vale, and they were friends for life. Eliza, later a journalist (and friend of Henry Irving) known as Mrs Aria, remembered meeting Mary at a party. A slim girl then, with chestnut hair and brown eyes, Mary sang a comic song, 'Did you see an oyster walk upstairs?' After 'unpleasantness at home' with one of her brothers, Mary vowed to be independent. For a singer of comic songs the obvious way was to go on the stage. Unlike Haidée, she had no voice-training, but she could sing, so she tried an agent who sent her to Talbot Smith of the Gaiety Theatre. Engaging her at once, he told her to come back next day to rehearse. When she did she insisted on having a contract—things she had heard about from Haidée—in order to prove to her mother that all was signed and sealed.

The first Gaiety was one of a bunch of theatres in a tangle of narrow streets behind the eastern end of the Strand. It had a large auditorium, and its management specialized at this time in operetta and burlesque. Mary Moore joined the chorus of *The Bohemian Girl* and *Little Doctor Faust*, an H. J. Byron burlesque in which Nellie Farren, Kate Vaughan, Edward Terry and E. W. Royce—known as the 'Gaiety Quartette'—were playing the leads. There could have been no happier start.

# II

*Pink Dominos* had settled now into its Criterion run, but on 10 June 1877 rumours of a possible lawsuit were printed in *The Era* under a bland heading, 'Theatrical Gossip'. Charles Wyndham and James Albery had disagreed over the amount Albery should receive for his adaptation, and the first sum mentioned—simply a gossip-writer's guess—was £100; in its next issue *The Era* made it £300, or thirty shillings a night for the run. Albery claimed £3 a night, and the matter went to arbitration with John Hollingshead (of the Gaiety) as referee. Though the antagonists accepted a compromise, £2 a night in London and £1 in the provinces, the argument continued to simmer, and *The Era* was hospitable. Wyndham asserted that Albery *had not even translated* the play, and this brought a quick and short reply:

> the truth is that [Wyndham] had it translated literally to *print* and *publish*, so that he might deposit it at Stationers' Hall to secure the copyright.

It grieved Albery that the £300 Wyndham offered came only when *Pink Dominos* was a certain success: 'He let me run the risk of getting nothing—or next to nothing—in the event of failure.' Wyndham replied that he had sent along an English version because Albery intimated that he did not understand French.

For all Albery's over-developed sense of injustice, his humour bubbled. In a final letter he was reminded of

> one of the most painful bores that ever worried unwilling ears. . . .
> Stranger after stranger turned away with some excuse from this bore. At last he sat down before Mr Walter Lacy [comedian] and opened fire.
> A smile and an expression on the comedian's face that did duty for a flag of truce—for it said plainly "Wait one moment"—caused the bore to stop.
> "Sir," said Mr Lacy, in his sweetest tones, "I shall be most happy to talk to you if we can agree as to terms."

The bore looked quite astonished, and repeated "Terms?"
"Yes, sir, terms; my charge for talking to you will be five guineas an hour—paid in advance."

He hardly knew on what terms he could correspond with Wyndham; personalities pained him more than dullness. However, they had met and reached an understanding, 'and so the unworthy warfare came to an end'. It would have been awkward if it had not, for they both wrote from the same address, the Criterion Theatre.

Within less than two months Albery entered the ring against an old opponent, Hermann Vezin, avuncular no more. He had been unwise enough to say in print that *Doctor Davy* was the joint work of Albery, Wills and himself. Briskly, Albery countered that, after he had remodelled and rewritten the plot in 1865 Vezin had said publicly that 'it might be called original . . . To him [Albery] therefore belongs the merit of having written this brilliant little play.' Letters multiplied in *The Sunday Times* and *The Era*: the pair gathered the threads of their old quarrel over translation, adaptation and authors' rights, and assiduously reworked them. At length W. G. Wills joined in with a dignified letter recalling that though he had made some important changes in the plot, 'the leaven and the life' of the writing were almost entirely Albery's. And Wills added

a grateful testimony to Mr Vezin's unselfish, generous zeal towards two obscure authors (as we were then), Mr Albery and myself; how he worked for us with managers and actors, for no benefit to himself, but out of pure friendship, sympathy, and hearty belief.

Albery was not pleased. Wills had gone too far in ardent praise of Vezin, 'no gentleman more truthful, honourable, and disinterestedly generous'. That was fuel enough for an ungracious letter (*Era*, 7 October 1877) in which Albery held that Wills had 'only seized an opportunity of proclaiming his superior magnanimity'. It is hard to accept that this was not a personal attack but bore only on the rights of authorship, when we find him ending with his own version of Congreve's lines:

> 'Tis sad that mirth should change to ire,
>     But Time may still amend.
> For still the actor I admire,
>     Tho' I deplore the friend.
>
> In days of mirth we oft have met,
>     That could no longer last,
> And tho' the present I regret,
>     I'm grateful for the past.

The personal side of the argument is plain. When Vezin kept silent Wills wrote again, saying 'what none but a friend could say when his [Vezin's] conduct was misrepresented.' At the same time he wished to be considered Albery's friend: 'I am certainly his sincere admirer.'

Just how much pleasure Albery got out of all this is arguable. I suspect that he enjoyed it. At a day when his original ideas were ebbing, he probably found it much easier to write a witty, vituperative letter than to concoct a scene. He seized another way of escaping from the playwright's discipline when H. J. Byron asked him for a 'sketch, comic essay, or indeed anything good' for the first number of a monthly magazine, *Mirth*. Byron, as editor, wished to know when to expect Albery's work, and assured him (to keep his spirits up) that he would be in good company. Albery obliged with contributions for the first three numbers, including a piece of political satire, based on current Civil List economies, in which a King is forced to retire to an almshouse. Byron asked (obscurely now) if he could use 'the story of the *single hair* which we once laughed at at the Albion', a Covent Garden tavern, haunt of actors, dramatists, managers and other theatre folk, from which Albery at one time was 'rarely missing'. At the Savage Club a member asked him why he had not written a new play lately. He picked up a menu card and scribbled on it:

> He revelled 'neath the moon,
> He slumbered 'neath the sun;
> He lived a life of going-to-do,
> And died with nothing done.

Yet, for all the hours spent at the Savage, the Arundel, and the Junior Garrick clubs, and at the Albion tavern, he got an astonishing amount done. And soon there would be a serious new distraction. He would fall in love at first sight.

# III

Mary Moore, at Christmas 1877, had reached a small part in the Gaiety pantomime *Valentine and Orson* (matinées only). Her mother fetched her as usual on Christmas Eve, and took her to see a business friend of her father's. There, playing cards, was James Albery, who asked her to join him and his friends. She did so, and when she lost and he offered to pay her debt she was furious. Her independence appealed to him; within a week he proposed. He was thirty-nine, and she was sixteen, so her mother asked him to wait for three months before announcing the engagement.

In February 1878 Albery's 'fanciful' operetta, *The Spectre Knight*, with Alfred Cellier's music, preceded Gilbert and Sullivan's *The Sorcerer* for six weeks at the Opéra-Comique. In this affair, echoing *As You Like It* and *The Tempest*, a banished duke who lives in a haunted glen with his

daughter and their attendants must fall back on his own resources. The
Lord Chamberlain explains:

> . . . and yet we make pretence
> Of being followed by a royal train.
> I am the royal train. I represent
> A dozen horses and some fifty men.
> 'Ere I was banished I'd to license plays;
> Potatoes I examine now, to see
> They are not blue, and carrots I cut up.

The daughter—called Viola but nearer to Miranda—has never seen a
young man until one arrives and promptly falls in love with her. She tells
him that she goes to bed at sunset for fear of a ghost on whom none must
look unless by the light of nine candles. The young man produces both the
candles and the spectre knight, who bursts into sub-Gilbertian song (with
a dreadful second couplet):

> I only mix with ghosts well known;
> With Caesar and Pompey I pick a bone;
> Among my friends the noblest *are* there;
> I'm on visiting terms with Hamlet's father,
> I haunt fair glens and respectable towers,
> And always go home at decent hours;
> For I am a ghost of high degree,
> And other ghosts take off their hats to me.

As Albery grew older and more dilatory managers and editors had to
plead with him to deliver his scripts. Richard D'Oyly Carte, who wrote to
say that they were withdrawing *The Spectre Knight* and using *Trial By
Jury* instead, put it all in a few words:

> *The Spectre Knight* has fully come up to what was expected of it, and, if
> they are unable to give it so long a continuous first run as they and you
> could have wished, it is because it was not delivered to them until 13 or
> 14 weeks after the time promised by you, although repeatedly applied for.
> Had it been delivered as it should have been, it would have had a run of
> over 100 nights.

D'Oyly Carte promised soothingly that it would return as partner to a
new Gilbert and Sullivan opera, *H.M.S. Pinafore*, and on 27 May this
happened. A week earlier *The Golden Wreath*, a ballet 'constructed' by
Albery, had opened at the Alhambra, Leicester Square: a resolute love
story of an Indian princess who throws the wreath into a sacred river,
hoping that the prince she adores will retrieve it and so be permitted to
marry her. Manfully he dives in, and finds himself in a sinister

underworld, kingdom of a fiend who also claims the princess's hand. A faithful slave rescues the wreath, and perishes. Albery pretended that he had based the story on an Indian legend, giving as his documentary evidence *Behudagi*, vol. II, 97. It was the sort of joke he enjoyed, and, anyway, erudite linguists were rare at the Alhambra. (Behudagi, at least according to Wyndham Albery, means folly in Persian.) The *Telegraph* said generously that for those lucky enough to see *The Grand Duchess* the new ballet would be a grand finale; even those late for the opera would be 'sure of a feast'. *The Golden Wreath* remained in the bill for five months.

# IV

This and *The Spectre Knight* were both running when, on 12 June 1878, Albery and Mary Moore were married. The difference in their ages caused the usual gossip, while *The Theatre* of 19 June was inclined to make facetious in-jokes:

> A cloud has fallen upon the Savage Club. Mr Albery was married last week to Mary, the youngest daughter of Charles Moore, of New Bridge Street, Blackfriars, and Park Road, Regent's Park. The principal members of the club feel their loss very acutely. Mr H S Leigh has not indulged in one joke or epigram since, and the sparkling raillery of Mr Gerald Dixon is no longer heard. Mr Halkett Lord, who has been away on a holiday for some weeks, will now return.

'It was not a happy wedding', the bride said long afterwards. She could have added that it was not a happy marriage, though in its early years they did exchange typical letters of the happily married, affectionate and slightly silly. The ceremony itself was a trifle marred by a meeting between the bride's estranged parents, and the fact that the officiating clergyman (her cousin) wept throughout. He thought the bride too young to marry. Even so, whatever she feared about her daughter's youth, Mrs Moore must have been pleased with the bridegroom's current income. He now had four shows simultaneously in the West End: *Pink Dominos*, *The Spectre Knight*, *The Golden Wreath* and (from 8 July) Irving's four weeks' Lyceum season of *Jingle*, Albery's version of *The Pickwick Papers*. This new, shorter text was the last production of Mrs Bateman's Lyceum management. After a tour had ended, Irving took over the Lyceum, which he would make so excitingly his own: first as Hamlet that December, with a new Ophelia, Ellen Terry. Two companies were travelling in *Pink Dominos*, which was visible as well in various parts of America, and in Australia, New Zealand and India; and *Two Roses* had lost none of its popularity at home or away.

During their engagement, when James and Mary were walking in Regent's Park, they had met Charles Wyndham—Mary's first introduction. Soon after they were married she saw Wyndham again briefly when her husband made a business call, presumably about an adaptation ('from the French') of Emile Augier's *Les Fourchambault* which Wyndham, once more on good terms with Albery, had commissioned.

Next, with the novelist Joseph Hatton, Albery wrote an unlucky melodrama called *No. 10; or, The Bastille of Calvados*; on at the Princess's in November, it was off in a fortnight. But no need to bother. In a few days, yet another Albery piece was opening. With *Pink Dominos* still thriving ('scandalously!' we can hear Blanchard's explosion) Wyndham had time to share in the Haymarket production, on 2 December, of *The Crisis*, Albery's carefully anglicized text of *Les Fourchambault*. Here two wealthy families discuss the possibility of intermarriage until one parent decides solemnly that 'marriage is the most degraded of human institutions when it is merely the union of two fortunes'. Mrs John Wood was a banker's extravagant wife, William Terriss had the Coquelin part of her worthless son, and Lucy Buckstone was her daughter. Did the author's wife, now pregnant and watching rehearsals, envy her bridesmaid, Miss Buckstone? Or did she find the discussions on marriage too open, too French, as some critics did? All we know is that a young actress was meeting her leading man of years ahead. Most people agreed that Mrs Wood was 'always funny'. The *Telegraph* said so, with reservations:

> There is no actress on the stage so comic as Mrs Wood, no one who more thoroughly appreciates the essence of fun or who can point a comic line so well, but this play was not a burlesque, and Mrs Denham was not intended as a caricature. It is not worthwhile to overdo everything, and this Mrs Denham was overdone from end to end. It was funny but not judicious.

Comic or not, judicious or not, *The Crisis* ran for four months, and came back for yet another in May 1879.

# V

When *Pink Dominos* at last trailed away at the Criterion Wyndham (now in complete control) followed it in February 1879 by *Truth!* a new label for Bronson Howard's *Hurricanes*, already acceptable in America. How much Albery did is not known; perhaps he failed to deliver his script in time; perhaps he and Wyndham had quarrelled again over terms. Whatever the cause, his name is not on the programme, though he must have worked on the play; almost surely he named one character Mrs Stonehenge Tuttle and set the scene in Honeysuckle Villa, Reading. When she acted in an 1885 revival Mary Moore wrote to tell Albery about the rehearsals:

> I thought of you so much all the morning, as the piece is so brightly written, and I recognised all your little jokes.

Wyndham in 1879 had many of these little jokes as a timid husband in a Quaker household. His formidable mother-in-law has reproached him for setting a bad example to two young men engaged to his wards—actually he has exposed one of them to the dangers of a fancy-dress ball. To extricate himself, he lies implausibly: one inept lie breeds another; and his wife refuses to forgive him until he accepts that truth is the best policy. And so on. Some people, as William Archer said, saw double-meanings where none existed:

> The audience had made up its mind to discover another *Pink Dominos*, and would have scented equivoques even if the play had been written by a bishop, and the Church and Stage Guild in solemn conclave had pronounced it free of offence.

The Criterion was now living on a contradiction. Simply this: the English public must be protected from risqué farces (usually from the French). Yet large numbers of the English public were willing, eager in fact, to pay to be shocked. So the works of Hennequin, Delacour, de Najac and the rest must be carefully anglicized; just enough, but not too much, of the original left intact. Here Albery, prickly fellow though he was, could be most artful—the reason why Wyndham continued to patronize him. Still, as it happened, the next Criterion adapter was F. C. Burnand, from Hennequin and de Najac. The play, *Betsy*, in which a piquante young actress, Lottie Venne, played a sly maidservant, had no part for Wyndham. Popular in spite of this, it would be a valuable Criterion stopgap later on. Burnand too had to devise an Anglo-French alliance. As a minor critic said priggishly:

> The French play in its original form was held to be too indelicate for our stage; and its adapter must have experienced some difficulty in expunging all that was unsuited to English tastes without the sacrifice of the mirth-producing power of the original.

We take the point.

Mr and Mrs James Albery lived first at Albery's chambers in South-ampton Street, Strand, where he was working on a more serious French play, Sardou's *Les Bourgeois de Pont-Arcy*, for the Bancrofts. On 12 May 1879 Mary gave birth to a son at her mother's house in Park Road, Regent's Park; and the Alberys moved a month later to Fairlawn, a house overlooking the Thames at Stone, in Kent, which was still a country village. When the baby's godfather arrived for the christening 'his striking appearance . . . impressed the inhabitants though few of them knew who he was.' He was Henry Irving, and the child was called after him. Of this Irving wrote:

My Dear Albery,

    The firm proof of your friendship has given me much happiness.

    I hope your boy may never need my protection but if he should (which God forbid) I'll be a father to him.

    That I promise you and your wife, to whom give my kindest greetings.

A cheerfully inveterate buyer of plays, Wyndham now asked Albery to take on the Meilhac-Halévy drama *Frou-Frou*, already adapted several times. Except for the Venetian scene (prudishly omitted in some versions because it is here Frou-Frou was living in sin), Albery, in his usual way, transplanted the piece to England. His work was useless, for in the end it remained on Wyndham's crowded shelves. Just how crowded they were George R. Sims discovered when he called at the family hotel off the Strand, now run by Mrs Wyndham. This was only the beginnings of the vast hoard of unproduced scripts that would accumulate during the whole of Wyndham's life. *Frou-Frou* was one.

No matter. In September there were two more Albery premières. *Two Roses* reappeared at its original home, the Vaudeville, with Thorne, James and Kate Bishop in their old parts and Henry Howe now as Digby Grant, Esq. *Duty*, the Sardou drama, would be the Bancrofts' closing production at the little Prince of Wales's in Tottenham Street. Very much in the mechanical Sardou manner, it turns on the idea that when the mistress of a recently dead man demands money, his son (for his mother's sake) pretends that the woman has been his own mistress, not his father's. Once the truth is known, the widow 'can still bless my husband for giving me such a son'. Squire Bancroft, Victorian of Victorians, liked Albery's text, though not (and this was Sardou's fault) the feeble love story and the 'unlocking of a skeleton from a dead man's cupboard'. *Duty* failed partly because the Bancrofts themselves were not in it; also, as William Archer said, it was 'literally killed by unappreciative criticism. Those who underrate the influence of newspaper criticism in England make an enormous mistake.' Burnand in *Punch* failed to appreciate the play:

Sir Geoffrey looks up at the portrait of his "awful Dad", and exclaims that what he has heard is "too horrible to be true." There is nothing whatever "horrible" about it. It is a disillusion—a painful disillusion perhaps—but nothing to scream and pant and tear one's hair about. "Fancy the poor old governor having gone in for this sort of thing," would have been a far more natural remark.

Not much encouragement there. And yet in *The London Figaro* that year a desperate versifier, attempting to answer the question 'Where are our dramatists? We cannot find 'em,' included a clumsy compliment:

"I" says Burnand, and Byron cries "I".
*Pink Dominos?* A Boucicaultization.
   Tom Taylor now's a solid, skilful man
Though he, we know, *reprend son bien partout*;
   That cynic Gilbert's got a simple plan
For humour—just to turn the world askew;
   James Albery? Not one since Sheridan
Has done such dialogue as he can do;
   But as for plot, such detail he despises,
And lets it worry through as heaven devises.

Sheridan again. Before long Albery would be giving up plots of his own altogether.

# CHAPTER NINE

# 'Decidedly the Fashion'
# 1879–1882

American plays no longer need changing; English audiences, educated by novels, the cinema and jet-travel, are expected to absorb the social differences. In the years after the Second World War, Albery would have been out of work as an adapter of Tennessee Williams or Arthur Miller. From a lecture by Bronson Howard at Harvard in 1886, we can learn exactly what Albery did to Howard's *The Old Love and the New*. Beginning life unpropitiously in Chicago as *Lilian's Last Love*, it was reshaped for New York, where it succeeded as *The Banker's Daughter*. Albery, 'one of the most brilliant men in England' (Howard told his Harvard listeners, with courteous exaggeration) was engaged to make the characters as nearly English as he could.

> Luckily, the American characters, with one exception, could be twisted into very fair Englishmen without a faint suspicion of our Yankee accent.

Howard grew fond of Albery: it was 'among the dearest and tenderest friendships I have ever made'. While they discussed international social questions, Howard got to know more about the minor niceties of social life in England than he could have learned in five years' residence. He seems to have been obsessed by children's noble acts on behalf of their parents. In *Truth!* a son lies to save his mother from disillusion; in the latest play a daughter, to save her father's business from collapse, marries a man she does not love. Reunited with her real hero, who is forced into a duel to defend her good name—more nobility—she confesses her love as he dies. Her husband, overhearing why she had married him, cries broken-heartedly: 'Duty! Honour! Who spoke of duty or of honour? I spoke and speak of love ... God help the husband whose honour is protected by duty alone.' (Estranged husbands and wives talked like this in the drama of the period.)

The duel was a problem. As Howard admitted:

> It is next to impossible to persuade an English audience that a duel is justifiable or natural with an Englishman as one of the principals. So we played a rather sharp artistic trick on our English audience. In the American version I assumed that, if a plucky young American in France insults a Frenchman purposely, he will abide by the local customs and give him satisfaction if called upon to do so. So would a young Englishman, between you and me; but the laws of dramatic construction deal with the sympathies of the audience as well as with the natural motives and actions and characters in a play, and an English audience would think a French count ought to be perfectly satisfied if Routledge knocked him down.

They got over the difficulty by making Routledge a professional soldier (on leave from India) whose opponent, Le Comte de Carojac,

> piled so many sneers and insults on this British officer and on the whole British nation, that I verily believe a London audience would have mobbed the lover if he had not tried to kill the Frenchman. The English public walked straight into the trap, though they abhor nothing on earth more than the duelling system.

(In these circumstances, what would have happened, I wonder, to the last act of *Three Sisters* if Albery had been called in to anglicize Chekhov?)

Writing before Howard's lecture, William Archer (who thought this was Howard's best play) had to guess who did what to the play in its English version. On the whole, he guessed right. Albery, 'master of dialogue', had revealed himself unmistakably once or twice. Archer also believed that Albery had suppressed one minor figure—a manifest advantage, though the character is talked about after his death. (So long, Howard said, as an English audience did not know him personally, they were ready to laugh at him.) When Albery suggested that the heroine's father and his partner should sell their banking business, not merely retire from it, he showed more financial wisdom than he ever did in life. 'An old-established business like that might be worth a hundred thousand pounds,' Albery told Howard. 'We must sell it to someone, not close it.'

Wilson Barrett, who had asked Albery for a play as long ago as 1870, now put on *The Old Love and the New* at the earlier Court Theatre (a converted chapel) where critics and public were respectful, though *The Times* considered that 'five long acts' needed cutting. Charles Coghlan played the husband; G. W. Anson the American tourist with no time to stand and stare—a type so easily recognizable. Yet Howard and Albery had wanted at first to make the man Irish, Scottish or English. 'We could not,' Howard said:

He remained an American in 1880, as he was in Chicago in 1873. He declined to change either his citizenship or his name,
G. Washington—Father of his country—Phipps.

The play, which lasted until mid-May 1880, was revived in the following summer at the Princess's, Oxford Street, with several of the same actors, and Wilson Barrett as the husband.

Bronson Howard's association with both the Wyndham and the Albery families would get closer. In the year of *The Old Love and the New* at the Court, he married Alice Culverwell, Wyndham's youngest sister. In the spring of the following year, 1881, the Alberys' second son was born (6 March), and he was christened Bronson.

# II

One January evening of suffocating fog (1880) the Bancrofts started their Haymarket régime with a revival of Lytton's *Money*, a title lucklessly appropriate. For economic reasons they had done away with the pit, and displaced playgoers showed their anger so loudly, so continuously, and so early, that Squire Bancroft had to come before the curtain and call for order. At the great disadvantage of being dressed for Sir Frederick Blount, with a foppish flaxen wig and pink complexion, he managed at length to quieten the house. Four months afterwards, at the Vaudeville première of Albery's comedy *Jacks and Jills*, playgoers in the pit—which still existed there—were unmerciful, especially towards the end. It was neither a good nor even an amusing piece. At home, Mrs Albery had foretold its failure:

> because it had no plot, to which Albery replied that the plays of the future would be written that way. He may have been a pioneer, but young as I was, I marvelled that James and Thorne accepted it.

The principals were called Bunbury; everything occurred in Bunbury's house. If, by remoter chance, it was from here that Wilde borrowed the name for Algernon's imaginary invalid in *The Importance of Being Earnest*, the piece at least performed some service. Nothing else could redeem its excruciating artificiality. The plot reveals itself in one sentence: love letters written to two sisters get into the hands of two spinster aunts. At a drunk scene—always dangerous when a night is going badly—the first audience wilted. *The Times* reported that 'even for a modern audience' it had been peculiarly generous, but Albery claimed from the stage that there was 'organized opposition,' and his speech alienated the stalls (and the critics as well). *The Times* notice ended:

> When an author, who has succeeded more than once, fails, it is right that his failure should be treated gently; but when he himself throws down

the gauntlet by attributing his own defects to the malice of an indulgent audience, sympathy retires into the background.

There were many similar disturbances during the 1880s (as indeed there would be seventy years on), though whether 'organized' or not is speculative; even Irving would not escape when he played Malvolio at the Lyceum. *Jacks and Jills* had only eight performances, the Vaudeville's third consecutive failure; hastily, for a couple of weeks, the management slipped in *Two Roses*, still happily blooming. Albery's life as an original dramatist was over; he had, however, some capable adaptations ahead.

His behaviour at *Jacks and Jills* had moved Wyndham to omit Albery's name as adapter of *Where's the Cat?*, the newest play at the Criterion. It was Wyndham's return—there had been no part for him in *Betsy*—and now, as an unlikely baronet, Sir Garroway Fawne, he had to spend the time flirting outrageously: on hearing that the girl of the moment is married, Sir Garroway exclaims: 'Damn it! Another platonic, and marriage would have been such a change!' Elsewhere he mourns: 'Whenever I see a lady I feel I could love, I am sure she's either my grandmother, some other fool's wife, or engaged.' The man must also pretend to know more than he does, and then seek wildly to extricate himself in the ageless routine of farce.

The comedy, adapted from the German, was originally called *Sodom and Gomorrah*, not a natural Criterion title. The new one, comically innocuous, referred to a bag made from a cat's skin and containing the savings of three young men who had sworn to meet after ten years and divide the money. One of them was a poet, played by Herbert Beerbohm Tree with more than a suggestion of Oscar Wilde. Albery set the play in the Lake District. His rendezvous was a remote hotel where Mrs John Wood, type-cast as the landlady, maintained a state of vulgar respectability throughout:

NAN [*the servant*]  Please ma'am, I'm so frightened I don't know whether I'm on my head or my heels!
MRS SMITH [*the landlady*]  No decent woman should be in doubt about such a subject as that.

(Delightedly shocked response from the audience.) Read coldly now, the plot is more tangled than any Restoration comedy. Despairing, its first listeners became restive, and Wyndham tried at the end to mollify them. 'Ladies and gentlemen, do you accept the piece?' he asked [here the house responded with a mixture of 'Yes' and 'No']. 'I wish to know whether you accept the piece in order that I may convey your verdict to the author, or rather the adapter, for it is a somewhat free adaptation from the German.' As the house was not entirely silent, he proceeded:

I am in a false position at the present moment. I did ask the adapter, believing myself that the piece would be a success, to be present tonight to receive his congratulations from you, but unfortunately I have to appeal to you on his behalf. Some little time ago he committed a mistake in the heat of disappointment, and candidly, he dare not appear before you—I allude to Mr Albery. He dare not appear here, but I think I may tell him that you do forgive him and that you accept the piece.

Cheering prevailed—no one could resist Wyndham's cajolery—and *Where's the Cat?*, for all its convoluted plot, and its obvious double meanings, ran for 150 performances. Even Blanchard, so much against Wyndham's selections, yielded to this one; indeed, he wrote in his journal: 'We find it an amusing piece, excellently acted by a strong company.' Only Albery himself was unhappy. In a letter to the press he rejected Wyndham's reference to the first night of *Jacks and Jills*:

I am certain that Mr Wyndham's heart was full of kindness towards me when on my behalf he responded to the call for author at the Criterion on Saturday night, but he unfortunately conveyed anything but my sentiments to his hearers.

If *Where's the Cat?*, in spite of Albery's improvements, did nothing at all for his own reputation, it fortified Wyndham's place as the day's most high-spirited comedian. The next Criterion play, *Butterfly Fever*, by James Mortimer, 'from the French', was a flimsy affair until its last act, when Wyndham had to go mad. While studying his part and going conscientiously mad in the open air, he was seen by two farm labourers who promptly fetched a policeman. Taken in charge, the only way he could prove that he was not an escaped lunatic was to give the police passes for the theatre. So he used to explain, but like many actors he was a self-indulgent raconteur.

# III

While sailing the North Sea in Alexander Henderson's yacht, Albery kept at work. Writing to his dearest Mary, he asked her to tell Wyndham that he was getting on with a version of a French comedy, *Femme à Papa*, and that he could do in a day what Wyndham wanted done to *Brighton*. In his absence Mary served as 'his most fair secretary'; her letter to Wyndham was admirable, and another letter she had written for him was 'such a masterpiece,' Albery said, 'that I have read it to Mr Henderson, feeling sure you would not leave me if he offered you an increase in salary.' Mary had dealt with Miss Newton (the original Ida in *Two Roses*), who wanted to produce *The Spectre Knight* at the Alexandra Palace: 'You did quite right . . . but £2.2s. would have done.'

During the year Albery wrote more than sixty letters to 'Middlie' (his nickname for her, because when asked how she was she replied

'Middling'). They were light, descriptive, affectionate letters, news of work scattered among the gossip. Wyndham, with his wife, son and daughter, and the actress Rose Saker, joined Albery on the Rhine, and the party went on to Wiesbaden and St Moritz. Being Wyndham's guest, Albery felt obliged to do some work on *Femme à Papa*, but really (he told Mary) there was

> nothing whatever to think about *here* but that leaves me more time to dream about my three little ones at home.
>
> Your affectionate lover,
> JIM

Wyndham himself was not idle; Albery thought he had the 'oddest way of taking a holiday—practically he is everybody's servant'. After a while he relieved Albery of *Femme à Papa* and instead put him on to a piece called *Le Petit Ludovic*. Albery had a notion that Mary would approve because it was 'not a bit like a French play', and would be 'almost original'. Wyndham discussed casting with him; 'we both anticipate a great go'. Mary was less sanguine: 'I cannot get it out of my head', she replied, 'but that it is that dreadful piece you read me out of *The Era*.' Not yet twenty, she already showed her theatrical good sense.

When they planned to move back to London they chose 11 Bentinck Terrace, facing Regent's Park, a district Mary had known since childhood. Albery's health that autumn had been tiresome; he had gone to recuperate at Ramsgate, whence most of his letter concerned fittings for the new house:

> In expending do not stop in the nursery. Anywhere but that. Let Maples cover the floor. I'll write five extra pages tomorrow and that will pay for it. In all things think first of them.

Touching; but in a postscript he asked how much she had spent altogether. Whether the move was wise is dubious. Mary might have felt that with a home so near the West End, Albery would be less likely to linger at his clubs. Between the lines of his letters from abroad, when he mildly reassures her about his drinking habits, we can see that she has been anxious. Instinctively, with precocious wisdom, she knew when his career was jeopardized. Years later she wrote:

> though highly ambitious, he lacked the power of concentration, and his Bohemian outlook on life prevented the full realisation of his hopes.

And again:

> It was Mr Albery's strange outlook on life that I think, prevented his plays from being the success they might have been. His writing was brilliant, but there was always a twist of some kind that pleased him, but

puzzled others. He seemed unable to concentrate on any work for long, and I have by me first acts of plays with clever and sparkling dialogue, which alas! he never completed.

From the first, she was eager about his work. He must have discussed it with her, and she copied scripts for him which he was invariably late in delivering. Once, because they needed the money so badly, she finished an adaptation herself—something Wyndham did not hear about for a good many years.

Marriage cannot have been easy for a very young wife. Albery's 'peculiar and original' ideas on the upbringing of his children upset her, and one episode in particular was agonizing. He had taught the eldest boy, Irving, to balance on a swing without holding the ropes, even when it was being swung rather high; when he wanted to go further, and to get Irving (aged three) to turn round while the swing was moving, Mary protested, and he replied that he would rather have the boy a cripple than a coward. So too with swimming lessons. Hiring a boat at Broadstairs, he tied a handkerchief round Irving's waist, slipped a walking-stick through it, and precariously held him up in the water while Mary from the beach watched in terror. Next, when he started to dress the boy, James fell overboard, fully clothed, and came ashore laughing at himself but wondering whether it had been the boatman's way of objecting to his teaching methods. At another time Mary was profoundly grateful to Arthur Pinero for offering to go out with James and the boy into deep water.

In the ebb of 1881 Wyndham started something different: *Foggerty's Fairy*, a 'whimsical extravagance' by W. S. Gilbert. Frederick Foggerty's good fairy has obligingly blotted out some unfortunate episodes from the past; the ensuing blank is richly comic, but the fairy, far too inventive, fills this with a new set of events as awkward for Foggerty as the others. Here was a magnificent part for Wyndham, but in spite of gratifying notices the play was too whimsical, too extravagant for Criterion audiences; it had the kind of subtlety better on the page than on the stage. First of all, Gilbert had written it for E. A. Sothern, who just before his death worked on the text with eager appreciation. On hearing Sothern read the script, Edgar Pemberton thought he would have made a success. But at the Criterion Archer intellectualized its failure, blaming the absence of Gilbert's remorseless logic and describing the fairy's idea of the past as an entirely arbitrary invention.

Something had to be done, and quickly. Like many actor-managers caught with a failure, Wyndham revived a former success—now *The Great Divorce Case*, first of the little French comedies that had done so well in 1876. Again he was the pitiable husband crushed by an unutterable mother-in-law; again, much battered, he would appear carrying a small corpse and murmuring mildly, 'I have had a difference of opinion with the dog.'

# IV

Irving's choice of a revival had nothing to do with failure. He proposed to open his fourth Lyceum season with a comedy, and with himself in a character part. So, on Boxing Day 1881, in the freshly enlarged and redecorated theatre, he acted in *Two Roses*, eleven years since his first famous portrait of Digby Grant, scrounger and snob. Once more during the last act, when he learns that he has inherited a fortune, Irving—the tall figure wrapped in a shabby dressing-gown—would condescendingly dispense with his long fingers 'a little cheque' to this creditor or the next. 'A little cheque' and the repeated 'You annoy me very much!' became catch-phrases. Only one 'original' was in the Lyceum cast, David James as Our Mr Jenkins. For the two suitors, Jack Wyatt and blind Caleb Deecie, Irving had to look elsewhere. H. J. Montague had died in America; Thomas Thorne was now in management. So 'Handsome Bill' Terriss played Wyatt, and for Deecie Irving chose an inexperienced young actor he heard of while in Scotland, George Alexander, currently a member of a Glasgow stock company. Irving offered him seven guineas a week; Albery received six guineas a performance. At the Vaudeville his fee was three pounds.

Disappointed by his return to Digby Grant, Esq., Irving resolved that this would be his last 'coat and trouser piece'. Notices had varied; some dismissed the play as dated and too slight for the Lyceum. Equally, a few held that Digby Grant had lost something in his transference from the small Vaudeville to the far larger Lyceum. Clement Scott championed the performance; for him, Irving seemed to deliver the catch-phrases with a new variety, and not in fact as if they were catch-phrases at all. 'Mr Henry Irving, in voice and manner was Digby Grant. His own individuality had disappeared.' This although, according to Laurence Irving, his grandfather must have been disconcerted when he lost half of his moustache and had hastily to remove the other half to restore the balance.

During the run of *Two Roses* Irving had a lot on his mind; he was evolving *Romeo and Juliet*, and Digby Grant had to be a kind of holiday before he opened as Romeo to Ellen Terry's Juliet in March 1882. That was a few days after Wyndham had tried another new play at the Criterion. In an effort to escape from farces so light they could have been played on tiptoe, Wyndham had gambled with *Foggerty's Fairy*; it failed, so he reverted now to something 'from the French'—an adaptation by H. J. Byron called *Fourteen Days* and with that familiar central figure, a husband with a roving eye. Peregrine Porter takes out for the evening 'another' woman—'of questionable character' said one critic primly—and gets drunk into the bargain. Missing a portrait of his wife, he suspects the woman, pursues her, and knocks down a policeman in the process. Hence fourteen days' gaol. The main sensation was the debonair Wyndham's entrance in prison uniform. Social realism, as in Galsworthy's plays, was a long time ahead. The Criterion was a drawing-room, and people in drawing-rooms seldom wore the broad arrow.

Albery was suffering that month from inflammation of the lungs; his health would be progressively poor, and writing much harder, but Wyndham, with a policy of stock-piling plays, kept him busy. He had finished one play (title unknown) for J. L. Toole, in management then at his own theatre in King William Street, off the western end of the Strand, but it was never produced and the manuscript disappeared.

Soon after *Fourteen Days*, Wyndham, released from gaol, left on an American tour, knowing that the Criterion would have to close for several months. The Metropolitan Board of Works, which originally hesitated about allowing it to be built at all, had had second thoughts and demanded certain structural alterations. When the theatre was built thirty feet below street level its ventilation problem was solved by drawing fresh air, through flues, into an antechamber beneath the floor. Ten years later the Board of Works decided that this was not good enough. The theatre closed and Thomas Verity, the architect, supervised the new system of direct-access ventilation shafts, which meant cutting into part of the restaurant above. New exits were made, electricity installed. Just as he was sitting down to Christmas dinner in Milwaukee, Wyndham received a cabled message that the Criterion was closing that week. 'What a pleasant appetiser', he wrote to Albery. 'I asked the ladies and gentlemen to charge their glasses and to drink with me in solemn silence to the memory of the departed and once more to the New Criterion. "*Le roi est mort–vive le roi.*"'

Recently, the Alberys had celebrated the birth, on 13 November, of their third son, Wyndham. Possibly, at Christmas, they toasted both Wyndhams: they had reason. Never more closely linked, Wyndham and Albery had become, in their different ways, king-posts of the theatre: Wyndham better known to the public; Albery's plays and adaptations performed through the English-speaking world. Their base was London. What was its theatre like in the early 1880s? According to that searching observer, Henry James, it was 'nowadays decidedly the fashion':

> People go to it a great deal, and are willing to pay high prices for the privilege; they talk of it, they write about it, and in a great many of them, the taste for it takes the form of a desire to pass from the passive to the active side of the footlights. The number of stage-struck persons who are to be met with in the London world is remarkable, and the number of prosperous actors who are but lately escaped amateurs is equally striking. The older actors regard the invasion of this class with melancholy disapproval. The clever people on the London stage today aim at a line of effect in which their being "amateurs" is almost a positive advantage. Small, realistic comedy is their chosen field, and the art of acting as little as possible has—doubtless with good results in some ways—taken the place of the art of acting as much. Of course the older actors with all

their superior science, as they deem it, left on their hands, have no patience with the infatuation of a public which passes from the drawing-room to the theatre only to look at an attempt, at best very imperfect, to reproduce the accidents and limitations of the drawing-room.

James went on to compare playgoing in London, Paris and New York. In spite, he said, of London's greater distances and 'repulsive streets',

you are better seated, less crowded and jostled than in Paris; you are not bullied or irritated by the terrible tribe of the *ouvreuses*. Your neighbours sit quietly and reasonably in their places without trooping out between the acts, to the deep discomfort of your toes and knees. You have a sense of passing an evening in better company than in Paris, and this, if it be not what you go to the theatre for, and if it be but a meagre compensation for a lame performance, may nevertheless, be numbered among the encouragements to playgoing.

'High prices' could mean: Stalls, 10*s.*; Dress circle, 6*s.*; Upper circle, 4*s.*; Amphitheatre, 2*s.* 6*d.*; Pit, 2*s.*; Gallery, 1*s.*; Private boxes, £1 11*s.* 6*d.* to £4 4*s.* This was the tariff for the Lyceum revival of *Two Roses*. But Wyndham himself at the moment was more concerned with the theatre in America, where his repertory would include various Albery texts. At home in Bentinck Terrace, with a shrinking income and an expanding family, Albery's situation would have been awkward indeed if Wyndham had not continued to commission him.

CHAPTER TEN

# 'Comedy! Bah!'

# 1882–1886

Wyndham had arranged to begin his New York season at the Union Square Theatre on 30 October 1882; but when he heard that Mrs Langtry had her première in *An Unequal Match* on the same date he paid generously for a box at the Park Theatre, and with the courtesy invariable through life, postponed his opening until the next night. Three hours before the Langtry curtain was due to rise fire broke out and destroyed the Park, killing two stage-hands. Understandably, Wyndham's house on 31 October was subdued; notices of *Fourteen Days* were less so, especially for its actors, though *The Spirit of the Times* was hardly gallant to the actresses:

> None of the ladies is a professional beauty. All are good looking and will become beautiful after a few months' stay in America has taught them how to make up and how to dress.

And again:

> There is one thing in the performance that could be advantageously cut, and that is the stay-laces. English women are far too fond of the corset.

Forgotten for twenty years, Wyndham's Civil War career was suddenly resurrected; legends of his military service began to circulate, and for some reason this might have helped with *Brighton*, which opened on 20 November. Knowing its American origin and popularity, he had been needlessly worried about it. New York applauded him, and he moved on presently to Cleveland, thence (3 December) to Chicago. There, less for his fame in the theatre than because of his war service and connection with the Great Fire years before, he walked into the centre of a civic

91

welcome. American tours enjoyed superfluous ceremonial, and Chicago had a well-cast, histrionic mayor. That day he was waiting, in full panoply, at Lake Shore Depot. As the players left the station two columns of the Illinois National Guard presented arms and the regimental band struck up; more soldiers lined van Buren and Dearborn Streets; and at Tremont House the mayor himself, who had inevitably been an amateur actor, gave an address which concentrated on his own war career rather than Wyndham's. Fellow-citizens, who had heard it all before, began to heckle him, but Wyndham's reply was tactful and brief. His season at Hooley's Theatre could not have started better, though he did have problems with the American agency, Brooks and Dickson. He wrote to the American dramatist and editor Howard Paul:

> I wish very much you were out here. I wish very much—*entre nous*—that I had come out here on my own hook and co-operated with you—my managers are remarkably nice people—most willing to please in every way—make concession after concession to my wishes—financially and otherwise—but somehow I think I was too modest when I put myself in their hands ...
> They are unfamiliar with the style of entertainment. Fancy, for instance, we go from here [Chicago] to Minneapolis and St Paul—three nights each—to play a company and repertoire that belongs *essentially* to a large blasé city. How I look forward with dread to the journey.

Paul failed to respond, and Wyndham had to continue with the agency. By Christmas he reached Milwaukee; on then to Detroit, and south to Cincinnati, St Louis, Indianapolis, Baltimore and Washington. Since his last tour the railroad system had developed and travelling was easier, though the company had quite a lot to say about the journeys. The *New York Clipper* was tart:

> John Dickson is the manager of the combination for Brooks and Dickson, and his heart is broken over the fault findings and complaints poured into his ear by the Britishers. Nothing is done to their satisfaction, or "like it is over the other side old boy;" and yet the company rides in palace cars [luxurious railway-carriages], puts up in the leading hotels, and carries enough luggage for a circus.

Too bad; but excellent box-office receipts must have pleased 'the Britishers'. From Washington they moved on (presumably in palace cars) to the Walnut Street Theatre, Philadelphia, where twelve years earlier Wyndham had acted in *The Lancers*, with Louisa Moore as his love. So back briefly to New York, and then back to it yet again after visits to New England and Montreal. When, at the Union Square, Wyndham did *The Great Divorce Case* for the first time during the tour his daughter Minnie, who had acting ambitions, took over a small part after a single rehearsal; she called herself 'Miss Curzon'.

That May the company travelled over the Rocky Mountains, across the grey deserts of Utah and Nevada, and saw distant snow on the Sierra before descending to the West Coast. For most of the players—they were the first English company to appear there—this was new ground, potentially fruitful: the local impresario had offered them 65 per cent of the gross receipts and a guaranteed minimum of 3,500 dollars a week. Audiences, alas, were quite unresponsive, both at the Bush Theatre in San Francisco (usually a vaudeville house) and, later, at the Baldwin. A heat-wave exacerbated things. Ironically, it was only during the last three nights that Wyndham had a 'sell-out' for a hurriedly rehearsed *Pink Dominos* (with an extra Sunday performance thrown in). Too late: the local manager lost 10,000 dollars. This failure, the only one on his tour, baffled Wyndham; but one cause, certainly, was resentment at the opening choice of *Brighton*, an English company in what had been an American play. New York and other cities had accepted it. The West Coast would not, and the *San Francisco Daily Reporter* did not try to hide its feelings:

> Comedy! Bah! It was farce from first to last—noisy, fussy farce. Everybody with the slightest pretension to dramatic taste was disappointed and not a few disgusted.
> Wyndham speaks so rapidly and indistinctly that one is compelled to strain every nerve to understand him.

There was a strong anti-British faction here, especially among Irish immigrants at a time when the Home Rule problem was being hotly argued. Wyndham remained discreet while in earshot of the local press, and the *Daily Reporter* had to admit that he

> speaks in a manly way of his failure here. He blames neither the press nor the public, but attributes it solely to the true cause—an ill-advised opening.

Diplomatic; but some weeks later, when embarking for home at Quebec, he did let himself go, rather eloquently, and his eloquence filtered westward. *San Francisco Music and Drama* published it:

> San Francisco! Why, it's the worst show town in America. Give them *Pink Dominos* and they are happy. Let them hear gray-haired jokes at the Minstrels and they crowd the house. Take them a first class opera troupe like McCaull's, an actress like Janauschek or Modjeska, and they give them the cold shoulder. Why, I had the best comedy troupe ever seen there, and I made a miserable failure of it.

In spite of this, the San Francisco manager afterwards offered him a return engagement on his own terms, a gesture that Wyndham (who had lost nothing himself) thought it best to refuse. Much had happened before this. At Salt Lake City the company had a week at Haverley's Opera House; poor audiences and a pursuing heat-wave. There was something unintentionally comic about Wyndham in the city of the Mormons, as Bob Sackett, a man with three fiancées. As he said to Albery, 'I cannot write you a long letter because I am diligently studying the Mormon question in all its branches.' The letter was to ask Albery for three extra characters for Act Two of *The Lancers:*

> My reason for desiring this is twofold. First, it will be impossible to get guests to look anything but cowboys in this country as we travel along, and next I don't wish to lose the names out of the bill but on the contrary to make it as full as my usual pieces. . . . You must be careful to make them all rather telling, especially Blakeley's part, so that they do not feel humiliated by playing them. . . . But do not in any way interfere with the plot. Let that remain just as it is. The Act is a perfect comedy act and only requires these alterations for my special necessities.

With some relief the company climbed into the cool air of the Rockies. At Denver it played for a week at the Tabor Grand Opera House, built by the Silver King, Horace Austin Warner Tabor, who had incensed local opinion by marrying his mistress, 'Baby' Doe, and bringing her to Denver. Unluckily for Wyndham, the Tabor family was in conflict with the *Denver Republican*, and the Opera House even announced on its bills that it did not advertise in the paper,

> which is not on the free list of the Opera House, and for that reason, we are informed the management of that paper have announced their intention of criticising adversely all attractions regardless of their merit, that may appear at the Tabor Grand Opera House. The Opera House management respectfully calls the attention of the public to the above facts, in justice to themselves and the combinations playing with them.

Firm, one would think; but, obstinately, the *Republican* paid for seats. After praising Wyndham and his company, it observed frigidly:

> Much discredit reflects upon the management of the house for its discourteous want of energy in allowing so strong an attraction to be so poorly attended.

There was more trouble. On Independence Day three county com-missioners were ambushed and killed by masked gunmen, found later to be leading citizens who objected to an increase in the rates. This too naturally affected the Opera House.

At length Wyndham's company travelled on to Quebec. Not far behind the train was another with the Governor-General of Canada (the Mar-quess of Lorne) and his wife, Princess Louise, aboard. When at the first stop Mary Rorke and Hamilton Astley got out to walk along the platform, they were mistaken for the Princess and the Governor-General, and this was repeated along the line, where other players joined in enthusiastically, curtseying and removing their hats. In Quebec Lord Lorne thanked them for sparing him much hard work, as the crowds had gone before his own train arrived.

# II

The company had just a month at home before returning to New York. Wyndham went to Paris, and thence wrote to Albery about *The Lancers* addition—still, it appeared unsatisfying: 'What an impractical man you are! If you read my letter you will see all I asked you to do for this piece.' Wyndham, it seems, had decided to be firm: 'Pray work hard for one day at what I want like a good fellow.' To a man of such enormous energy as Wyndham, Albery's growing lethargy must have been inexplicable. Yet, obviously liking the man and his work, he continued to employ him.

Back in America during September, the company went into a new season at Union Square with *The Great Divorce Case*, followed by *Pink Dominos*. Only the women's clothes failed to please. Thus, the *New York Mirror:*

> The ladies . . . are all clever. Their acting might be studied with profit by many of our native comedy actresses. But in the matter of dress they are simply barbarous. A more ugly, ill-fitting, unharmonious, unsightly collection of female garments than those worn by Mr Wyndham's female assistants it would be well nigh impossible to gather together. But we can forgive the English women their ignorance of dressing on account of their knowledge of acting. Contact with their American sisters should teach them how to remedy their gaucheries.

Wyndham could have extended his stay, gaucheries or not, but because Henry Irving and Ellen Terry were coming at the end of October he decided to move on, a tour rather less exhausting than the first, with fewer stops and a longer engagement at each place. New England success in what were then risqué plays thoroughly astonished them. Indeed, during six splendid weeks at the Bijou, Boston, they added to their repertory *Pink Dominos, Where's the Cat?* and *Butterfly Fever*, enjoyed to the full, double-meanings and all. When they did *The Lancers* (with characters at last added by Albery) Wyndham revived local memories, for he had played the same part there in 1870. A Philadelphia clash with Irving and Ellen Terry, who were at the Opera House, did not harm their Walnut Street business. And receipts had been so good at Hooley's, Chicago, that they were invited to return: gratifying, for some people in Chicago had found offence in *Pink Dominos*, the local *Tribune* among them:

Mr Wyndham's company acted with a refinement which partly redeemed the suggestiveness of the comedy ... *Pink Dominos* was an unsavoury dish served up on a plate of silver.

We gather from a notice in the *Chicago Times* that unprofessional conduct on stage was not unknown:

The members indulge in no lapses from the business in hand—they do not seem to be peering about in search of acquaintances in the audience, or nodding and smiling to unseen people behind the scenes, or engaging in whispered converse with each other on matters foreign to the play, or, indeed, doing any of the thousand things of the kind common to most of our companies.

*Inter-ocean* broke the news that Wyndham might return to Chicago regularly:

To those who admire finished work in comedy ... we can present the agreeable information that there is a fair prospect that Mr Wyndham's company may become something more and better than an incident of occasional seasons.

In fact, nothing happened. The tour continued, to the deep South and back. There had been talk of a return New York visit, but Wyndham decided against it. He had heard that alterations to the Criterion were now ready, earlier than expected, and he was anxious to reopen the theatre.

# III

In America he had Albery in mind, commissioning several adaptations from both the French and the German; constantly he was urging Albery to 'lose no time', 'my plans depend very much on a prompt delivery', 'I beg you to do it immediately.' He did receive one script, Albery's translation—hardly more—of *Ihr Ideale* by Heinrich Stobitzer, of which Wyndham wrote to him from Chicago:

*Ideals* has come. Life is a mixture of fortune and misfortune. I fear to produce the play. I am afraid it would be howled at. Now and then you have touched to my mind the right chord, but then you seem to have gone off the line again. The piece is inconsistent in its character. I am waiting anxiously for *Beaten Track*. Excuse more. I am killed by hard work and lack of time to do it in. I play 2 pieces each performance and act 8 times a week. As I am my own manager, my own secretary—[*illegible*] being too busy on other matters—I have my hands full.
    Kind regards to Mrs Albery

*The Beaten Track* (originally *Paul and Virginia*) was also from the German; though Wyndham hoped to produce it in America, he did not get the finished version in time. From Chicago (February 1884) he wrote to tell Albery of 'an odd thing . . . by which I hope to secure you a tolerably good sum.' He had discovered that the Wallacks intended to produce a play they had had in stock for ten years, a script unnamed and unsigned. When Wyndham heard the plot he recognized it at once as Albery's *Married*, in which he had acted at the Royalty in 1873; now he asked the Wallacks to let him have it if it was a success. He needed a play: as he said to Albery, 'having given up any definite hope of getting a piece from you in time to play over here, and in London.' Negotiations with the Wallacks were tricky; they claimed that, ten years before, Sothern had given them the script with full rights, and Wyndham asked Albery—without much hope—to look over his papers to see whether he ever did give or sell Sothern a copy of *Married*. Whether Albery received anything from this source is doubtful.

Wyndham had done extremely well in America; he never gave up trying to help Albery (late scripts or not). He wanted also to get Mrs John Wood for a part in *Featherbrain*, the next farce he was planning for the Criterion. The idea of having 'Ma' Wood came to him in America; and he wrote from New Orleans asking Albery to look over the part and to put in some lines for her:

> Think it over and if you agree with me tell Smale [acting manager and treasurer] to open negotiations with the lady . . . I am willing to encounter the extra expense for the sake of the fun we shall gain by it.

As he was still uncertain about the piece, he wrote rather desperately to Albery, 'If any good lines occur to you, pray put them in, for believe me they are needed.' Before *Featherbrain* opened Wyndham appeared on 16 April at the refurbished Criterion in *Brighton*, the first play he had done there. This was wise; he was not in *Featherbrain*; few things did so well there without him, and he had been unable to engage Mrs Wood. Though Albery kept fairly close to the French original, *Tête de Linotte*, he did make one change to avoid giving offence. A married man who tells his mistress he is a bachelor, became simply a bachelor. A few days before the first night—23 June—Wyndham sent Albery a cheque

> as a slight souvenir of our wrangles, dispute, and hearty work. If the piece turns out well I shall still remember practically my indebtedness to the English author.
> I am bound to admit however that I am afraid of it. It seems to lack the one great essential for all these light pieces, "go." I hope I am mistaken. We shall know I suppose on Tuesday.

*Featherbrain* lasted two months; the Criterion closed for the summer, and then the play came on again for another seven weeks. Wyndham's

97

doubts were realized, for it had nothing like the life of the usual Criterion farce. Mary Albery attended *Featherbrain* rehearsals. At one of these Wyndham did suggest that she should take the place of an actress who had failed to please him. Greatly tempted, she would not accept: 'I was too shy in those days, so I lost my chance.'

In spite of Wyndham's easy control of the Criterion, he was not in any way complacent: he knew too much about the theatrical seesaw. His next choice, called *The Candidate*, had failed in Paris, and he himself had little faith in it. Rehearsed in ten days, it opened on 22 November without an author's name on the programme. Eventually (one of those revelations that delight the press) the dramatist was found to be Justin Huntly M'Carthy, Irish politician and historian, who had worked on a piece, *Le Député de Bambignac* by Alexandre Bisson, which had the type of milieu he knew intimately. As one critic said:

> Politics just now form the most popular topic of conversation, and, here, whether we be Conservatives or Radicals, we find our politics ready-made and to hand. At clubs, at balls and dinner-parties, they will be discussing Viscount Oldacre and Mr Baffin, his secretary, and their adventures at Easthampton.

M'Carthy enjoyed his chances for political satire just as much as audiences enjoyed the current (and transparent) allusions. This was adaptation with a difference; it had nothing whatever to do with Mrs Grundy.

Wyndham (as a Lord Oldacre) again had mother-in-law trouble, a light comedian's occupational hazard. To escape from it, Oldacre plans to contest an election at Easthampton. Then, sending his secretary to impersonate him, he goes up to town, heedless that the secretary is a Radical while he is a true-blue Conservative. (If he had once thought about it, the play would never have existed, but in the period's convention—in frivolous comedy through the ages—one had to allow for extremes of fantasy.) When the secretary arrives at Easthampton he is all but lynched by a Radical mob and forced to make a speech with a left-wing slant. Predictably, he is elected; and, on returning home after a fortnight's delicious freedom the horrified Oldacre learns that he is now a Radical Member. The secretary excuses himself: 'Advocate the preservation of the Peers with a water-butt close by!—it was not to be done for a moment.' The character was said to have been based on Charles Bradlaugh, Member for Northampton (hence Easthampton), who was known as 'the working man's friend'.

As usual, Wyndham himself triumphed. So did George Giddens (who had been in the American company). For this production two innovations: no orchestra, and to indicate curtain-rise the traditional *trois coups*, the three knocks of the French stage. Wyndham also dispensed with the call-boy; artists were called by an electric bell. However, these measures had little to do with the success of *The Candidate*. Hurriedly put on, it lasted for 285 performances.

# IV

Now Albery's health deteriorated. Early in 1885 it broke down so seriously that he could no longer write. As Mary said 'It paralysed his pen'; what the trouble was is not plain; certainly he drank too much, but this could not have been the entire story. He had problems with his sight, and he had hurt his right hand. At his marriage Albery had been at the crest of his popularity, with a good income from performances in England and abroad: an income lost to him because he had invested heavily and unwisely in the family business, a rope walk that, under his partner and brother-in-law, Usher Back, was no longer flourishing. With a wife, three children and a dwindling income, he was in a dilemma. Looking into the family finances, Mary saw they were worse than she feared. On top of everything else, James was in debt. She had to do something quickly, so she sold up their home in Bentinck Terrace, and packed off Albery, the children and a faithful nurse to lodgings in Ramsgate. With no one to turn to in the immediate family—soon after her marriage her beloved mother had died—she sought an old friend, Alice Howard, in England then with her husband Bronson for the production of his play *Young Mrs Winthrop*.

Young Mrs Albery was in desperate need. Would Alice give her an introduction to her brother, Charles Wyndham? Mary had acted briefly, and the stage seemed to be her only hope of employment. Moreover, the Bronson Howards were close friends; Albery had anglicized Howard's *The Banker's Daughter* (in London, *The Old Love and the New*); their second son was called Bronson, and the Howards were his godparents. Alice did come to the rescue, and the forlorn Mary Albery presented herself at Boscombe Lodge, Wyndham's house in Finchley Road. She was nervous, all the more so because Wyndham averted his eyes from her throughout the interview. A kind man, he wanted to help, but as he told Alice it would be hopeless to put Mary on the stage—she looked so old and worn. (She was twenty-three.) In the end he compromised by engaging her at £4 a week for *The Candidate* tour, understudying Isabel Eveson, an American actress who played Lady Dorothy. She was told that Miss Eveson would leave the company in three weeks; this did not happen, but after a month while they were at the Prince of Wales's, Liverpool, Mary had to go on suddenly for a matinée; the manageress of the theatre, Fanny Josephs (who had been in the Criterion *Pink Dominos*), assured her that although she lacked the American girl's experience, she was 'more the English lady'. That was hopeful; but when Isabel Eveson returned Mary knew that Wyndham did not intend her to act. Guaranteed a weekly wage as an understudy, and nothing more, she saw that this would never do, and resolved to go up to London at once to confront Wyndham. After she had reported at the Prince of Wales's, and ensured that Isabel Eveson was on, she took an evening train to London, arrived at the Criterion as the curtain was falling, and went behind. When Wyndham saw her he asked what she was doing: 'You ought to be in Liverpool.'

Boldness was the only course. It all depended on him, she said, whether she returned or not: 'I have discovered your kind ruse to *give* me a salary, but this will be of no use unless it is going to help me to *earn* one in the future. I must be allowed to play one of the parts to see if I am going to be any good.' When she had got him to understand how strongly she felt he agreed that she should go back to the tour and he would arrange a part for her. Next morning, as she looked from the train window, her hat, her only good hat—it was trimmed with an ostrich feather—blew off. She draped a shawl over her head, and with customary good sense consoled herself that at least it had not happened on her way to London. Soon she received the small part of Lady Oldacre, played until then by a former amateur actress who did not need the money and who knew Mary's plight. Though Mary did not like taking the part from her, they would always remain good friends.

To get acting experience was not her sole worry. Albery's illness and his inability to work must have been sorely on her mind—just how much this letter from Liverpool shows:

My dear Jim,
Many thanks for your letter. It certainly looks very shaky, but still it is a beginning, and I hope you will persevere, for I can always read your writing, and I would rather have a nice long letter from you, like you used to write me, however shaky, than the best written letter that you could dictate.

Besides, if you keep *writing* every day your hand will soon get steady. It is dis-use that makes it so unsteady. Now do like a dear boy, try and finish *The Beaten Track* there is so little to be done to it, and I am sure Nannie would write it for you, at dictation. If you would only try and rouse yourself, you could have everything your own way. You ought to be feeling better by now dear, for you have been at Ramsgate for two months now. Don't forget to answer all the questions I asked in my last, in your next letter. Be very loving and kind to the dear little boys. God bless you all,

Yours affectionately,
Mary

For the last week of the tour the company was in Brighton. Mary received a telegram inviting her to a party next Sunday at Wyndham's new house in St John's Wood. That summer his daughter Minnie had been married to a barrister; the young couple had taken over Boscombe Lodge, and Wyndham and his wife had moved into the large Manor House at 43 St John's Wood Park, on the edge of the original wood. The road, which ran between Wellington and Avenue Roads, widened into a triangle and then narrowed again. From his bedroom in Finchley Road, Thomas Hood had watched the houses going up in the 1840s: styles varied between stucco hunting-lodge and Italianate villa. Wyndham's Manor House, standing alone behind a stone balustrade, was massive and imposing, with a tower room at its centre. There were trees everywhere: great oaks, planes, sycamores, and lilacs, laburnums, may. During the eighties and nineties arches spanned St John's Wood Park at the Adelaide Road end. (They were pulled down in 1914.) A procession of Victorian figures moved across its shaded pavements and knew its secluded charm. Dickens walked down the road on his way to W. P. Frith's house to have his portrait painted, (Frith had tried through four years to talk him out of being painted with a moustache.) Mrs Henry Wood wrote *East Lynne* there ('dead, and never called me Mother'); Jean Gravelet ('Blondin'), fresh from Niagara, walked a tight-rope strung across his lawn; Hengler, the showman who built a permanent circus where the London Palladium stands, lived at No. 13; and later Ralph Partridge the antique dealer would drive in one of his many carriages from No. 25 to his business in St James's Street: he kept eight horses, and when he changed to cars after the First World War the coachman became his chauffeur. They talked too in the Park of a haunted house; perhaps the ghost of Little Willie from *East Lynne*? During the 1930s Owen Nares lived at No. 2, a tall white house opposite Dennis Wheatley at No. 8; but the leases were running out, and the land reverted to the Eyre Estate; the houses crumbled, once neat gardens became hopelessly overgrown; and the demolishers moved in.

As, in the distant Eighties, Mary had 'nothing to wear' for the occasion—her good clothes were in store—a friend lent her a dress which they altered to fit. On her arrival at the Manor House, Wyndham—who was in his element when called on to stage-manage a large party—drew her hand through his arm, took her into the ballroom and stayed with her until she was surrounded by friends.

She went back to the company for the autumn. Wyndham had decided to play the fortnight's return visit to Liverpool with the Criterion cast; 'Lady Oldacre' became ill and Mary (nervously) succeeded her— nervously, because she had to act with Wyndham, who cheered her by saying that she was to come to London. At this time another young actress had joined the company: May Whitty, whose daughter Margaret Webster would write, sixty years later, that on the short tour her mother learned the valuable lessons of clarity, precision and pace:

> Wyndham played comedy with mathematical exactness, but his smooth, light dexterity made what he said no more than the natural and spontaneous expression of his thought. He did not teach much by direct instruction; you watched and tried it out and became a little better at it.

101

Mary was quick to pass on theatre news to Albery:

> I think Bruce at the Princes would be your best plan, or Mrs Langtry who
> I hear has got a failure . . . and wants a new play badly. . . .

For herself, she had got on very well, and she 'liked it'—acting, we
suppose. All the same, if she had £500 a year she would not bother.
Though she had not yet heard from the Criterion, they generally did
things in a hurry, so she would not be surprised to be recalled to town any
day. She assured Jim that she was not 'quite jolly' without him. The fact
that he could read (even large type) was a very good sign. Next she wrote
to tell him they were going to do Bronson Howard's *Truth!* for a week,
and that she had been cast as the young wife, the best part she had had: 'I
thought of you so much all the morning as the piece is so brightly written.'
(Albery had adapted it for the English stage.) Presently, recalled to town,
she acted at the Criterion for the first time—in *The Candidate*—on 26
October 1885. She was also in the curtain-raiser, *Cupid in Camp* ('I am
afraid my performance was not of the best but . . . my head was in a whirl
at my sudden access to good fortune').

Exiled in Ramsgate and urged by his wife—'it would be such a comfort
to have that done at last'—Albery managed to finish *The Beaten Track*,
and he also revised his play *Fortune*, renamed *Judy Morris*. In these
months his only contribution to the family purse came from a *Two Roses*
tour, a revival of *The Crisis* (rechristened *The Denhams*) at the Court,
and a few small amounts from Usher Back towards the cost of the
business Albery had sold to him. The children's nurse had to go without
wages for more than a year.

During the long run of *The Candidate* (which ended on 16 January
1886), Wyndham had pondered on his future, and the future of his
theatre. Which way next? Interminably, it seemed, little French farces.
Though he had established the value of treating farce seriously, he
showed how restless he was by producing other kinds of play at the
Crystal Palace Theatre. Yet he could not quite break his attachment.
While on holiday himself he arranged for *The Man with Three Wives!*
'from the French,' to enter the Criterion bill, and Mary had a tiny part in
it, experiencing for the first time the invisible attentions of an admirer.
He sent notes and flowers—that was all, but it was enough for Lytton
Sothern, whose taste for practical jokes derived from his father, E. A.
Sothern, to pretend that the man was dangerous and after her. No
wonder that Mary 'regained my youth', and looked on life with hope
renewed. She still earned £4 a week; of this she sent £2 to Ramsgate;
weekly board and lodging with a friend of her mother's in Mornington
Crescent cost her fifteen shillings; and somehow she managed to pay the
fare (about seven shillings) to Ramsgate every Sunday. She might protest
to Jim that she was not 'quite jolly' without him; but she was happy: 'to be

young and feel that your foot is on the ladder—that indeed is happiness.
Success had not come to me at this time, though it was very near.' When
Wyndham decided to break from farce and to try something new he swept
Mary with him—up several rungs of that invisible and inevitable ladder.

# CHAPTER ELEVEN

# 'Listen again'
# 1886–1889

Back from the Riviera, Wyndham went to see how *The Man with Three Wives!* had fared. Seeing that Mary Moore looked so much younger and prettier, he told her he had a good part for her in the next play: exciting news, and there would be another excitement ahead, her first experience of acting in the enormous Crystal Palace Theatre (not much like the Criterion), where the company gave a matinée of *The Man with Three Wives!* The next play was a farce, *The Circassian*; from the outset, its rehearsals were tiresome. To get the best from his actors Wyndham lost his temper frequently (and not always genuinely), passing storms that while they lasted had Mary in tears: uncertain as she was, she was terrified of losing her job. One day, after being especially harsh, Wyndham ordered tea. The other actresses called him a darling for having thought of it:

'Mrs Albery doesn't think so.'

'Mrs Albery hasn't said what she thinks.'

Wyndham took the hint, and thereafter behaved more gently until the production was ready and its opening date fixed. Now tired of farce, he probably regretted doing another; only two days before the first night he decided to scrap *The Circassian*. Possibly it lacked the essential 'go'. Whatever its faults, he knew in his producer's bones that it would fail. He needed to do something entirely different—a costume play, *Wild Oats*, from the late eighteenth century. When he had first played Jack Rover in the Royalty Theatre revival of 1873 it was a part he had been longing for since the days of Samuel Phelps. Dismayed, Mary heard of the death of *The Circassian*, and when told that Wyndham had asked to see her she thought he must be going to say there was nothing for her in *Wild Oats*. But there was: a leading part, Lady Amaranth. Wyndham amused her by saying that her personality suited a Quakeress.

It would be an event. For the first time at the Criterion Wyndham put on a play whose long theatrical history had begun at Covent Garden in 1791. The author, John O'Keeffe, was Irish. Formerly an actor, his sight failed in his early twenties. Whenever a play of his was performed his son would lead him to a door beside the stage, where he listened at the keyhole for any sound of the reception. If he heard hissing he would press his fingers to his ears until applause burst out, and his son would tug his arm and say, 'Now, Father, listen again!' Mrs Inchbald's study of the man whom Hazlitt called, with some exaggeration, 'our English Molière' had a sequel at the Criterion after ninety-five years. If the blind author had come to the première he would have had to deafen himself to noises outside the theatre. The difficulty was that all scenery (eleven changes) had to be carried through the front of the house, lifted over the footlights and put together there. Stage-manager and master-carpenter held that it was impossible to be ready in time. No scenic rehearsal took place until an hour-before the curtain should have risen. It was bound to be late; when impatient sounds had been volleying outside the theatre for some time Wyndham ordered the pit and gallery doors to be opened; an angry crowd surged in as, not yet dressed or made up for Jack Rover, Wyndham came in front of the curtain, and announced that before the rest of the house was admitted he was going to say something 'in confidence'. After explaining the difficulties of getting an 'elephant into a bandbox', he asked forgiveness for any hitches and waits to come (as it happened, there were few). His charm was sovereign. On that night, 29 May, the audience responded faultlessly.

While Wyndham talked to pit and gallery the new leading lady was in her dressing-room, being helped into her costume by Mrs Labouchere (formerly Henrietta Hodson, with whom Wyndham had once acted Rover at the Royalty Theatre). It had been his idea that Mary should ask Mrs Labouchere to coach her; the result pleased him, and saved any scenes at rehearsal. Mrs Labouchere even lent Mary the French-grey silk dress she had worn in 1873, and added a lace shawl; Mary's neat figure showed off the costume perfectly, and she must have realized how it suited her. This, the older woman's kindness, and Wyndham's encouragement, combined to send her on without (she said) 'the paralysing nervousness that has always seized me since on every other first night'.

Wyndham too looked handsome in knee-breeches fastened with silver buttons, a satin waistcoat, lace jabot and cuffs. As he made his entrance on 'I am the bold Thunder!' he was foretelling a thunderous reception to come. Rover, the strolling player, scatters quotations like thistledown—the opening line comes from Buckingham's *The Rehearsal*, and in itself sets the plot going. Mistaken for Sir George Thunder's son who has run away from school to join a group of actors, Rover is dragged to the house of Lady Amaranth, a wealthy Quakeress to whom Sir George hopes his son will be engaged. Repeatedly, Amaranth addresses the young man as 'my pleasant cousin', a catch-phrase to which Mary Moore (said one of the next day's notices) gave 'a musical intonation'. She was duly discovered as a 'coming actress', and Wyndham told her he would raise her salary; she had just signed a contract for three years at £4 a week during the first year, £5 in the second, and £7 in the third. She told him now that she owed him everything for having trusted her. 'The result', she wrote later, 'might have been the other way round, when he would have had me on his hands for three years—*for I should not have released him.*' (This was Mary's true voice.) They agreed in the end to vary the terms, so that she would be leading lady at the Criterion for two years, with £5 for the first and £7 for the second. Wyndham also paid her (and she was most grateful) during the summer vacation, a gesture rare in those days.

*Wild Oats* did everything Wyndham had hoped. As Mrs Inchbald had written of it in 1808 (and as the Royal Shakespeare Company would discover in the 1970s):

> soon after its first production that source of a new kind of mirth, termed by some exquisite nonsense, of which he [O'Keeffe] was the first discoverer, made the town so merry that, like good wine, he might have sold it at any price.

The truth that most people had no idea where Rover's quotations came from hardly mattered. Wyndham himself was on delicate ground. A line of celebrated actors had played Rover down the years—William Lewis, R. W. Elliston, Charles Mathews the Elder, Phelps—and comparisons were natural:

> Mathews had not the *élan* of Wyndham, nor had Wyndham ever quite the easy elegance of the repose that marked the most mercurial flights of the elder Charles.

Thus the historian Barton Baker. If Wyndham ever read that *History of the London Stage* it would have pleased him to know how Baker recognized his depth, passion and pathos, 'whereas his famous predecessor, away from the lighter vein of comedy, was not distinguished.' Wyndham was anxious to prove definitively that he was more than a featherweight farceur: and *Wild Oats*, though a comedy, undoubtedly helped.

On 8 October he did what he had contemplated for some years: he changed his name from Culverwell by deed poll which described him as 'a comedian', and in which he affirmed:

> Whereas for many years past I have but rarely used my family name of Culverwell and am desirous of absolutely abandoning and disusing the same. . . .

106

His son Howard, then at home on leave from his Colorado ranch, was now twenty-one, and had no objection. It seemed to be a proper moment to become Wyndham legally.

## II

So much for the newly ratified Wyndham. Little enough during 1886 had happened to Albery: a benefit performance, for David James, of *Tweedie's Rights* and *Chiselling* at the Gaiety; a revival by Hermann Vezin of *Doctor Davy*; and some plays in touring engagements. Wyndham, determined to keep Albery working, asked him to repolish the dialogue of *David Garrick*, the next Criterion choice, in T. W. Robertson's version which E. A. Sothern had used twenty-two years earlier. Albery's notion of cutting Squire Chivy's intrusion towards the end of the play was an improvement, one that made it easier for Wyndham and Mary Moore's Ada to sustain the emotion of their last scene. Albery wrote too a new line for Garrick, 'a good woman is an understudy for an angel', which Wyndham seized in future for any autograph album.

Anxious to have the best possible text, he engaged two other play-doctors as well as Albery. Clearly, after the reception of *Wild Oats*, he would welcome another period comedy: he looked his best in eighteenth-century costume—remember his Charles Surface—and the notion of playing Garrick appealed to him as it would to any leading actor. Robertson's son wrote to wish him success 'in a part most admirably adapted to you'. A magnanimous thought, for young Robertson must have known that Wyndham, on his Criterion summit, would make a great deal out of a play that poor Tom had sold to a publisher for ten pounds.

Mary was not altogether in key with Ada Ingot, the lovesick maiden whom Garrick disillusions by pretending to be a drunkard. She was not surprised to be ignored or only faintly praised: Ada is essentially a feed for Garrick himself:

> really the least effective character in the piece. The old maid Araminta is a far more grateful part, and often when Mr Wyndham told me [wrote Mary] I was not looking well, I would answer lightly "Never mind, I can always play Araminta."

Although Mrs Labouchere helped her again, Mary was initially too inexperienced to cope with the mannered style. Wyndham himself could not fail as Garrick, though some older playgoers—as always on these occasions—had seen Sothern and were disappointed in the new man. Presently they had another chance for comparison when Edward Compton brought to the Strand a production that had gone briskly out of

107

town: yet another text, William Muskerry's *Garrick: or Only an Actor*.
Wyndham tried to get an injunction against this. He failed, and so did the
play. Compton had soon, and aptly, to substitute *The Rivals*.

At the Criterion dress rehearsal of *David Garrick*, Ben Farjeon, the
novelist and Wyndham's old friend, suggested that the second-act curtain
should immediately follow the drunk scene, and this change Wyndham
made. He respected Farjeon's judgment, and after every first night used to
say, 'Now, Ben, tell me the truth.' When all was said and done, with the
help of Albery, Alfred C. Calmour (author of *The Amber Heart*), and
others, the old piece was better-shaped when it opened at the Criterion on
13 November 1886. Wyndham and Mary Moore would play their parts
hundreds of times in what was at once a triumph, a valuable stop-gap and
easily their most famous production.

Physically, Wyndham was far more handsome and imposing than the
real David Garrick. He had his show-piece in the already historic drunk
scene, but the part also needed subtlety when Garrick must both indicate
his dislike of behaving as he does, and yet persuade the girl that he is a
drunkard. In time Mary satisfied herself; thenceforward their partnership was never in doubt. Ironically, though Wyndham had freed himself
from the clatter of farce, yet both he and Mary would be bound to what a
later critic, Willson Disher, called the 'story of a heart of gold wrapped in
a player's hide'. It so happened that in the year he first played David
Garrick he was elected to the exclusive Garrick Club (where his portrait
by the Academician John Pettie now hangs). Unlike Albery, he was never
an inveterate clubman—there was no time—and because he always
walked home to St John's Wood after the theatre he could not attend
supper parties. Still, the new honour pleased him.

On 7 January 1887 at 10 p.m. (local time) Wyndham gave *David
Garrick* for the Prince and Princess of Wales at Sandringham House in
Norfolk. It was the first play performed there, and on so small a stage the
quick scene-change in the last act was testing. At the Criterion they could
manage this with a whole battalion of stage-hands, and now as many as
forty of them went up to Sandringham when the Prince assured
Wyndham that he wanted everything done as it was in the theatre. But
where could such a large gathering have supper? At the local inn,
Wyndham thought. Not at all: the Prince insisted that everyone should
come to Sandringham: 'They would like it.' They did; and he looked in on
the men during their meal. The players supped with the royal party in the
conservatory; a nervous Mary sat beside the Duke of Clarence, who held
her fan, made appropriately of three ostrich feathers. After the night's
excitement (for which Wyndham received a silver loving-cup) she found
the drive in the sharp air over the snow to King's Lynn wonderfully
calming.

The Command performance was splendid publicity, and *David Garrick*
flourished still further, though the part was so much Wyndham's own

that when a heavy cold prevented him from going on performances were cancelled: a secondary Garrick would have been unthinkable. Following custom when caught in a long run Wyndham planned ahead. He had thought of doing *Passion Flowers*, an adaptation by T. W. Robertson of Alfred de Musset's *On ne badine pas avec l'amour*, in which Madge Kendal had once played the heroine. Now she was called in to coach Mary, a part by no means suitable ('being of an imperious description'), and as Mary, like most people, stood in awe of Mrs Kendal, little progress was made and Wyndham abandoned the play.

That June a German theatrical agent called Bernstein saw *David Garrick*. Knowing Wyndham spoke German, he talked of a visit to the Residenz Theatre in Berlin. It was a pity, he said, that Mary could not come as well: 'If only she could speak German.' Mary, who did know a little, promptly addressed him in German, and Bernstein, delighted, insisted that she and Wyndham would be an enormous success together in Berlin. It was settled; they would appear with a German company at the end of the year, and Wyndham himself translated the play.

Mary spent the summer vacation with the Bronson Howards in America where she met William H. Crane and Stuart Robson, the two comedians who had been so prominent in *The Henrietta*, Howard's satire on high finance. Because she knew she would need a refresher course, she travelled home by a German liner: a scheme which appealed to her practical nature, but failed because during a rough passage 'the doctor was my only chance. Unfortunately, he also had the idea that it would be good for his English to practise on me, and the weather being all in his favour he won easily.' In the circumstances she went to Berlin during September in advance of Wyndham. Bernstein, who met her, had booked her into a Friedrichstrasse *pension* where she was able to study with the daughter of the house, a governess. To help with pronunciation, Wyndham summoned an expert, a professor, who opened his exceptionally large mouth so wide when he articulated that Mary could not help watching him, and the object of the exercise was lost; more helpfully, she accompanied Wyndham to the Berlin theatres.

The *pension* was not at all expensive, so she sent for her sons and their nurse, Ann, who got her out of an absurd situation. Like many players, she was intensely superstitious, and when she saw the new moon shining through her window—traditionally, a month's bad luck—she rushed to tell Wyndham that she could not appear; she knew she would fail. Reasonably, Wyndham was annoyed; if she were going to be as foolish as this she would have to go back to England. Fräulein X, a German actress in the first piece, could play Ada. In tears Mary returned to the lodgings, where Ann was candid with her. If she went home without playing she would be unhappy. Then why not stay and take the chance? It was unanswerable, and she wrote at once to Wyndham to say she had changed her mind, an incident that somehow fortified her for the ordeal.

109

All was not yet plain sailing. Herr Lautenberg, manager of the Residenz, was unpredictably doubtful, and told Wyndham he wanted to break the contract. Wyndham would have none of this. He had already announced the news at home, and it was essential for them both to appear. Without a word to Lautenberg, he consulted Bernstein and contrived to organize a provincial try-out. As Herr Synthal and Fräulein Maurel they played *David Garrick* with a stock company at Liegnitz in Silesia (the modern Legnica), and though they were somewhat disturbed by the Continental system of audible prompting from a box at the centre of the footlights they were hugely popular, and invited to stay for the rest of the week. Booked already for two nights at Frankfurt-on-Oder, they could do no more than return to Liegnitz afterwards, where houses were sold out, and the local press wrote like this:

> Seldom have we seen the Liegnitz audience, which is generally considered very cold, so enthusiastic. And they were right. Mr Wyndham is a great artist. Miss Moore, who played the part of Ada Ingot, charms through her tender, pure appearance—through her sweet face, with the large speaking eyes. . . . She possesses very touching tones, but she has more difficulties to master in the German language than her companion . . .
>
> LIEGNITZER TAGEBLATT

> Nothing was to be seen of the usual theatrical gestures; it was all so natural, so artistically simple, that the moderated method [restraint] of the accomplished actress astonished us.
>
> LIEGNITZER ZEITUNG

Having discovered where they were, Lautenberg sent Edmund Reicher, his leading actor, the potential Simon Ingot, to tell them he was firm; their contract was to be cancelled. But seeing the impression they had made in Liegnitz, Reicher persuaded Lautenberg to relent, and after all they opened in Berlin. Wyndham's daughter heard someone in the theatre say that he had come to see the English clowns, which was hardly encouraging, and when the first piece was greeted by hisses and abuse Wyndham begged Fräulein X not to tell Mary; instead she ran to the dressing-room and said that the audience was in splendid form. Wyndham's resolve to play there was justified; the opening night was so exuberant that after Mary's first exit the audience would not let the play proceed until she had returned to take a call. Edmund Reicher met her in the wings, he clasped her in his arms and kissed his *süsses Kind*. At the end of the second act the press sent a unanimous tribute (scarcely a custom with English critics). And while Wyndham and Mary were at supper after the show Lautenberg called at their hotel to apologize for his want of faith. Next morning the notices were good. 'Miss Moore', said one, 'does not speak our language as well as her talented companion, but with what consoling charm!'

They were fêted and toasted and expected to reply in German—a cue for Wyndham to begin truthfully: 'Accustomed as I am . . .' One evening at a supper-party he mischievously told the guests that in his family Miss Moore herself always responded. Unluckily for him, she had just prepared a speech which she delivered fluently—and in German. She had it ready because on the previous night Wyndham's daughter, Mrs Spencer Bower, who had been educated in Germany, was asked to speak, and—nervous and unprepared as she was—could get out very little. It made Mary determined not to be caught but to have something in hand. Another experience was less cheerful. Invited one day to a luncheon, her hostess begged her to bring the children (who had been kept a secret from press and public), and Mary agreed to bring Irving, the eldest boy, on condition that they were alone. On arrival she discovered a large gathering that included a well-known critic. Seeing her consternation, the hostess introduced the boy tactfully as Mary's stepson, whereupon at the end of the meal the critic murmured, 'Mees Moore, the next time you have a stepson, don't have him so like yourself.'

When they left Berlin Colonel Swaine, military attaché at the British Embassy, saw them off. Soon after they had got back to England they were invited to act before the Tsar of Russia in St Petersburg, so early in January 1888 they set off again, stopping a night in Berlin, where Colonel Swaine warned them that in St Petersburg the *Garrick* script would probably be taken away and kept for several weeks by the censor. Why not seal it inside the diplomatic bag at the British Embassy? He would take it on to the Embassy in St Petersburg, where it would be returned to Wyndham. To undertake the mission Colonel Swaine was made a Queen's Messenger, and the script arrived in formidable secrecy. On their first morning in St Petersburg Wyndham and Mary met Major Edward FitzGerald Law,[*] the British commercial attaché, who became a great friend. No, he said, when Mary decided to explore; it was too cold to walk, she must drive. 'How ridiculous!' she thought, and took no notice until after a few yards her petticoats froze to the waist. (No wonder Wyndham hired sledges for the rest of their stay.)

Without any of the teething troubles of Berlin, they acted, in German, at a principal St Petersburg theatre; Royal carriages took them to and fro, and Tsar Alexander and the Tsarina came to a performance, preceded by the Imperial Chef and his staff. Asking why, Mary heard that the Chef had to make the pastry for the Imperial family (no doubt to eat in the interval?) After three weeks they went on to Moscow and the Paradise Theatre, and the manager (who seemed to be in tune with the title) proposed to Mary: she heard that his two previous wives, both actresses,

[1]Major Law, afterwards Sir Edward, became in 1900 Financial Member of the Governor-General's Council in India. He resigned after a publicized difference of opinion with the Viceroy, Lord Curzon; during his last embittered years Wyndham and Mary met him frequently in London.

111

had died—presumably of overwork. They saw a Russian play which so affected the audience that everyone sobbed audibly when the young hero was exiled to Siberia. (Much impressed, Mary had the play translated; but Mrs Kendal, who she had thought would be ideal as the mother, returned the script, saying it was too painful.) One Russian memory was sad. Mary had managed to save from her salary (now £8 a week) three sovereigns which she hid carefully in her room. When she was ready to leave she could not find them:

> Even now I dream of that room and the place where I had my money; it worried me so much at the time. Little things like that mean much to us when we are young and struggling.

Being, as they say, of a careful disposition all her life, it would still mean much to her when she was old and rich.

# III

While they were abroad a revival of *Two Roses* ran for twelve weeks at the Criterion with William Farren as Digby Grant and David James as 'Our Mr Jenkins'. Ellaline Terriss, aged sixteen, understudied one of the Roses. When her father, 'Breezy Bill' Terriss, or 'Handsome Bill' (the names are interchangeable) took her to the theatre, Wyndham offered her a three-year contract, starting at a guinea a week. Albery meanwhile completed a long sketch for a play which he sent to David James, but heard nothing more.

In February 1888 Wyndham and Mary reappeared in *David Garrick* at a Criterion adorned with laurel wreaths, playbills and other mementoes from Germany and Russia. The wreaths remained until they disintegrated and only the ribbons were left. Soon after returning Wyndham laughed when Mary showed him excitedly a formal request to call at the Russian Embassy. He had had one himself: 'It is Johnny Toole's handiwork, I feel sure. He knows of the joke Sothern and I played on Bruce, and now he is having a turn at us.' That was an elaborate practical joke by Wyndham and Sothern in which a bogus Russian Ambassador arrived at the Prince of Wales's, run then by Edgar Bruce. The visitor, who presented the gullible Bruce with a souvenir of their meeting, said the English theatre had so impressed him that he wanted all its best actors to go to Russia.

Glumly, Mary agreed that the 'ambassadorial' letters must be from Toole. But only a few weeks later, Wyndham heard from a supper-party neighbour that everyone at the Russian Embassy was puzzled that he and Miss Moore had not called for the Tsar's presents. Next day they did call; it was well they did, for after Wyndham's anxious apology he found that the Tsar had sent him a ruby and diamond ring, and to Mary a ruby and diamond brooch.

He had no need just yet to ferret among his growing pile of scripts. *David Garrick* ran until the summer vacation and on 10 August reached its 376th performance. A Russian critic visiting London made some candid remarks about the theatre—unaware that they would be translated—and one of them concerned the Criterion: 'Charles Wyndham and Miss Moore, known in their famous roles of the past winter in St Petersburg, are both talented . . . Miss Moore is still young but her playing is too sentimental.'

Towards the end of the run Wyndham received a letter from Hall Caine, the novelist, valuable simply because it suggests that Wyndham should play more serious parts:

> I expected a fine performance, and I find it a great one. Such acting makes it a distinction to write for the stage. With so much power and pathos, your sermon parts ought, I think, to be more numerous. May you get another as good as this. The lady is most lovely, and her delivery of the line "Do with me as you will—you are my master," had a great thrill in it.

We may assume from this that Hall Caine had heard some gossip about Wyndham and 'the lady'. During the year she made the separation from Albery more apparent by bringing her children back to live with her in London, and Albery moved into rooms in St Martin's Lane, very close to the theatre that is now named after him.

Ellaline Terriss understudied Mary in *David Garrick*, and played the part at a 'flying matinée' in Brighton for which she got 1s. 3d. extra. (Wyndham had invented the flying matinée, a rapid visit by a West End cast; though a trial to the technical staff, it was an idea that attracted other actor-managers.) Ellaline played Ada Ingot again one afternoon at the Crystal Palace where crowds gathered round the stage door after the show to see Wyndham leave. Taking her by the arm, he whispered, 'Smile—smile—smile at them—*smile!*' She remembered his advice for the rest of her career, and much more than that from her Criterion apprenticeship. However long a run, or however well a play was going, Wyndham always called the company together once a month to rehearse the laughs; an astute lesson in actor-management.

Albery about then gave to Mary his interest in some of the Wyndham adaptations. To legalize this, Wyndham—wary at last of ambiguous verbal agreements—wrote formally to 'Dear Mrs Albery' confirming that for *Welcome* (from *Le Petit Ludovic*) she would get £2 a night up to £300, and from *Their Ideals* £2 a night until £200 had been reached. Through a previous arrangement, *The Beaten Track* had become her entire property. Albery, who from now until his death did little more, retained the *Two Roses* rights. He was ready to let them go for practically nothing

113

to the manager William Duck, until Mary begged Duck not to buy.

Gossip never affected Mrs Wyndham's attachment to Mary. When Mary's health gave trouble the two women, with Mrs Bernard Beere (who was to act in the next Criterion play), went to Monte Carlo. It was Wyndham's idea, and at Christmas, after he had arranged his next revival, *Still Waters Run Deep*, he joined them. On this holiday Mary had her first and last night at the gaming tables. She had just read *As in a Looking Glass*, F. C. Philips's best-selling novel, in which the heroine is a lucky gambler. Now Mary had a startling example of high bidding from Mrs Bernard Beere, who would make an entrance to the Casino, sensationally dressed. One day Mary herself crept surreptitiously towards the roulette tables where she began rapidly to win. She lost just as rapidly, and she had the strength of mind to stop. (Never again, she said, and it was so.)

Back in London, she and Wyndham opened on 1 February 1889, in *Still Waters Run Deep*, one of Tom Taylor's most durable plays. Those who saw both the first production (1855) and the Criterion revival noticed that Wyndham had raised the social scale:

> The modest villa is changed into a luxurious "boudoir", with all the wealth of colour and ornament that Messrs Liberty can introduce. Japanese monsters, china plates, and etchings, adorn the shelves and walls, and Mrs Sternhold and Mrs Mildmay are in keeping with their surroundings and appear in "Worth" costumes that only the richest could command. A corresponding change takes place in the character of Mrs Sternhold. She is evidently the society dame ... Yet with these changes the play is so well written that all seemed perfectly natural.

Wyndham was now John Mildmay, the husband, instead of Captain Hawksley, the lover, which would have been a natural choice. But, in his latest and more serious mood, Mildmay, who waits coolly and cleverly for the right moment to assert himself, was certainly the better part. Mary, looking 'very lovely', was that weak little creature Mrs Mildmay.

Because there was still plenty of life in *Two Roses*, Wyndham put it on for Wednesday matinées. When he heard that she was going to play Lottie, Albery wrote to her:

> I cannot see you quite equal to Fawsitt in Lottie, but you may nearly reach her, and certainly pass her in refinement. Her great forte was comicality, without effort. She was in the play gentle and tender from beginning to end. She never seemed to make a point, or rather the audience seemed to make them for her—except when she was hiding behind the curtains (in Act II). Then the way in which she threw her power over her Father came close upon tragedy. She so carefully prevented Jack seeing her. This was the point of the play.
>
> The lovingness of the sisters is its charm if there be any. Do not miss it. I trust you will score.

Even more moving than Mary's Lottie could be was Wyndham's reason for reviving the piece—to help Mary pay Albery's debts (some incurred before they were married). He was still seeking to help in any way he could: first, by engaging her; then by giving Albery as much work as possible while he was still capable of doing it; and now by reviving *Two Roses*. Wyndham knew, as Mary realized, that creditors continued to pursue her.

Developing a serious cough, she had to leave the cast of *Still Waters* for three weeks, and Wyndham took her to see Sir Richard Quain, the specialist, who ordered a sea voyage, a matter in which Wyndham again showed his concern and generosity. Because his sister, Alice Bronson Howard, was returning to America, she could accompany Mary on the outward voyage, but in order that Mary should have a companion on the way back he sent his cousin, Edith Heather Bigg, as well. Though the Atlantic was rough, Mary sat grimly on deck, protected by a tarpaulin, for nine hours a day in extreme discomfort, until towards the end the weather changed: almost cured, she reached New York, where Albery's adaptation *Featherbrain* happened to be on with Minnie Maddern (Fiske), who would later become known for her work in Ibsen—very far from a woolly French farce which ran for little more than a month.

In London Mary returned to the foolish Mrs Mildmay. The play lasted until the summer, but she had no part in its successor, Burnand's *The Headless Man*. Instead Wyndham engaged her collie, Boy, who during a rehearsal ran after him as he left the stage in a dog-cart. The Farjeon children were delighted: Boy's appearance was something from their side of the curtain. (They were close friends and neighbours of the Alberys.) Wyndham played a solicitor, outwardly methodical and fond of telling everyone that method was what they lacked. Actually he is a muddler—hence the title. Owing to his eccentric filing system, a bride receives counsel's opinion that her innocent bridegroom is a bigamist. An old gentleman who wishes to revive a claim to the peerage is told to read books on the fishery laws. There was much else besides in a part Burnand wrote for Charles Mathews, who died before he could play it. Sothern, who was to have taken it over, quarrelled with the author. (Hence Burnand's addition to the text, a version of his meeting with Sothern in Garrick Street. Momentarily, they greeted each other warmly; then, realizing they were not on speaking terms, abruptly parted.) Wyndham's Sam never remembered what had happened the moment before, or what had taken him to a particular place; a curious irony, for these were exactly the misfortunes that overtook Wyndham in old age. *The Headless Man* did not please everyone; at the première a man in the gallery shouted his discontent—not at the play but because programmes were charged for—and Wyndham, identifying him as 'the man in the white hat', merely increased the uproar. As a souvenir of his disturbance the man left his hat in the theatre, where it was preserved for some time. Boy, a dog star in the making, was most disappointed when the play came off.

On the last night before their holiday (followed by an American tour) Wyndham and Mary gave a single performance of *Wild Oats*, in which they had begun their partnership. 'No one,' *The Theatre* observed snobbishly, 'would have imagined, from the string of carriages outside the theatre that the London season was over and the fashionable world out of town.' This time Wyndham spoke in his most winning manner, recalling the *Wild Oats* première when he had pleaded with the audience to bear with him. During the latest season the public had borne with him so generously that he had had to push *The Headless Man* and *Wild Oats* into the dog-days, and relegate Holcroft's *The Road to Ruin* to some shadowy future. (In fact, it was never done; Albery's alterations were probably the last work he ever did.)

They were going to America on a five months' tour, said Wyndham that night:

> Ladies and gentlemen, kindly imagine for a moment that this theatre is a railway station; that you are on the platform and we in our carriage. The guard gives the signal for separation, and as we vanish from your sight, please imagine that I grasp you all by the hand, and tender you an affectionate and grateful adieu.

Mary's social activities came as naturally to her as her professional life; she enjoyed playing the hostess, something that came less easily to Mrs Wyndham. As Charles loved to entertain his band of friends, he took over a large room in the Criterion building, decorated it with portholes and lockers to look like a cabin, and called it The Yacht Room. Inviting puzzled new guests, smart or Bohemian, he would explain breezily, 'Oh, I always keep it moored at Piccadilly Circus.' It was there through the next decade.

That summer the Wyndhams were going to St Moritz, which he called the healthiest of resorts, and Mary started out with them. They had got as far as Italy when she received a telegram telling her that James Albery had died on 15 August; and at once—with Mrs Wyndham loyally accompanying her—she returned to London.

# CHAPTER TWELVE

# The Only Dramatist
# 1889–1892

When James Albery died of cirrhosis of the liver he was only fifty-one. Mary's sister Fanny, who registered the death, sent telegrams to Mary in Italy, and to the Farjeons on holiday in Margate. Albery's death was Eleanor Farjeon's first sharp recollection of a telegram; when her mother explained what it meant, that Papa was leaving for London because Mr Albery had died, the child realized that Aunt Mary, prettiest of all their courtesy aunts, would have to wear black: 'She won't look nice, Mama.' 'She'll look beautiful', Mama assured her; and she did. Soon after the funeral, which took place from Mary's house in Melina Place, St John's Wood, Mary had to seek Ben Farjeon's help. A good many obituary notices had appeared; and one newspaper in particular published an article which accused the wife of neglecting her ailing husband. In old age she would write: 'Alas! we had been separated for practically four years . . . I would gladly have done anything in my power to help; but, as all my intimate friends knew, it was impossible to do more for him than I did.' Ben Farjeon advised her to consult a solicitor and to ask for heavy damages. Instead the solicitor blandly arranged a meeting between her and the writer, and suggested an apology which was duly printed. As a bonus the offender wrote to her penitently, confessing that her 'sad little face' haunted him. This may or may not have been a consolation.

For Mary, James Albery's death had to be an anticlimax, for the marriage had already died. She had long been responsible for their sons, who during the past two years had lived with her in London. Albery's death meant something different to theatre people; William Archer, one of his ardent admirers, read the placard with sincere regret, though above all, and candidly, he did regret that his feelings were not more poignant. If Albery's promise had been fulfilled, how deeply he would have mourned.

In fact, Albery's life was a sequence of ifs, his character a series of contradictions. *Two Roses* had made him; played all over the English-speaking world, it was revived several times in London. Materially his greatest feat, in later years he must often have cursed it. Any new play he wrote faced instant and unfavourable comparison—here Archer, never a *Two Roses* man, was in a minority—and at length Albery simply gave up and, in an obituarist's phrase, 'glided into the ranks of the adapter'. After his sudden fame, and that astonishing efflorescence of the early 1870s, he had slipped gradually away. His original work in the four years after *Two Roses* included six comedies, two farcical comedies, a 'poetical fairy play', an extravaganza, a comedy-drama and a one-act farce, not to speak of the *Pickwick* adaptation for Irving. Obviously, such a pace as this had to slacken. Moreover, his social life and his drinking habits scarcely helped. A *Daily News* obituarist said gently that nights at the Albion tavern in Covent Garden were 'hardly conducive' to sustained work by day.

He was a witty talker in a style transiently popular. Certainly, long after he died they remembered his repartee at the Savage Club, to which he had been elected in 1871 and where quick verbal improvisation counted for much. Agreed, what he said can seem disastrous in print: one ought to have been there to have listened to this alert, handsome man and caught the gleam in his prominent eyes. 'If you ever go to heaven', he told a peppery Savage, 'you would kick up a row with the angels because your halo didn't fit.' As he left the club one night a stranger asked if he knew a gentleman with one eye of the name of Walker? 'Ah, let me see', Albery replied, 'and what is the name of his other eye?' Yes, a trifle disheartening, and possibly not Albery's at all; but Archer misjudged when he refused to put Albery among the wits whose sayings pass from mouth to mouth until the authorship is forgotten, and 'men in their anecdotage attribute them to Sheridan'. (Albery's early dialogue was often matched with Sheridan's.) More likeably, he is said to have got up towards the end of a bad and interminable play at Webster's Adelphi and asked politely, 'Excuse me, Mr Webster, shall you be very much longer? I want something to drink and then go home to bed!' Probably he found it far easier to talk than to think out a plot—always his weakness.

Pinero observed wisely (as one dramatist of another): he could begin, but he could seldom finish. *Two Roses* and *Apple Blossoms* were the best:

> In his other original plays there was the sparkling promising first act;
> and then came the slackening of grip and the signs of infirmity of
> purpose. Yet . . . none failed to reveal a keen insight into life, and often a
> vein of genuine poetry.

To adapt for an English audience those wicked French farces—this at least was something he could manage with comparative ease and even a kind of distinction. We can imagine how he revelled in making the frivolous affairs acceptable to London. Barton Baker said of the most notorious:

> *Pink Dominos* was the first English piece that broke down the icy wall of insular respectability, and induced the Mrs Grundys to flock to hear naughtiness in their native tongue—in French it was always quite another thing.

Archer, who at that time took drama so gravely, was sad that a man of extraordinary talent should descend to *Where's the Cat?* Yet 'some of his hack work . . . was so marvellously well done that it almost seemed worth doing. When such a man dies, one feels something like remorse at having missed the opportunity of knowing him face to face and studying his art in the light of his personality.' From mood to mood this personality was a study in contradictions. He could turn 'white with anger' on the only occasion Archer saw him, the unhappy first night of *Jacks and Jills* which finished him as an original playwright. According to his widow, he could be 'kind and amiable'; he was also a 'great quarreller', as men who were good to him, such as Vezin and Wyndham, soon discovered. Even a boy could recognize Albery's two sides. Irving Albery (only ten at his father's death) was fond of him, but never forgot how terrifying he was as a swimming teacher. This man who could appraise Victorian hypocrisy and adjust Parisian farces to suit it would dust the powder from his wife's face before they went out together. His attitude to women emerges in his comedies where he idealizes the young and satirizes the old (W. S. Gilbert had a similarly disturbing trait). His late marriage to an extremely pretty girl of sixteen was in keeping. Although Mary played none of his heroines until much later, when they first met she must have been for him the embodiment of Lottie in *Two Roses*, Jennie (*Apple Blossoms*) and Rose in *Forgiven*. No doubt because the ideal woman continued to elude him, he was most at home in his club, where he would be appreciated for his swift flashes, so easy to remember, and not for the bitterness he must reasonably have felt after a run of failure.

Even during a brief life, his achievement as a dramatist was blurred. Again, the facts fight each other: he was unlucky enough to succeed at the very beginning of his career, when he had the good luck to get Irving as interpreter and protector. Digby Grant, Esq., helped to put Irving on a royal road; but, having written *Two Roses*, Albery would never be allowed to surpass it. His plays are shelved; only the version of *Pink Dominos* lived on into this century. But we can see now that the comedies, like Robertson's, freshened the contemporary stage. The historian George Rowell has said truthfully that 'in catching and refining Robertson's style, however briefly, Albery stands alone'. He stands alone too as the only dramatist of his family. Though his distinction may have waned, he deserves to be the frontispiece in the family album: as husband, father, grandfather and great-grandfather, he would head a famous theatrical line.

## II

Now, in the autumn of 1889, and after a few provincial weeks, Wyndham and Mary Moore set off for their first American tour together; it was six years since Wyndham's visit. On arrival he accompanied his wife and Mary to a New York matinée of Bronson Howard's war play *Shenandoah*; that night they dined with the Howards, and Wyndham (whose idea of fun could be the elementary practical joke) hastened to describe the plot of a new play that was running in London and closely resembled *Shenandoah*: Howard seems to have survived the evening. On 14 October the company opened the new Tremont Theatre at Boston, with *David Garrick*, which also survived—here the almost blinding brilliance of the electric light. Asked about it, the electrician guessed he was merely showing Boston what really good lighting meant. *Garrick* disappointed New York audiences, so Wyndham (determined to show what really good acting meant) tried *The Candidate*, *Wild Oats* and *The Headless Man*, with which he and Mary played William Brough's little French Revolution drama *Delicate Ground*, familiar to Charles but Mary's first shot at Pauline, Vestris's old show-piece. It was during this New York season that Wyndham was elected to the Players' Club, the American counterpart of the Garrick, established in Edwin Booth's old house in Gramercy Park.

In Chicago at Christmas, where he believed *Garrick* might be unpopular, Wyndham chose a double bill of *The Candidate* and *Delicate Ground*, to which the public and the *Chicago Tribune* (in the language of its period) responded:

> Mr Wyndham is a rare actor. In rollicking farce characters or in those more serious bits of society comedy of which Mr Augustin Daly's company are the daintier American exemplars, he is equally good to see and to hear.

*Garrick*, some said, failed in America owing to patriotic loyalty to Sothern, and the fact that Wyndham was expected to play in farce. There could hardly have been an antipathy to costume plays. *Wild Oats* flourished, even though in Chicago Wyndham was warned by letter that he would be sued for infringing an American author's rights. Apparently someone had written quite a different *Wild Oats*; but neither Wyndham nor the ghost of John O'Keeffe would be troubled. (There has never been any central clearing-house for play-titles.) Much seemed to be happening in Chicago. The Italian tragedian Salvini was there. When (18 January

1890) he and the Wyndhams and Mary Moore were entertained at the Twentieth Century Club, Wyndham wished that (as Garrick) he could have had his old friend Samuel Johnson at his elbow to make the speech. But his own was good enough. He talked of the nature of acting and its development, qualifying Salvini's view that it was constantly improving. A prophecy about the development of the problem play might almost have looked ahead to his own work during the next decade:

> Comedy-drama in these exciting days of thought and discussion will no more be able to resist absorbing such questions than plants can help absorbing the quality of the rich dirt in which their roots lie hidden.

After Chicago, the Grand, Cincinnati (Mary adored 'the wonderful trams in which you drove along the street and suddenly found yourself in an immense lift which took you bodily up to the hills'). Then Baltimore, Washington and, on a return visit, Palmer's, New York, where the manager (no diplomatist) suggested dropping *David Garrick*. Wyndham asked him not to slight the play: 'Why should New York be the exception?' (This was a little disingenuous.) Finally, though Philadelphia accepted *The Candidate*, it still thought of Garrick in terms of Sothern, and Wyndham was forced to substitute *Still Waters Run Deep* and Robertson's *Ours*, which he had last played nearly twenty years before.

# III

London again in March 1890. There, after *David Garrick*'s almost statutory return to the Criterion, Wyndham planned to do *She Stoops to Conquer* as a farce, a revolutionary notion for critics and public. A. B. Walkley was pained and admonishing:

> None could play Goldsmith better than Mr Wyndham. If he would but treat Goldsmith's lighter moods a little less in the spirit of Palais Royal farce, and his heavier moods with a little less of the hysteric fervour of *David Garrick*. . . . I admire Mr Charles Wyndham as well as they [the Criterion public] but
>
> > I could not love thee, Charles, so much
> > Loved I not Goldsmith more.
>
> It is not . . . the Caucus race in *Alice in Wonderland*. . . . You are playing an artificial play, written for an artificial age. Be then yourselves artificial.

Wyndham promptly asked two rhetorical questions: 'How am I to cast the mantle of antiquity over the antics of Tony Lumpkin?' and 'How am I to laugh without a nineteenth-century ring in my voice, or by what alchemy can I stay the trickling of an anachronistic tear?' In the event, he must have satisfied himself and most of his admirers. We can divine the result from a few phrases by the critic Archibald Haddon as late as 1922: 'In living memory, among the most important performances [of eighteenth-century comedy] have been Sir Charles Wyndham's Young Marlow, acted with a Palais Royal rattle at the Criterion 32 years ago . . . and the Kate Hardcastle of Mary Moore.' *Autres temps*. Now, after ninety years, if photographs are evidence, it looks as if Wyndham, as handsome as he was gracious, and Mary Moore, adorably demure, could hardly have failed, however much they 'rattled'.

No one minded when Wyndham rattled through the amorous Bob Sackett in yet another revival of *Brighton*, though during this one he had his first—if brief—experience of strike action by stage hands whose ultimatum he had refused. One evening, when he entered his dressing-room, he found sitting there an unknown man who announced that (a) he was a union official and (b) unless Wyndham yielded there would be no performance that night. Furiously, Wyndham ordered him to leave the theatre. Once outside, the man called a strike; only a group of old faithfuls remained; Wyndham's dresser clutched a fly-man's legs to prevent him from climbing into the flies and cutting the curtain cords. The scene was already set for Act One; but there had to be three changes. Called hastily together, the company was told what had happened, and the men volunteered to change the sets, and the women to move the furniture and properties. The show went on, and seldom better, finishing only ten minutes later than usual; next day the stage-hands, who had waited morosely through the evening in Jermyn Street, all asked to come back, and that was that.

No industrial action afflicted the next play, an indifferent comedy, *Sowing and Reaping*. Wyndham had another Bob Sackett part, though this time the man pursued only one woman—a married woman—and was trapped into marriage himself. A critic expressed what by then was common form in saying that the actor had just the 'light and airy touch' to carry off the baseness of an intriguer and make his conduct amusing. Before long Charles and Mary were on holiday in St Moritz—a stay she remembered because while they were crossing a glacier she broke a parasol lent to her by Princess May (later Queen Mary), a disaster that became a story for all occasions. Back at the Criterion *Welcome, Little Stranger*, Albery's adaptation of *Le Petit Ludovic*, was running briefly, his last new work to be produced, with his name alone given as the author. There were no protests from anyone.

At home in London during those busy years Ben Farjeon and his wife kept watch on the Albery boys while Mary was on tour. The Farjeons lived in Adelaide Road, not far from Melina Place; the families passed on nurses and governesses to each other, and Eleanor was sent to stay with the Alberys while her brother got over whooping cough. She and Irving

Albery (known as Button, because he swallowed one when he was a baby) were childhood sweethearts. Mr and Mrs Wyndham, who lived just round the corner, invited Eleanor to frighteningly enormous children's parties. Though in later recollection she saw Mrs Wyndham as 'a kindly, homely little person', she was terrified as a child of making a fool of herself on the highly polished floors. Worse, when she heard Mrs Wyndham whisper, 'Nellie, I'm sure you know a little piece to recite to us' she started, got it wrong, forgot what came next and cried. To her chagrin, Bronnie Albery had just said Longfellow's *A Psalm of Life* without forgetting a word (Tell me not, in mournful numbers/Life is but an empty dream!') One of the period's most uplifting exhortations—now with a familiar phrase in almost every line—it had become an essential party piece: the applause for Bronnie was a salute to convention as much as to his faultless memory.

# IV

Home from holiday, Wyndham chose a challenging revival. Like the earlier *Wild Oats*, Dion Boucicault's *London Assurance* was a tempting actor's play but not an assured classic. (Indeed, one day it would fade from the repertory for a good fifty years.) With a cast of Criterion quality, its style and liveliness were sovereign, and Wyndham inherited fluently the part of Dazzle, eternal hanger-on, which at that time went to the leading actor. Charles Mathews had created it in 1841. Now the Criterion revival would be the first to dress the play in the costumes of its own period, the men wearing frilled shirts, flowered waistcoats and strapped-down trousers, and the women short-waisted dresses with voluminous skirts and flounces, all 'faithfully reproduced by Messrs. Nathan'.

Writing to the *Daily Telegraph*, Oscar Wilde suggested that Wyndham's costume might be used as a basis for a departure in men's dress. The choice of colour of the evening dress coat would be left to the wearer, useless buttons would be used for their decorative value: 'When a thing is useless it should be made beautiful.' The use of a frill to a shirt 'prevents the tediousness of a flat polished surface of stiff linen'. Commending the cloaks worn by Wyndham and Arthur Bourchier ('We must wear cloaks with lovely linings. Otherwise we shall be very incomplete'.) Wilde continued in his fashion-plate manner:

> Of the moral value and influence of such a charming costume I think I had better say nothing. The fact is that when Mr Wyndham and Mr Bourchier appear in their delightful dresses they have been behaving very badly. . . . But if one is to behave badly, it is better to be bad in a becoming dress . . . and it is only fair to add that at the end of the play Mr Wyndham accepts his lecture with a dignity and courtesy of manner that can only result from the habit of wearing delightful clothes.

The play had been staged so often within London memories that comparisons could be heated, and were. But Wyndham's style was precisely keyed to Dazzle, an ingratiating bluffer who manages to keep himself favourably placed while remaining on the edge of the main plot. That plot is, simply, a contest for Grace Harkaway's hand between an elderly rake, Sir Harcourt Courtly, and his son Charles. Boucicault reveals Dazzle's character in an early scene with Grace's father (Max), who mistakenly thinks the fellow knows Sir Harcourt, a mistake Dazzle is in no hurry to correct.

MAX  Sir, if you are not otherwise engaged, I shall feel honoured by your company at my house, Oak Hall, Gloucestershire.
DAZZLE  Your name is—
MAX  Harkaway—Max Harkaway.
DAZZLE  Harkaway—let me see—I ought to be related to the Harkaways somehow.
MAX  A wedding is about to come off—will you take part on the occasion?
DAZZLE  With pleasure! Any part, but that of the husband.
MAX  Have you any previous engagement?
DAZZLE  I was thinking—eh! Why let me see. [*Aside*] Promised to meet my tailor and his account tomorrow; however, I'll postpone that. [*Aloud*] Have you good shooting?
MAX  Shooting! Why there's no shooting at this time of the year.
DAZZLE  Oh! I'm in no hurry—I can wait till the season of course.

But other characters cannot wait for ever to know his real identity. Before the end of the play he has to declare himself, and how Wyndham must have enjoyed the declaration:

Simple question as you may think it, it would puzzle half the world to answer. One thing I can vouch—Nature made me a gentleman—that is, I live on the best that can be procured for credit. I never spend my own money when I can oblige a friend. I'm always thick on the winning horse. I'm an epidemic on the trade of a tailor. For further particulars, inquire of any sitting magistrate.

The showiest part is Lady Gay Spanker, a horsey young woman whose name is a clue, and whose description of the hunt had long been an isolated aria: at the Criterion she was Mrs Bernard Beere, and William Farren was the elderly Narcissus, Sir Harcourt, a part that his father, 'Old' Farren, had originated at Covent Garden. Mary played that rarity an intelligent heroine, though the young Boucicault had dangerously obscured her intelligence with such speeches as this:

I love to watch the first tear that glistens in the opening eye of morning, the silent song the flowers breathe, the thrilling choir of the woodland minstrels, to which the modest brook trickles applause: these, swelling out the sweetest choir of sweet creation's matins, seem to pour some soft and merry tale into the daylight's ear, as if the waking world had dreamed a happy thing, and now smiled o'er the telling of it.

Boucicault, after all, was only twenty when in 1841 he supplied the play to order. Charles Mathews had wanted a five-act comedy for Covent Garden and, with some help from an actor-friend named Brougham, Boucicault wrote it in a month. During rehearsals it was much altered and severely cut; Mathews amplified his own part of Dazzle, and the author (the last person to be considered in those days) was not mentioned on the bills until success had been established. Though the night of the première in March 1841 was cold and wet, and theatregoers stayed away, those that did come soon cheered the company. Even if the massive Theatre Royal, Covent Garden, and the tiny casket of the Criterion could hardly have been less similar, both Mathews and (half a century later) Wyndham knew how to carry the house. Each of them did so with a passage towards the end of the play:

SIR HARCOURT   Charles, who is Mr Dazzle?
CHARLES   Dazzle?—Well, I don't exactly know who he is. I say, Dazzle, excuse an impertinent question.
DAZZLE   Oh, certainly.
CHARLES   Who are you?
DAZZLE   I have not the slightest idea!

At both theatres he might have replied, with truth, that he was an expert comedian.


# V


The more expert he grew, the less Wyndham liked criticism. It rankled when New York rejected his most recognized play; and in London, after so much applause, it shocked him to be told that he had taken 'astounding liberties' with *She Stoops to Conquer*. We can understand why, foolishly, he was moved to write to a theatrical paper, threatening not to invite the critics in future. But he should have guessed that at once Clement Scott would dive into battle, here suggesting light-headedly that critics should preserve their independence by paying for their seats. ('Just imagine what a scramble there would be!' observed *The Theatre*.) This is one of the arguments that recur and fade; but it was odd that Wyndham should be involved, for he was not naturally peevish or small-minded. As for Scott, though he asked why Wyndham 'impetuously resented criticism', he was soon declaring typically that Wyndham's next Criterion part, Charles Surface, was incomparably the best he had seen.

After the Goldsmith affair, Wyndham would be suspected of tampering with Old Comedy. *The Theatre* notice of *The School for Scandal* held firmly that he had 'Criterionised' Sheridan's play: 'By this I mean that he has made it, as he thinks, more acceptable to the patrons of his theatre.' There followed a catalogue of grumbles: 'At Lady Sneerwell's a pavane is danced by extra guests and not by characters in the play', and so on. As for the acting: Wyndham himself was in the right spirit of comedy, but Mary Moore, though a gentle, loving Maria, was intensely melancholy, and Mrs Bernard Beere's Lady Teazle was what Sir Peter described her—'a woman of fashion and nothing more'. Ellaline Terriss, who played the maid, was about to leave the company—Wyndham had released her to get experience in a larger theatre, but she never forgot the Criterion Sir Peter, 'a courtly old gentleman', William Farren, who delighted in chaffing the Careless (George Giddens) for the sake of seeing him lose his temper.

It was during this run that two unknown dramatists took the Criterion for a single matinée of a play, *Richard Savage*, set in the eighteenth century, and conveniently adapted to the *School for Scandal* décor. The authors were Marriott Watson, a journalist and popular novelist, and a young Scot, J. M. Barrie. Their collaboration was by remote control: Barrie wrote his 'bits' in Scotland, and Watson his in London; then they rewrote each other's. Much later, Barrie remembered his only historical play as dark and gloomy. As it had gone the rounds without luck, they subsidized a performance themselves. There were eleven speaking parts and extras (members of the Kitcat Club); Bernard Gould (stage name of the future *Punch* cartoonist, Sir Bernard Partridge) played Savage, poet and satirist; and Cyril Maude—the evening's Benjamin Backbite—was Richard Steele. (Did he wear the same costume? Possibly.) W. E. Henley contributed a prologue in twenty-three rhyming couplets. 'We were so anxious', said Barrie, 'not to be diffuse that we polished off the love scene in about twenty lines. This was the only occasion on which I took an author's call.' Not a dignified manœuvre: Watson was tall and Barrie short, and the newspapers next morning described them as the Long and the Short of it. *The Times* said resignedly, 'The spectator is enabled to witness the poet's magnanimous suicide, not only without a pang, but even with some measure of relief.' Nothing more happened to *Richard Savage*, but at any rate it gave Barrie a taste for the stage.

That autumn in Wyndham's revival of *Brighton* an actress named Mary Ansell played one of the girls; Barrie immediately wanted her for his new farce at Toole's, *Walker, London*, for which he needed only a girl who was 'young, beautiful, quite charming, a genius for preference, and able to flirt'. Apparently Mary Ansell would do: later she became his wife. Although Wyndham himself never did a Barrie play—and, indeed, few of the characters would have suited him—several were first acted at his theatres.

# VI

When, during April 1892, Lillie (Lily) Langtry was starred at the Criterion in *The Fringe of Society* (yet another piece 'from the French'), she was already an experienced actress but still primarily a fashionable Society beauty. Once Wyndham would be unsure of her professionalism. This was on the evening she telephoned calmly to say that she was at the Savoy Hotel and would be late: could the curtain be kept down for a few minutes? Coldly, Wyndham said no. Penitently she rushed to the theatre, but as the curtain had risen as promptly as ever she had to go on in the evening dress she was wearing, though in the first act she was supposed to be in day clothes. She had just time to put on a hat, with a cloak that disguised her dress. The cast waited tensely for the curtain: Wyndham, who had been playing a bored man of the world, would surely explode into an angry actor-manager. On stage, awaiting their call, the players heard Mrs Langtry say, 'Do you know what you deserve?' Before Wyndham could reply, she said, 'This—and I'm going to give it you.' At which she kissed him soundly, her arms around him, and tension slackened in startled laughter.

She had too a butterfly sense of humour. Entering one night, Wyndham accidentally trod on her toe; though he had not hurt her, she got her dresser to fetch a basin of water, and in the wings and visible from the stage, she assiduously bathed the bare foot. Much worried, and beginning to fluff, Wyndham hurried through his scene before rushing off to ask her needlessly—and to her gently malicious pleasure—to forgive him. As it turned out, she did not have to restrict her engagements to suit Wyndham's programme: in a few weeks the play had faded.

Aged eighteen, George Grossmith junior had his first part at the Criterion in *Haste to the Wedding*, Gilbert's version of *An Italian Straw Hat* (which has had almost as complicated a genealogy as *David Garrick*). The operetta failed; Gilbert without Sullivan lacked the better half. Still, 'G.G.' both fell in love with his leading lady, Marie Studholme, and helped his manager out of a hole. On the Saturday night at the end of the first week he was going to spend the week-end with his parents in Brighton. Reaching the Victoria ticket-office he saw in front of him, arguing with the ticket clerk, a flustered Wyndham who had apparently left his money behind: 'I am Charles Wyndham. I'll give you a cheque.' Charm did not work; the clerk said they were not allowed to take cheques. Turning away angrily, Wyndham spotted Grossmith: 'Hullo. Have you a sovereign on you?' Grossmith had. His first week's wages. He handed it over as if it had been one of a hundred, and took a bus back to his home in Dorset Square. No Brighton for him; but on Monday night he found the sovereign awaiting him—and an invitation to supper with Wyndham and Mary.

127

Wyndham was now fifty-six: still slim, energetic, youthful-looking, he knew that at last he must consider such middle-aged parts as the dignified person he had played in *The Fringe of Society*. Certainly, work at the Criterion would have more weight, and there would be no return to the froth of *Pink Dominos*. This was the year 1893, the start of his famous association with one of the first names of the London theatre, Pinero's friend and rival dramatist, Henry Arthur Jones.

## CHAPTER THIRTEEN
# The Long Sermon
# 1893–1897

'Always experimenting, learning, improving his art ... he has kept himself plastic and progressive.' To a point, this could describe Wyndham in the early Nineties. It is in fact Max Beerbohm on Henry Arthur Jones. A change in Criterion method was due; Jones was to supply one in *The Bauble Shop* (the only play he ever wrote 'to order for a manager') in which Wyndham, conquering a new kind of part, crossed the gap between farcical lover and middle-aged, though still attractive, moralist. The actor H. A. Saintsbury recalled the two Wyndhams:

> I grew to know and love Wyndham as I watched him through a long series of light comedies. I think of him now as two distinct persons; the dashing touch-and-go comedian of military carriage, with crisp brown curly hair and fair moustache—what verve! what easy grace! what perfect aplomb and control! what irresistible fascination!—and later as the middle-aged *raisonneur*, clean shaven and grey, with unmatchable charm and a curious break in the voice that added effect to a manner that no woman could withstand.

Wyndham's new dramatist was quite unlike his Criterion predecessors. Having secured himself in melodrama (predominantly *The Silver King*), he turned to social problems, a serious approach to the theatre that must have surprised, even disconcerted, Wyndham, whose world had been the theatre of entertainment, and light entertainment at that. Jones (1851–1929), a farmer's son, self-educated, had been a draper's assistant and commercial traveller. Through life—through lectures, prefaces and pamphlets—he was a campaigner; above all, he wanted to take drama into literature. While publicly denigrating Ibsen and his followers in the 'lob-worm symbolic drama,' he was palpably influenced himself, even to trying a 'commercial brand' of the style he despised. A difficult man, then. It says a lot for Wyndham's patience that the friendship endured the toil of rehearsing five productions.

In the first of these, *The Bauble Shop*, Viscount Clivebrooke, the Prime Minister (Wyndham, of course), has an arch-enemy, Stoach, M.P., a name Swinburne, who was an authority, thought was 'matched only by Balzac'. Clivebrooke is about to introduce a Public Morality Bill when Stoach, discovering that he has been visiting a shopgirl late at night, touches off the 'scandal' in the House. The Bill is thrown out; Clivebrooke's career collapses. He marries the girl. So unlikely a tale could hardly placate the critics. Logically, William Archer suggested that, through two acts and a half,

> we waited longingly to hear Viscount Clivebrooke bid Mr Stoach, M.P., 'go to the devil!' and had he used an even curter formula to the same effect I don't think the Censor would have objected—instead of taking this simple, obvious and probably effectual course, the noble Viscount ... grovels, writhes, whines, abases himself to the dust before a contemptible scandalmonger at whom in the circumstances stated the country would simply have jeered.

Archer agreed that recently two political careers had been 'blasted by the breath of scandal'; but there the circumstances were more serious. As for the Bauble Shop girl, 'no more wooden lay-figure was ever presented to a confiding public ... Beside her, Little Nell seems positively human.' Having disposed of Jones, Archer conceded that Wyndham's vigour and conviction carried the play through to popular success ... his portraiture of the pitiable Clivebrooke was by far the strongest piece of serious acting he has yet given us', and Mary Moore was 'pretty and sympathetic' as the poor little toy-shop girl with a drunken father.

Wyndham, given to surprises, astonished even his ardent admirers by his 'passionate invective, dignity, tenderness, love ... from that night Charles Wyndham ranged himself among the most finished actors in europe'. Jones's admiration, firmly engaged, would remain. Acknowledging Wyndham's gifts, he was impressed too by the relative tranquillity of rehearsals, minor skirmishes aside. Also—and primarily important to him—Wyndham never took liberties with the text. ('He was a model for that.')

Both men were annoyed with critics who queried parliamentary detail. Jones had taken special care over this; moreover, besides having the Prime Minister's room in the House and its furnishings copied, Wyndham had consulted Viscount Duncannon (later the Earl of Bessborough), then the Speaker's secretary and a Whip. Duncannon came to the Criterion to rehearse the 'Ayes' and 'Noes' heard off stage; and in gratitude Jones and Wyndham presented him with an inscribed silver bowl.

Ellis Jeffreys, in the minor part of an earl's daughter who shocks her parents by imitating music-hall songs, shrank at first from a number she was supposed to sing so realistically. She had already appeared in musical plays; but Wyndham had to persuade her how to put her song over with the proper brassiness:

> I'm a maiden up-to-date, I'm a pal for any mate,
>> And the boys they just freeze on to me.
> In the Row, in the Park, I'm a demon for a lark,
>> And my life is one eternal spree;
> Yes—I—am—all—there! and there's nothing I don't know
> You—bet—your—life, dear—Boys! This Maiden's all the go!
> Yet, though I show my paces, I'd ne'er kick o'er the traces!
> Oh! dear—me—No! At least—not often!

There were tears; Wyndham persevered quietly until the right gusto emerged—so much of it that later he had to warn Miss Jeffreys to hold it back a little. Still (in Jones's experience), rehearsals were calmer than usual: he probably realized that he could be difficult himself, and occasionally Wyndham's even temper could flare. Thus when he found there were no spoons for his tea-party scene with the heroine, he cried, 'How can I possibly act without spoons? Dismiss the rehearsal!' Literally a storm in a teacup, and need for much tact all round. Here Mary helped. 'A very clever woman', Jones called her, 'and a very clever actress.' In the end *The Bauble Shop* ran for 135 performances, and a mutually rewarding partnership began.

## II

Wyndham's choice of play could waver; *An Aristocratic Alliance*, by an aristocratic dramatist (Lady Violet Greville), angered critics because its derivation from Sardou's *Le Gendre de M. Poirier* was ignored. An actor in a small part, the chef, stole the show, which ran only two months. Wyndham had swiftly to bring in *The Candidate*, where his improbably named Viscount Oldacre was as victorious as ten years before, and Justin Huntly M'Carthy inserted some fresh topical gags. It was then that Wyndham, essentially and candidly a commercial manager, had a flattering request from the *avant-garde*. Bernard Shaw, a voluble red-haired writer, music critic and publicist, not yet a drama critic, wanted him to stage a comedy called *The Philanderer*. Wyndham was not interested in the idea, which had arisen after the enthusiastic Dutch expatriate J. T. Grein had put on the more polemical *Widowers' Houses* for his newly founded Independent Theatre. Shaw believed that *The Philanderer* needed a management with greater resources; further,

131

admiring Wyndham as an actor, he held him to be the only man in England who could play the title-part of Charteris.

Henry Arthur Jones, who never stopped writing, had failed with his fourteenth-century tragedy *The Tempter*, much of it in alarming blank verse ('Ocean, voluptuous destroyer, help!') but he did carry off 'the new and original modern play' of *The Masqueraders*, put on by George Alexander at the St James's. Mrs Patrick Campbell, fresh from Paula Tanqueray, was her highly volatile self at rehearsal, and we can be certain that Jones was glad to return to the less ruffled atmosphere of the Criterion. True, before his comedy, *The Case of Rebellious Susan*, could open, he and Wyndham had their differences. In the exceptionally fine summer weather Wyndham put up a stage in his St John's Wood garden where the company rehearsed—not too seriously at first, and breaking off for the summer holidays which Wyndham took as usual at St Moritz. But by that time one aspect of the plot had begun to nag at him. The play's theme is in Sir Richard Kato's not too gracefully phrased speech, 'Believe me, what is sauce for the goose will never be sauce for the gander. In fact, there is no gander sauce.' Sir Richard (Wyndham) would say this when trying to get Susan to remain with her erring husband. Susan, however, is resolved to go off and prove that the woman is as much entitled to licence as the man. The trouble was that Wyndham (and, we assume, Mary Moore) did not want to suggest that Susan, when she left, had actually had an affair. Jones, in a long dedicatory letter 'to Mrs Grundy' in the printed text, demanded that everyone—Mrs Grundy, audiences, and certainly this time, his actor-manager—should 'look at life'; in other words, no excision of lines which confirmed Susan's guilt. Wyndham, as actor-manager, thought above all of the effect on his public, and affirmed that unless certain lines were cut 'my participation in the piece will not only be useless but positively dangerous'. Jones proposed that he should go out to St Moritz to discuss views that Wyndham called 'utterly irreconcilable'.

Knowing that Jones was so earnest and dedicated, and fearing that their friendship might be damaged, Wyndham wrote a long explanatory letter. Briefly, as a broken marriage is eventually mended, Susan's romance should not be 'vulgarised down to a commonplace and unworthy temporary intrigue':

> I am astonished at a practical long-experienced dramatic author believing that he will induce married men to bring their wives to a theatre to learn the lesson that their wives can descend to such nastiness, as giving themselves up for an evening of adulterous pleasure and then return safely to their husband's arms provided they are clever enough, low enough, and dishonest enough to avoid being found out?

Whether or not Susan is found out depends simply on the length of a sermon preached at an English church in Cairo.

Jones wanted to stick to his script; it was his duty, he said belligerently, to brush away hypocrisy wherever he found it. But Wyndham had reacted as a Victorian would; probably Mary had also objected to the incriminating lines; her personal situation could have made her particularly vulnerable. At length the two friends reached a compromise. The scene which Wyndham had found so repulsive could be taken either way, and one experienced playgoer has recorded for us the way in which he took it. William Archer, who liked *Rebellious Susan* (which had mixed notices in October 1894), wrote that:

Jones offers us that rarest of commodities in the theatrical market, a pure comedy. There are one or two scenes in which it deflects a little on the side of farce, but they are quite episodic; where is the comedy-writer who has never availed himself of a little reasonable license of caricature? English literature assuredly knows him not. At no point does Mr Jones's play trend towards drama. Great problems, great passions, great sufferings, do not enter into its scheme. Society is regarded from the ironic point of view.

Here, and shrewdly, Archer (once so pained by the girls in *Brighton*) realized what had disturbed Wyndham:

A jealous wife rides the high horse for a certain time, threatens, and even attempts, vengeance in kind, and then climbs down more or less ingloriously—that is the whole story.

He added a footnote:

How I came to say "attempts" I do not know. In the theatre, I fully understood the author to imply that she not only attempted but accomplished the retaliation she threatened; and I actually noted in my tablets the two speeches in which the fact is conveyed.

On reading this, Wyndham must have wanted to tell Jones 'I told you so!' But, no doubt, admitting the success for them both—*Rebellious Susan* would have 164 performances—he wisely let the matter go. Husbands were seen ushering their wives down the sinuous Criterion staircase; a few mothers may even have dared to take their daughters. On Max Beerbohm's evidence the play created a demand for artificial comedies of 'smart' life as opposed to the old-fashioned 'high' life. Jones's *The Liars* and R. C. Carton's *Lord and Lady Algy* would supply some of the demand.

When he wrote from Switzerland Wyndham told Jones that, though he did not think Sir Richard Kato, Q.C., gave him any special chances, the 'uninitiated' might regard it as a good part. In fact, his Kato proved—and not only to the uninitiated—that it was a splendid part, rich in lines that he could endow with individual charm, as in his whimsical speech to the estranged husband and wife: 'And if there is any little natural disinclination to make each other's acquaintance, let me give you a formal introduction.' Clement Scott said of this performance 'It looked nothing, and still was everything; no flurry, no bustle, no attempt at point-making.' An amateur, but experienced, critic felt similarly. Kate Terry Gielgud, Sir John's mother, who attended the first night, wrote to a friend that it was, of course, an incalculable advantage to have Mr Wyndham as Sir Richard. He

> represented an admirable part of an harmonious whole, not a bit of character-acting elaborated into such proportions that everyone else was dwarfed thereby. He had all the plums in the author's pudding, yet pulled them out so unobtrusively that he was never beyond the frame of the picture. Miss Moore pleased me more than usual; but she had not to enlist sympathy. Her Lady Susan was throughout the silly, spoiled child, who thought it a very fine thing to fly off in search of romance and chivalrous devotion, and fondly imagined that she could defy convention and yet escape the whisper of scandal.

Escaping from her invariable Dresden-china heroines, Mary had borne off her first important modern part; and when temporarily she had to leave the cast with throat trouble, business dropped. It picked up on her return. In consequence, Wyndham raised her salary from £16 a week to £20. She had been royally received in two senses. On being presented to the Prince of Wales (no Victorian) in his box after the performance, she found him quick on his cue: 'Now tell me, what *did* you do during that long sermon?' he asked. Mary could only reply, 'I am afraid, Sir, you must ask the author.' Here Jones had no royal command.

Shaw had wanted Wyndham for *The Philanderer* ('I had written a part which nobody but Charles Wyndham could act'); but at the Criterion in the Nineties?—no: it was a play 'impossible in his theatre'. Two other dramatists would have been more natural choices—Pinero and Wilde. There is no evidence that Wyndham, incorrigible buyer of plays though he was, ever had on his shelves anything by Pinero (never a writer for the shelf), but he did buy—and for £300—*The Importance of Being Earnest*, which Wilde had shown already to George Alexander with the note: 'Of course, the play is not suitable to you at all; you are a romantic actor; the people it wants are actors like Wyndham and Hawtrey.' No wonder Alexander was discouraged. When, early in 1895, *Guy Domville* failed miserably at the St James's, and he needed a new play at once, he remembered Wilde's farce. *The Case of Rebellious Susan* looked like running until the summer vacation, so Wyndham released *The Importance* without asking Wilde to return the advance, but stipulating only that he should have the next new play. (There would be a poignant sequel.)

Almost on the day that Wyndham 'gave' *The Importance* to Alexander, business at the Criterion began to fall. He needed a new play himself, and on 5 May 1895 he opened in R. C. Carton's *The Home Secretary*,

'Trust me, henceforth, to make you what a wife should be.' Wyndham as John Mildmay in a late revival of *Still Waters Run Deep*

Wyndham's Theatre, 1899, drawn by the architect, W. G. R. Sprague. Now listed as an historic building, its façade is of cream-coloured Portland stone

The New Theatre, St Martin's Lane, 1903. W. G. R. Sprague's impression of his thirtieth theatre. Renamed the Albery in 1973

'She's going to smoke!' Sensation in *Fourteen Days*, H. J. Byron's adaptation 'from the French', at the Criterion in 1882

obviously more attracted by its satirical dialogue than by the clotted romance. All the same, he and Julia Neilson (as his wife) had to cope with a style heavily metaphorical: 'The estrangement you have built up between us has received its coping stone' [he to her]; 'I have turned the lens of truth upon my own heart' [she to him]; and 'When you first gave me your name I hung round it my garland of wild flowers' [she to him]. Lewis Waller (not yet the matinée idol who inspired KOW—the Keen on Waller society) had to be gallant (that was obligatory); as a flighty Mrs Thorpe-Didsbury, Mary Moore revealed 'a very pretty feeling for comedy'. Critics tetchily dismissed the plot—a question of a stolen dispatch box. In another Carton play, *The Squire of Dames*, which he took from *L'Ami des Femmes* by Dumas *fils*, Wyndham was again a *raisonneur*; but the piece (November 1895) suffered in translation. For Puritan England its central idea, turning on the separation of a married couple, had to be changed; the marriage must not be consummated—an absurdity at which Archer was inclined to be waspish. Even so, Queen Victoria desired to see Mr Wyndham; in January 1896 she commanded a performance of *The Squire of Dames* at Osborne; plans were made and programmes printed for 27 January. Then Princess Beatrice's husband, Prince Henry of Battenberg, who had joined the Ashanti expedition, died of fever, and, after all, the performance was cancelled.

# III

Wyndham, as sole manager of the Criterion for twenty years, and now with Mary Moore as his business partner, decided to celebrate on 1 May 1896 with an afternoon-and-evening marathon. To begin, a Lyceum matinée which included the first act of Lytton's *Money* (the Bancrofts leaving retirement to appear), and after this the last three acts of *The School for Scandal*, Wyndham as Charles, William Farren as Sir Peter, Mrs Patrick Campbell as Lady Teazle and Mary in 'the thankless part' (as she called it) of Maria. From the profession Wyndham received a gold cigar-box. That evening at the Criterion, after two short pieces, he gave *David Garrick*, himself and Mary in familiar parts they could have played in their sleep, followed by the second act of Sheridan's *The Critic* 'hopelessly ruined by its silly gagging', someone said. The Prince of Wales came that evening, and, altogether £2,452 6s. 4d. went to the Actors' Benevolent Fund. Nor was this all. Later in the year Wyndham's old friend Henry Irving, back from America, presented him with an affectionate address from the Fund of which Irving was President: 'Like Garrick with whom your name is linked for all time, you have contributed to the gaiety of nations by the unapproachable spontaneity of your graceful comedy.' After Wyndham had finished acting on the crowded 1 May he and his wife entertained 1,500 people at the new Hotel Cecil in the Strand, which had not yet opened to the public. On hearing the number, the manager had said resignedly that he was sure they would be content with a buffet. Mary, with her innate business sense, replied, 'Well, Mr Wyndham will be quite satisfied, and no one will expect anything else—but think what a fine adertisement it would be for your hotel if it were known 1,500 sat down to a hot supper!' The manager concurred, and it was at the end of a hot supper that Lord Russell of Killowen, Lord Chief Justice (one of the few political appointments their host never filled on the Criterion stage), proposed Charles Wyndham's health. A guest, who said he neither attended celebrations nor ate supper, was Bernard Shaw (then critic for *The Saturday Review*); he went to shake hands with Wyndham and could not get near enough.

Fifteen days later, Charles and Mary began a new Criterion play, *Rosemary*, by collaborators later practised, Louis N. Parker and Murray Carson. This was a romance, and therefore a departure. The idea was Carson's, an actor who had appeared frequently with Wilson Barrett. He and Parker sent the last act—a monologue—to Wyndham, and strangely, though nervous about appearing as a man of ninety (which he had to do in the last scene), he was interested enough to ask for the complete text. Having sent it, the authors disappeared to France. Within two days Wyndham had joined them. Did they want a lump sum, he asked, or would they take royalties? Wandering in the woods, they argued together. Should they gamble, or take the bird in hand?

WYNDHAM    Well? What is it to be?
PARKER and CARSON    We think—perhaps an inclusive payment.
WYNDHAM    For ever and for everywhere?
PARKER AND CARSON    Yes.
WYNDHAM    How much?
PARKER AND CARSON    We thought, perhaps, h'm, a thousand pounds.
WYNDHAM    Oh, not all at once! £500 now and the rest on the hundredth night.

He wrote the cheque in mid-forest, and departed. They had sold *Rosemary* for ever and for everywhere.

This time rehearsals could hardly have been worse. Everyone begged Wyndham not to go on with the play. No one believed in it—no one except Mary. Dolly was her favourite part. Having what she thought was a dazzling idea, she called together Wyndham and the authors. In the dreaded last act Wyndham, as Sir Jasper Thorndyke remembering that when forty he had fallen in love with a girl on her wedding morning, had to say, 'I can see her now standing in the doorway with the flowers in her hands and the sunshine on her hair. . . .' At this moment Mary, possibly visualizing another entrance for herself, proposed that the walls should become transparent so that the audience could see what Sir Jasper remembered. As she explained her idea in the Yacht Room, Wyndham and the two dramatists broke into laughter and refused to take her seriously. Four cast changes added to the trouble; Alfred Bishop resigned because he found Professor Jogram's character contradictory, and was given the postboy's part instead. When chronic asthma obliged Edward Righton to retire, Bishop again switched his parts, and James Welch was brought in for the postboy. Annie Hughes joined the cast in place of an actress originally engaged and unsuitable. J. H. Barnes, now the Professor, founded one scene on Samuel Phelps (with whom he had acted as a young man), and for him at least *Rosemary* was a happy episode.

Everyone at the dress rehearsal except Mary—and presumably Barnes—was in despair. Wyndham believed the play was too quiet. On the first night Parker and Carson walked up and down the neighbouring streets, not daring to enter until someone ran after them and insisted that they should take a call; the audience was shouting for the authors, and loudly enough not to be denied. Presently, when Mrs Tree, lion-hunting, invited them to supper, they knew they had succeeded. Mary, in this unashamedly sentimental affair, and still looking incredibly young (she was thirty-four) with her hair in ringlets, thought she had never looked better on the stage. Early Victorian costumes suited her; but there was a second reason. Her mind, reflected in her face, was 'in a very gentle and softened condition'. After a serious disagreement, she had been on the edge of leaving; but a friend urged her not to, reminding her what she owed to Wyndham, and that she could never forget his goodness in the dawn of her career. So she stayed. When she realized she had done the right thing it gave her enormous pleasure: 'This no doubt reflected itself in my face and softened it.'

Wyndham, unused to an ageing make-up, had reason to be nervous of Sir Jasper's monologue; in H. A. Saintsbury's opinion, he could never be an old man 'though he must have been close on seventy' when he played Jasper: actually, he was fifty-nine. (He was seventy when a rising critic, James Agate, saw him at Manchester in a revival, and noted sourly that 'he played an old man of 90 with the hands of a boy of twenty'). The last act was the problem. Earlier in the evening, and aided by the curious break in his voice, he could move an audience even with those embarrassing speeches. *Rosemary* ran until 25 July 1896, and returned after the summer break. When Wyndham sold the American rights (and the authors must have cursed themselves for choosing a lump sum) there were inflated reports of the amount. Forty or fifty thousand pounds, rumour reported. Mary believed it to be more like five thousand.

At Christmas she went to the Riviera with Wyndham for a short holiday; meeting Henry Arthur Jones in Paris on their way home, they heard him read his new play, *The Physician*, and in this, after a few more weeks in *Rosemary*, they opened on 25 March 1897. The physician, a specialist named Lewin Carey (Wyndham), tries vainly to cure a dipsomaniac. Marion Terry (considered by some to be a better actress than her sister Ellen) appeared as a woman who throws over Carey; at last, and obligingly, the dipsomaniac dies, and his fiancée (whom the specialist has loved all the time) is free to marry him. Not, on the whole, a transcript from life; few believed in it, and, unusually for a Jones-Wyndham play, it did not last. Wyndham went in July to Berneval-sur-mer to see Oscar Wilde, and to get him to translate and adapt Scribe's *Un verre d'eau*. It was a wasted journey, though Wyndham stayed for three hours and Wilde (who never wrote for the theatre again) seemed happy with the idea and the possible cast. In September he wrote from Dieppe: 'I have been obliged to decline Wyndham's offer. I simply have no heart to write clever comedy, and I feel it is best to tell him so. It is a great disappointment to me, but it cannot be helped.' While in prison Wilde had assured his agent, More Adey, that he intended paying his debts by instalments. He mentioned Wyndham as one instance out of 'alas! too many' to whom he owed £300 for literary work never done. 'My trial of course prevented it. I must pay him half if possible.'

# IV

So to the final Jones play at the Criterion, *The Liars*, a small masterpiece of English social comedy. Wyndham, as Sir Christopher Deering, had the most satisfying of his *raisonneurs* (today we should call the man a marriage-guidance counsellor). Jones never wrote more wittily, or for him more elegantly; the comedy was often compared with *The School for Scandal*, and the historian Allardyce Nicoll has said that it 'evoked the kind of laughter heard rarely in the theatre since Goldsmith and Sheridan'. Without question, it was superbly made: Jones the technician at his most redoubtable. The first act introduces members of a house-party; in the second most of them converge upon a Thames-side house and interrupt a tête-à-tête; in the third act they are all plausibly brought together so that they can get Lady Jessica out of the mess that threatens her marriage. These are the liars of the title which some critics objected to as tasteless. (Jones's original title was *The Triflers*; Wyndham got him to change it, and at once the advance booking increased.) Jessica has flirted outrageously with Ned Falkner—not because he attracts her, but because she is bored, and her husband neglects her. Early, we learn all we need to know about the marriage:

GILBERT   What's all this tomfoolery with Falkner?
JESSICA   Tomfoolery?
GILBERT   George says you are carrying on some tomfoolery with Falkner.
JESSICA   Ah! that's very sweet and elegant of George. But I never carry on any tomfoolery with anyone—because I'm not a tomfool, therefore I can't.

138

GILBERT   I wish for once in your life you'd give me a plain answer to a plain question.

JESSICA   Oh, I did once. You shouldn't remind me of that. But I never bear malice. Ask me another such as—if a herring and a half cost three ha'pence, how long will it take one's husband to learn politeness enough to remove his cap in his wife's presence?

GILBERT   [*instinctively takes off his cap, then glancing at her attitude, which is one of amused defiance, he puts the cap on again*]   There's a draught here.

JESSICA   The lamp doesn't show it. But perhaps you are right to guard a sensitive spot.

GILBERT   I say there's a confounded draught.

JESSICA   Oh, don't tell fibs, dear. Because if you do, you'll go—where you *may* meet me; and then we should have to spend such a very long time together.

Like Kato in *Rebellious Susan*, Deering is a bachelor; each has been knighted for services to his country or profession; both uphold the conventions, the sanctity of marriage, man's—and more especially woman's—duty to society. In his resolve to prevent Lady Jessica and Falkner from going away together, Deering in a famous fourth-act speech tells them to remember

the brave pioneers who have gone before you in this enterprise. They've all perished, and their bones whiten the anti-matrimonial shore. Think of them! Charley Gray and Lady Rideout—flitting shabbily about the Continent at cheap *table d'hôtes* and gambling clubs, rubbing shoulders with all the blackguards and *demi-mondaines* of Europe. Poor old Fitz and his beauty—moping down at Farnhurst, cut by the county, with no single occupation except to nag and rag each other to pieces from morning to night. Billy Dover and Polly Aitchison—cut in for fresh partners in three weeks. The old idiot, Sir Bonham Dancer—paid five thousand pounds damages for being saddled with the professional strong man's wife. George Nuneham and Mrs Sandys—George is conducting a tramcar in New York, and Mrs Sandys—Lady Jessica, you knew Mrs Sandys, a delicate sweet little creature, I've met her at your receptions—she drank herself to death, and died in a hospital.

In this way Jones began to unwind the thread that Somerset Maugham with Lord Porteous and Lady Kitty in *The Circle* would unravel even further. To justify his marital views, Deering himself has an autumnal romance with a widow who yields to him in the last act while he is packing to accompany Falkner to Africa. In late Victorian and Edwardian comedy the Empire, as far-flung as possible, was an indispensable background: where else could Falkner (and other broken-hearted lovers) go? Where else could duty call so insistently?

Jones recognized Wyndham's gifts as *raisonneur*: 'a perfectly trained method, so rare on our English stage today; a fine and swift economy of speech and glance and gesture; every word and look and movement delivered with intention and restraint'. His period description of Lady Jessica—'a very bright, pretty woman, about twenty-seven, very dainty and charming', also describes Mary Moore; she was thirty-five, but as Irene Vanbrugh, who played Lady Rosamund, Jessica's sister, generously admitted, 'she held without effort after a number of years the title of the perfect *ingénue*'. The affinity between Mary and her part was reasonable; Jones, after all, had become a house dramatist at the Criterion, and she played three of his heroines. Irene Vanbrugh (who was married to the younger Dion Boucicault) watched Wyndham, fascinated:

> It was an experience and a delight . . . to note the vibrant vitality with which he came on to the stage. Part of his method was to stand in the wings for some minutes before his entrance, concentrating mentally and exercising physically. Then, when all his powers were well assembled, he entered like a vital spark illuminating the whole stage and unerringly focussing the attention of the audience.

For some reason, Shaw, an admirer of both Jones and Wyndham, did not get his press ticket, so *The Liars* was ignored in *The Saturday Review*. Mary wrote, asking him to come to a later performance. Though he intended to accept, he fell from his bicycle, and injured his face so badly that 'people swooned in all directions when they saw the wreck of my beauty'. Even when patches and plasters were off and stitches out, he would not risk the chance of Mary spotting him in the bandbox of the Criterion. A loss to everyone, especially to the historian.

Another critic, Archer, dismissed the play as insubstantial, something 'in which the Criterion public should find a pleasant relaxation after the painful intensity of *The Physician*'. He did recreate one moment that should be in every manual of English acting:

> Mr Wyndham, as an actor, has one great fault from the critic's point of view—he is too persistently good. . . . Here is a little problem for an aspiring actor: a piano is heard off the stage, there is a pause in the conversation, a lady asks "Is that not Mrs Ebernoe?" and a gentleman answers "Yes"—how is the gentleman to convey in that one word "Yes" the fact that he is devotedly, chivalrously, adoringly, in love with this Mrs Ebernoe whom, be it observed, we have not seen and of whom we know nothing? Don't ask me how it is done but go to the Criterion and see Mr Wyndham do it. The "Yes" certainly deserves to rank with Lord Burleigh's nod in point of concentrated expressiveness.

Let Irene Vanbrugh, herself about to be a leading lady, sum up: 'In the last act he [Wyndham] had a very long speech. I was standing on the scene during this, and nothing has ever taught me more than listening to him night after night; the variations, the sincerity were a revelation.' Wyndham now had entirely expunged the light comedian. While he pleaded with Jessica that Falkner's interests, duty, honour, all lay 'out there . . . Send him out with me to finish his work' the speech began to sound like a sermon. A compelling sermon, if a long one—Henry Arthur, bred in the Theatre Theatrical, saw to that.

# CHAPTER FOURTEEN

# Wyndham of Wyndham's
# 1898–1901

On the anonymous publication of *The Ballad of Reading Gaol* in 1898 Oscar Wilde said he wanted Wyndham among others to receive a copy. We do not know how Wyndham responded, for he had further preoccupations, but he never lost touch with Wilde during a maze of complicated plans which needed all his stupendous energy and Mary's business sense. Their Criterion partnership was about to develop.

The story behind the building of Wyndham's Theatre was as theatrical as anything the pair had ever acted. Joseph Pyke, a business-man negotiating for a Charing Cross Road site where some old houses stood, approached the ground landlords (the Salisbury estate) and told them he wanted to build a theatre there. The Marquess of Salisbury, currently Prime Minister, was firm; no theatre should be built on his land, he said, unless it was built for Charles Wyndham, whose acting he admired. So Pyke came to Wyndham with a proposal: if he (and his partner) would secure the site and clear it (at a cost of £10,000) Pyke would advance the money for the building, charging them 6 per cent on the loan, and holding as security a mortgage on the cleared site. Unable to find the capital—he had lost heavily on his South African shares—Wyndham agreed that Mary should raise the £10,000 among her friends. Though she disliked the idea of borrowing and could offer no security, she formed a syndicate of ten friends, each of whom guaranteed to her bank a thousand pounds for one year while she paid the interest on the loan. Once the theatre was built they could increase the mortgage and repay the bank.

Never revealing her friends, she did admit that there were millionaires among them. Very likely they included Alfred de Rothschild, Leopold de Rothschild and Sir Ernest Cassel. One man, a prominent financier whose name excited the bank, was anxious to be among the ten. The bank had stipulated that if the money were needed and any guarantor failed to produce it or went bankrupt, Mary would have to provide it herself. Surprisingly, the financier did go bankrupt; but though she replaced the missing £1,000 she never had to call in any of the money. Negotiations had begun in 1897 when she and Wyndham asked Lewis and Lewis, their almost regal solicitors, to draw up an agreement, one that specified the amounts each of them should find and affirmed that, should the theatre be let or sold, the proceeds would be divided equally. At first Lewis and Lewis were not at all sure that Mary was doing the right thing. In July 1898 they wrote to her:

> We cannot regard the position of the matter as at all satisfactory in your interest, and we repeat the advice we have already given you that you are incurring very great risk in advancing the £10,000. We understand however that you desire to go into the business notwithstanding all risks.

The site was duly cleared; the architect, W. G. R. Sprague, produced the plans, the contractor received a first payment of £2,000. Meanwhile, the show had to go on. Perhaps Wyndham's temperamental restlessness obliged him to try parts of so many kinds. Certainly his two attempts at romantic costume drama failed; he had never been a man for tushery. Anybody who neglected to read the notices—and more people are in outer darkness than drama critics realize—probably thought Parker and Carson's *The Jest* (10 November 1898) was a comedy. Regular playgoers liked to laugh—indeed, expected to laugh. Now Criterion farce had ended; they had got used to Wyndham moralizing in Jones's comedies; and, having laughed a good deal before that, they did not mind. If Wyndham moved them—not to tears, but to a few serious thoughts scattered about the last act of the comedy—this was excusable. One thing he must never do was to embarrass them, and that is what he did in *The Jest*. Moreover, he died—and what was even more unbearable, he had a long dying speech. Even at this remove we can imagine fingers loosening starched collars and women looking down at their laps. In *The Jest*, as an Italian nobleman attacked by a lunatic, Wyndham died only after he had crawled painfully towards a balcony, feebly waving a banner to catch the eye of someone described class-consciously as 'a rough soldier'.

Only that spring, when Shaw had retired from dramatic criticism, vowing never again to cross the threshold of a theatre—'The subject is exhausted, and so am I'—Wyndham had commented, 'Now the playwright may sleep in peace, and the actor take his forty winks without anxiety.' He spoke much too soon. Max Beerbohm, Shaw's successor on *The Saturday Review*, spent an uncomfortable Criterion evening. He was as unhappy about Mary's performance as Wyndham's:

Her prime quality, sense of humour, she had to suppress. Her talent for sentimental acting did not carry her far.

He went on to an impression of her acting style:

All her pretty mannerisms—drooping her head on one shoulder and gazing pensively into space and chanting her words down the scale—were of no avail.

In fact for him the play depended upon its single set: a terrace, a colonnade, and an orange grove:

I have never seen a more beautiful scene on the stage of any theatre . . . it gave one the illusion that the characters . . . whenever they walked from the terrace, had really passed into a long grove of trees, beyond our sight.

When a critic praises a set at some length it must be a suspiciously poor play. And this was by no means the last Wyndham would hear from Max.

## II

Early in 1899 a small, dapper man read his new comedy to Charles and Mary. The comedy was *The Tyranny of Tears*; the dramatist Haddon Chambers, an Australian who had already had various plays in London, among them *Captain Swift*, which Tree did at the Haymarket and in New York. But Chambers, who had now written specifically for Wyndham and Mary, was baffled when they told him which of his characters they would prefer. At the centre of the play is Clement Parbury, a mild husband governed and intimidated by his wife's 'tyranny of tears'. When she orders the dismissal of his secretary Hyacinth for kissing his photograph he actively rebels. She leaves him, only to return at the last in a conventional pairing-off exercise when the husband's old friend (Gunning) takes charge of Hyacinth. Though it had seemed clear that Wyndham and Mary would choose husband and wife, they insisted upon friend and secretary; Chambers had to use every coaxing gift to explain that he could conceive of no one else as the Parburys, parts he had always designed for them. At length they agreed. Later, in his room at the Hotel Cecil, Chambers had no trouble when he read the play to Frederick Kerr (Wyndham's final choice for Gunning): Kerr was so impressed that he willingly sacrificed a season's engagement with John Hare and gambled on *The Tyranny of Tears* having a long run.

At this point—and worried, probably, about progress in Charing Cross Road—Wyndham was less sanguine. He wondered whether the play was too slight. Its plot, as with *The Case of Rebellious Susan*, rested on the wife's departure, but there the likeness ended. Mrs Parbury is spoilt and lachrymose; when she leaves her easy-going husband the latter celebrates his freedom with Gunning; and, unable to face breakfast next morning, they turn to champagne. Night by Criterion night, Wyndham and Kerr drank a harmless and unpalatable concoction labelled 'Sparkling Saumur', but at one performance during what proved to be a long run Wyndham for some reason had ordered real champagne. According to the text, Alfred Bishop, on his arrival as the wife's father (Armitage), had to say 'Champagne in the morning! Dear, dear!', whereupon Wyndham would pass the bottle and he would drink with feigned disapproval and secret zest. On this exceptionally hot night Wyndham and Kerr finished the bottle before he entered: Kerr liked to recall Bishop's expression as he tried to fill his glass from an empty bottle and then noticed the lordly label. Here the rueful Armitage had to describe the situation at home:

ARMITAGE   We supped in the kitchen at two. It's amazing how emotion stimulates the appetite. No, Clement, her indisposition is of the mind. She wept.

PARBURY   All the time?

ARMITAGE   All the time. [*Then he adds with a sigh*] I had a rather trying night of it . . . my dear daughter is, of course, always more than welcome to my home, but I trust you will not misunderstand me when I say that I require notice. Since I regained my liberty—I mean since the death of your wife's dear mother, I've drifted into my own—er—little ways. This has deranged my plans; without being indiscreet, I may tell you I have had to send telegrams.

Though Beerbohm believed that more should have been made of Parbury's position as a popular novelist, he conceded that Wyndham revelled in the relative simplicity of his part, playing it with the absolute assurance of a tight-rope dancer crossing a road. Kerr too could be perfect without exerting himself. Mary Moore was 'very feminine'—to be feminine was the most important thing—but as the secretary Hyacinth, Maude Millett (one of the 'Two Roses' in the Criterion revival) marred an amusing portrait by wearing three highly elaborate dresses, out of tune with her impoverished youth in a country vicarage family of thirteen. Mary supervised the dresses: she frequently went to Paris to study fashion.)

Like Henry Arthur Jones, Haddon Chambers received 10 per cent of the receipts, which often rose to £1,600 a week. This meant that West End dramatists were now rather better off than James Albery, who got three guineas a performance for *Two Roses!* Chambers wrote other plays, though none quite so fruitful, and *The Tyranny of Tears* would be revived at Wyndham's Theatre. When he died in 1921 Somerset Maugham remembered him spitefully, warts and all:

> Since he wrote plays I suppose he must be counted as a man of letters, but surely there can have been seldom a man of letters who cared less for literature. I do not know whether he ever read: certainly he never spoke of books. He attached no great importance to his plays; but it exasperated him to have his best play, *The Tyranny of Tears*, ascribed to Oscar Wilde.

There were rumours to this effect, though Maugham could not understand how after Alexander had taken Wilde's name off the bills, 'such a notion could ever have been as widely spread as it certainly was'. Maugham was right at least in thinking that if Chambers were remembered at all it would not be for any particular comedy but for his phrase (from *Captain Swift*) 'the long arm of coincidence', which lives still in anthologies of quotation.

So, with a success, Wyndham ended his twenty-three years at the Criterion: *The Tyranny of Tears* sent them out laughing. But for his final night he chose *Rosemary* in aid of the Prince of Wales's Hospital Fund. The Prince himself was present to hear Wyndham say that normally the house held £220 when full; that night had brought in £1,474. Then, in one of his familiar long, warm speeches he remembered three people who had been with him for more than fourteen years: the late William Blakeley; George Giddens; and

> the lady who has played at this theatre without a break when, by your favour, *Wild Oats* and *David Garrick* inaugurated that period during which the theatre has achieved and maintained its highest financial prosperity. I refer to my friend and my family's friend ever since she was a little girl—Miss Mary Moore. Not only by the exercise of her delicate art, but in a thousand other ways, of which the public can have no direct knowledge, my fellow-worker's zealous services, keen instinct, and sound judgment have materially contributed to the success of my management.

It was a grave moment, he said, when a man left the place which had been his professional home for over twenty-three years. Grave, yes, but not sad.

# III

Work on the new theatre continued rapidly. By July the contractor had received £15,000, and the decorators their first instalment. Today, on the façade of his theatre the architect, W. G. R. Sprague, is commemorated in a simple panel:

> Wyndham's Theatre was built for
> Mary Moore and Charles Wyndham
> in 1899
> Architect        W. G. R. Sprague

146

No other London theatre remembers its architect like this; Sprague's elegant building was the first in his line of small West End theatres: the New, now the Albery (1903), the Strand (1905), the Aldwych (1905), the Shaftesbury Avenue Globe (1906), the Queen's (1907), the Ambassadors (1913) and the St Martin's (1916). Wyndham's now seats 769. When it opened it held 1,200: 540 on satin-upholstered tip-up chairs, the rest in private boxes and on undivided pit and gallery benches. Like the Criterion's, the stage is flat; but it is larger—60 feet wide and 30 feet deep. The architect—who had to fit his theatre into a space of 7,000 square feet—had a gift for intimacy. As Ian Albery, Mary Moore's great-grandson, would say, 'Ask any actor. You stand on the stage of Wyndham's, and you have the house in your hand.' But Sprague was versatile; when he was designing Wyndham's he was also working on the Balham Hippodrome, entirely opposite in style, size and purpose. Large and brash, this was for music-hall audiences; Wyndham's for smart Edwardian society. It remains an island of turn-of-the-century elegance; apart from the Palace in Cambridge Circus, the only free-standing theatre building in the West End: nothing else touches its walls (except a recently constructed upper bridge that links it with the neighbouring Albery). From the opposite pavement in Charing Cross Road Wyndham's curiously delicate exterior can be seen as a whole, unspoilt, and as it was in 1899.

The façade is of cream-coloured Portland stone, restored in 1973; there are classical decorations, and a stone balustrade surrounds the roof. Wyndham, passionately fond of the open air (he had tried, unluckily, to rehearse *Rebellious Susan* out of doors), hoped to turn the flat roof into a winter garden; a lift to take people up to it was planned—the shaft still exists—but the London County Council refused permission. The roof was undeniably used once, during the midsummer of 1916 at the heart of the First World War. Then an all-star cast (justifiable phrase) assembled for a quick rehearsal of *The Admirable Crichton*, and to hear Barrie read from his text. This was in preparation for a King George's Pension Fund matinée at the London Opera House in Kingsway. So many celebrities were on Wyndham's roof that morning—Ellen Terry, George Alexander, Lillah McCarthy, Gerald du Maurier, Arthur Bourchier (the Crichton) and a crowd of others—that if there had been a Zeppelin raid London would have lost most of its leading players. Bernard Shaw was there as well (an unnaturally quiet spectator). Mary Moore (in a group photograph wearing one of her familiar large 'Gainsborough' hats) would be a silent lady's maid—one of the staff in a comedy that, Squire Bancroft once said gloomily, 'deals with the juxtaposition of the drawing-room and the servants' hall, always to me a very painful subject'.

Inside, the Wyndham's of 1899 would look as its audiences expected a theatre to look: all in muted good taste, its colours, cream and turquoise, glinting here and there with what a newspaper called 'judicious gilding';

147

the dress circle and upper circle curving gently inwards; curtain and boxes hung with looped and fringed satin; and the proscenium as a complete picture-frame with the footlights hidden. Fashionable London was Francophil, and the decorators responded. Their inspiration, they said, was from the Louis Seize period; ceiling pictures derived from Boucher; tapestry panels brightened the saloon. In the original decorative group, still above the proscenium, two allegorical winged figures gaze at a bust reputed to be of Mary Moore. That is reasonable enough—though the likeness is not startling—as on either side of her in gilded frames are portraits of Goldsmith and Sheridan, in whose plays she had acted.

By 12 August 1899 the Electric Brush Company had received a first payment (£500). Cream-silk shades softened the house lights; and soon furniture and draperies would arrive from Shoolbreds. Messrs Osler provided a crystal chandelier (£95); potted palms filled the corners; woodwork was fireproofed. The final cost reached £37,000. In mid-autumn Sprague's building had begun to look like a theatre; and on 16 November 1899 its doors opened to—naturally—*David Garrick*, preceded by Leo Trevor's *Dr Johnson*, a sound partnership. The Boer War was on, so the proceeds at this charity performance—£4,000—went to the Soldiers' and Sailors' Families Association. Again the Prince of Wales—greatest Francophil of all—attended, and on the stage the band of the Coldstream Guards played the National Anthem: French décor; British patriotism. The idea had been to keep *Garrick* on for a fortnight, but because playgoers cling to something familiar it ran for four months. To swell charity takings, illustrated first-night programmes signed by the company were offered at a guinea each. The regular programme cost, less opulently, twopence. Prices of admission were: Private boxes £1 11*s*. 6*d*.—£6 6*s*.; Stalls, 10*s*. 6*d*.; Dress circle, 7*s*. and 5*s*.; Family circle, 4*s*.; Pit, 2*s*. 6*d*.; Gallery, 1*s*.

Now Wyndham (whose nephew, Percy Hutchison, was the stage manager) would have to juggle to keep two theatres moving at once; he still leased the Criterion, at first with Charles Frohman and (quite like the old days) a 'from the French' comedy, *My Daughter-in-Law*. Wyndham conducted rehearsals which a new member of his cast, the young Seymour Hicks—himself an outstandingly glib speaker—found alarming. One day nine people and a dog surrounded Wyndham, who was eating ham and eggs:

> Wyndham talking as rapidly as I ever have in life, which is saying a good deal: "Capital, my dear Hicks, capital, capital, capital—very good, but I should be a little less serious—brighter, brighter. (*A manager arrives*) What's that? Rand mines are 6¼—buyers, that will be all right. Ask them what Jumpupfontein B's are going to. (*To an actress*) Oh! my dear lady, no; if you wear a dress that colour what's to become of the two armchairs? We have two green satin armchairs in this scene—two armchairs I say!! (*To one of the actors*) Cross right, my dear fellow; go

over and kiss your mother when she comes on; good. (*To a messenger*)
What's that? Tell the man to wait. Where's that bit of bacon? Oh, when
you take hold of a girl's hand, dear old man, do it gently; you'll never get
a woman to love you if you take her hand like—I never did—and I know;
no, no! (*To a manager*) Buy the five hundred and take a profit at once.
Hi! You furniture people, why on earth do you bring curtains that colour?
Do you want to frighten all the old ladies in the stalls? (*To himself*)
Now I've dropped the egg! (*To an actor*) No, no, kiss her, my boy, kiss
her as if you meant it. (*To a furniture man*) What a carpet! no, we won't
have that! (*To an actor*) Take her face in your hands and tell her you
want—(*To a waiter*) Another cup of coffee, please. (*To an actor*)—her
father—(*To a manager*) What's that? oh! Well, sell the things. (*To the
actor*)—to give his consent to—(*To a manager*) What's that? Hang the
City, I wish I'd never seen it! (*To a messenger*) Tell the lady to wait.
What's that? (*To a secretary*) No, I can't dine at Lady Crowbrough's on
Tuesday. (*To an actor*).Squeeze her, my boy, squeeze her! That's it, look
lovingly into her eyes, and say—(*To a waiter*)Another pat of butter,
please. (*To an upholsterer*) Ah, that's the colour, my boy; why didn't you
bring it before? (*To an actor*) That's it, give her the rose and exit.
Capital. Come back and do it once more. Lie down, Fido. (*To a lady*) That
dog wants washing. You know I spoke to you about it last week.

Another time someone leant over Wyndham's chair and, so Hicks felt,
whispered something about himself, not at all kindly. Interrupting the
rehearsal, he complained that he could not go on while people criticized
what he was doing. Wyndham, all charm, replied, 'You're mistaken. . . .
They were only saying you were wonderful—delightful, so fresh and
bright. The only little thing they did suggest was that you are like me on
the stage, just like me, so natural that sometimes the points don't carry.'
Really, there was no answer to that: Hicks did not record one.


# IV


Arthur Bourchier, always a full gale of a man, began his two years with
Wyndham at the Criterion in February 1900. At first he repeated his
performance of Dr Johnson which he had played in a curtain-raiser at the
Wyndham's opening—something a critic found so real that he wanted to
put his arm in the Doctor's and 'take a walk down Fleet Street'.

Though at Wyndham's *Garrick* could have run for months, a revival of
*Dandy Dick* had already been booked—Pinero's farce about the Dean and
the racehorse—and Wyndham went on tour in *Cyrano de Bergerac*, a
completely misguided choice. When the original Cyrano, Coquelin the
elder, came to the Lyceum in 1898 Paris-conscious London swooned.
Wisely, Irving (who had bought the English rights) thought twice about
it. An English version, so soon after Coquelin's triumph, would never do,
and it did not. William Archer had adored the play (in French): 'A literary opera, with the instrumental accompaniment omitted, but with

149

recitatives, arias, duets, trios, concerted pieces, even choruses, all in due form. Max Beerbohm said firmly:

> I wish all my readers to see *Cyrano*. It may not be the masterpiece I think it, but at any rate it is one's money's worth. The stalls are fifteen shillings a-piece, but there are five acts, and all the five are fairly long, and each of them is well worth three shillings. Even if one does not like the play, it will be something, hereafter, to be able to bore one's grandchildren by telling them about Coquelin as Cyrano.

That was exciting; but Rostand's relishing use of language would defeat most English translators. *Cyrano*, with its duelling and gasconading, is above all an audacious adventure in language. Rostand enjoyed it, but few English translators have expressed his enjoyment; the race of images and epithets has been muffled in cotton-wool. Moreover, few actors have had the temperament, the larger-than-life personality, to respond. Neither the version by G. Stuart Ogilvie and Louis N. Parker which Wyndham used in 1900—only two years after London had heard Coquelin himself—nor one by Gladys Thomas and Mary Guillemand, which Robert Loraine transformed in 1919 and 1927, got very close to Rostand's spirit. Brian Hooker's translation, used by the Old Vic at the New in 1946, came off intermittently—it hinted very seldom at what Humbert Wolfe had called 'the vast efflorescence' of Rostand's alexandrines. Wolfe himself, in the mid-1930s, translated the play with much of the fitting bravura for a Charles Laughton film which Alexander Korda was to make, but never did. No English translator genuinely opened a theatre door to *Cyrano* until Christopher Fry, for the Chichester Festival in 1975, recognized the luxuriance of the imagery in a version always consistent and written in chiming couplets that never worried the listener or impeded the action.

When Wyndham bought the English rights from Irving an admirer proposed that the narrative, mid-seventeenth-century, should be put back to the Elizabethan world, and that Cyrano, the Gascon, should be Irish. Wyndham argued politely that though an average audience would find the play more intelligible, the change might upset people who already thought of it as a classic. Cyrano is much more than a man whose nose is long enough to be a cruel joke. He is idealist, wit and swordsman; above all he loves Roxane, and when her dull, handsome suitor wants to serenade her Cyrano takes his place, knowing that in the darkness beneath her balcony he and his nose are invisible. Character, situations, panache, poetry, wit—no wonder Wyndham could not resist the part. On tour he and his company went fairly well; but in Dublin they found themselves expected to give a 'State' charity performance commanded by the Lord-Lieutenant and attended by the Duke and Duchess of Connaught. Charles and Mary, invited to a Royal reception, had swiftly to borrow a Court suit and the regulation veil and feathers to make a show.

Perhaps Mary Moore had this picture taken in Russia to remind her that on her first day
in St Petersburg (January 1888) her petticoats froze to the waist

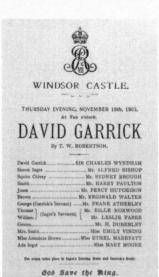

During the State visit of the King and Queen of Italy in 1903, Wyndham and Mary gave *David Garrick* in the Waterloo Chamber at Windsor. The choice of play bored Edward VII—he had seen it seven times. The programme was printed on fringed silk

In their surest standby, *David Garrick*, which they played on countless occasions between 1886 and 1913. Mary regarded Ada Ingot as the worst part in the play

Soon, on 19 April 1900, *Cyrano* opened at Wyndham's. As with *The Jest*, it was not what people expected. The audience, or most of it, had no wish whatever to see handsome Mr Wyndham, master of the social graces, as a figure of fun with a grotesque nose based on the Duke of Wellington's. They did not want elegant, ageless Mr Wyndham to die. He might make a long speech in the last act; it might have a moral; but most assuredly he should not die. Max Beerbohm, angry at the mere thought of an English version, could see what the play should have been—actors could not. All they saw was the chance of playing Cyrano:

> Mr Wyndham happens to be the man who ultimately got it. But as the part does not, from a critic's standpoint, exist, how am I to praise his performance of it? How, as one who revels in his acting, do aught but look devoutly forward to his next production?

After this Wyndham must have regretted his light-hearted relief when Shaw retired from criticism.

Such a theatre enthusiast as Sir George Arthur was engaged at the time in the Boer War: a dreary business, he said years later, but at least it saved him from seeing the failure of one of the most adroit comedians the English stage had known. Kate Terry Gielgud too was both disappointed and surprised: before *Cyrano* she had believed at heart that Wyndham could express much of the quality of French technique. Towards the end of the run the company had an experience common to most London theatres that night. The scene has been described (with small differences) by several actors. At Wyndham's *Cyrano* had reached the Balcony scene when Charles, sensitive to movement in front, felt that something unusual was happening. Edging to the wings on the dark stage, he asked the prompter, who told him that Mafeking had been relieved. Newspaper-boys could be heard in the street outside; inside, restlessness increased, so Charles stopped the performance, had the lights turned up, and announced the news. Once the applause had died down—and that took some time—they began the scene again (said Mary) 'as though nothing had happened'.

There it was: on 1 June they finished the run. Wyndham, as usual, spoke. The play had met with a peculiar reception—numbers liked it, numbers did not: to the former, his congratulations, to the latter, his condolence. Actors have always been endearingly ready to find external reasons for failure, and Wyndham did his best: after the relief of Mafeking bookings had slumped—probably, he thought, because the time was too exciting, people were too full of emotion, too full of sadness, for so sad a play. He hoped to revive it . . . but he never did. Someone had an ingenious notion why *Cyrano* failed. Nothing to do with acting or translation: simply that in the English mind a big nose goes with a comic character: Mr Punch, Ally Sloper, Cyrano. It was a logical progression, but from Wyndham no comment.

151

# V

On now to a richer occasion and a major drama of its period which might have had as its epigraph Paula Tanqueray's line, 'The future is only the past again, entered through another gate.' In *Mrs Dane's Defence*, staged by Wyndham during the autumn of 1900, Henry Arthur Jones was back indignantly at his old theme: one law for the man, another for the woman. As always, society's harsh injustice affected him strongly—so strongly that his audiences would sympathize with the unfortunate woman: a feat at the turn of the century, when heroines had to be innocent. (Mrs Dane was not.) A woman with a past—all those things that shocked Edwardians so enjoyably—she was not even Mrs Dane, though Sir Daniel Carteret (himself a judge, and a man who could have extracted the truth from Munchausen), had to cross-examine her for three-quarters of an hour before he proved she was lying. It was vital for him to know. His adopted son, on the verge of a brilliant career, had fallen in love with the woman, already a victim of gossip. When Sir Daniel questioned her relentlessly the audience stayed on her side. At first it looked as if she might escape; her tale seemed invulnerable. Then, by using 'we' instead of 'I', she made a fatal error and toppled into headlong confusion:

SIR DANIEL    When Felicia Hindemarsh left Tawhampton, where did she go?
MRS DANE    I don't quite know.
SIR DANIEL    But you had letters from her. Where did they come from?
MRS DANE    Let me think—it was some seaside place I think. (*Pause*)
SIR DANIEL    You don't remember?
MRS DANE    No, I'm getting so terribly muddled, I don't know what I'm saying. I—I—you frighten me.
SIR DANIEL    I frighten you?
        [*His manner throughout has been calm and kind but very firm*].
MRS DANE    Yes. I know you're very kind, and that I've nothing to fear, but I feel—I feel as if I were being thumb-screwed, and if you ask me one more question I must shriek out for help. [*A little pause*] I'm sure it would be better for me to go and write it all out when I'm alone [*making a movement to go*] Don't you think so?
SIR DANIEL    [*arresting her with a gesture*]. No.

At the première (9 October 1901) this scene held the house in taut silence. When the curtain descended on Sir Daniel's 'I say you're lying! You are Felicia Hindemarsh!' it was several seconds before applause burst tumultuously. If Henry Arthur had kept to his first draft, suggested by a newspaper story, this would not have happened. A perfectionist, he had realized that because of an earlier passage where Sir Daniel interrogated a detective, he had let the audience know that the woman was guilty. This would have ruined her long scene with Sir Daniel. Jones went alone to

Switzerland, and there he got it right, finishing the scene in four hours of white heat and stopping only for a moment while he watched a funeral procession in the street outside. (Literary detectives will look for the point in the script where this occurred.)

At the time Wyndham engaged Lena Ashwell for Mrs Dane (in a play that had no title until one of the cast, Alfred Bishop, suggested it), she was an experienced actress, not yet a star. During rehearsals a certain despondency clouded her:

> I was a dark horse, and Mrs Dane was a woman with a murky past, and heroines should have virtue on their side. Even if for a time circumstances were against them, they should be proved innocent in the end. I felt encouraged when I heard two scene-shifters discussing Mrs Dane, and one said: 'Love her! Why, I'd marry her myself.'

She learned from Wyndham much about the essence of timing and judgment. Whenever, according to directions for her third-act exit, she became hysterical he stopped her, explaining that the moment of climax was over. This had come with his discovery that she was Felicia Hindemarsh; nothing she could do would recapture that special moment of tension, and it would be more effective if she went out quietly. She found that it was: so much so that she was almost inaudible. Again, Wyndham insisted that Mrs Dane must dress simply, though this contradicted an old theatrical idea that clothes should bring out a woman's character.

Sadly, the period demanded a fourth act. As so often elsewhere, the play fell to sentimentality and anticlimax; Felicia Hindemarsh exiled to Devon (and an uncertain future); and two marriages foreshadowed: Sir Daniel's to Lady Eastney (Mary Moore), and his son's to her niece. Notices concentrated on the acting, even if J. T. Grein good-humouredly tried to redress the balance:

> We in England are apt to forget this; we print the actor's name in gigantic capitals, while the author's comes lower down in tiny letters. . . . We are mostly not alive to the fact that the author creates, whereas the actor illustrates; that the very existence of the actor is dependent on the author.

With everyone else, the third act overcame him:

> as bold and intense a piece of work as has ever sprung from the prolific mind of this thoughtful dramatist . . . The effect of this scene is—without exaggeration—colossal; at least such was the impression it made on me. I felt the moral torture so intensely, the cunningly devised phrases of the author, the insinuating force of Wyndham's dulcet manner, of his screwing, digging, exploding voice, the terrible mortified face of Miss Ashwell—all that concentration of influence to destroy the new life of a

153

woman!—it made me almost implore aloud for mercy. It was painful
physically as well as mentally. Yet I do not complain, for author and
actors between them had but reproduced an episode of real life, and,
in placing it before us, they had, if anything, softened its awful veracity.

Now sixty-three and grey-haired, Wyndham did not look his age. In Sir
Daniel he had a character less sympathetic than some—a man who
admits that when young he had resolved to break up a marriage and only
an accident had prevented it. For all that, he could upbraid a woman for
her youthful 'crime'. It was a superb acting part; Beerbohm swore
Wyndham had done nothing better. Lena Ashwell made her name, and
promptly appeared on picture-postcards. She had time to study Charles
and Mary on and off stage. His knowledge, she decided, was as great as
Irving's but different in kind. He was irresponsible, and had little idea of
the value of money; she was worldly-wise with a fine brain for finance and
a strong sense of 'what people will say'. If her stage scope was limited, she
was neat, accurate and attractive.

Dedicating his published text to Wyndham, Jones repeated his
insistence that while they worked together failure was impossible, a 'most
confident belief of mine' that there had been too few chances to test.
Above all, he admired Wyndham's voice: only two notes in it, but
everything could be done with them. In old age he liked, as an example of
Wyndham's articulation, to speak Sir Daniel's 'There was a child?' in a
piercing whisper as if it were one word only, yet every syllable was clear.
Wyndham once said to Irving, 'We haven't got much of a voice, you and I.'
'Thank God we haven't,' Irving answered.

Wyndham told Lena Ashwell that the applause after his cross-
examination was the most tremendous he had known. To the author he
said, 'You could lean up against it.' His new theatre was in for a run—209
nights. Soon after the opening Oscar Wilde died in Paris at the age of
forty-six. This must have saddened Charles, who never ceased to hope
that he would get a play from him. Earlier that year Wilde had written to
apologize for delay in answering a letter: he had been ill with blood
poisoning because of insanitary conditions at the Hôtel d'Alsace, which
he wanted urgently to leave, but could not until he had paid his bill: he had
only fifty shillings a week. In his letter he mentioned a possible version of
a play by Dumas *père*, adding that though he would rather do original
work, money troubles gave him no peace.

Wilde had said once, 'The first rule of playwriting is not to write like
Henry Arthur Jones; the second and third rules are the same.'
Wyndham's box-office manager would have denied this. Audiences loved
Mrs Dane. Though Mary was out of the cast for three months, the piece
was still running when she came back. She had been to South Africa,
where her eldest son, Irving Albery, then a soldier, was dangerously ill
with enteric fever. Though warned that there was no chance of recovery,

she and her sister Fanny immediately set sail; the voyage was agonizing, and when they reached Madeira they discovered cables begging them to return. Ignoring them, Mary completed her mission: Irving on her arrival was emaciated and apparently dying, but miraculously he recovered, and she went home in May to resume her part of Lady Eastney; she was quietly gratified to know that receipts—which had begun to drop— immediately rose again. Wyndham had paid her full salary during her absence, a cheque she never cashed: instead (possibly to his astonishment, even if little could have astonished him then), she had it framed.

Content though she had been with her secondary part in *Mrs Dane*—indeed, she enjoyed it—she was back in the lead when they revived *The Case of Rebellious Susan*, and had a flattering letter from Henry Arthur:

> Your Susan was as near perfection *as possible* seven years ago. Now she has swallowed up even that margin, and is nearer perfection than is possible.

A handsome Italianate young man who took over from Fred Kerr was Harley Granville Barker (without a hyphen in those days). In the theatre he wanted, rather humourlessly, to be with 'creative artists', and this was to be his sole appearance with Charles Wyndham, the kind of 'gentleman actor' from whom he wanted to escape. History has room for them both.

# CHAPTER FIFTEEN

# 'The Comedy Widow'
# 1901–1904

With 1901 a new reign, and for Wyndham and Mary the beginnings of a new theatre. Behind Wyndham's there was still some land to spare, and prospective buyers for it; but when negotiations fell through the partners decided to build another theatre themselves. During the summer they discovered a contractor who bargained to have the theatre ready for them in nine months. Good; then just as they were about to go on holiday they received a demand for £2,000, commission for their introduction to the building firm. Believing this to be far too much, Wyndham on principle refused to pay. Though Mary, with her instinctive business sense, held that it might cost them even more if there were to be a further delay and they should forfeit the use of the theatre for another year, he maintained that it was an intolerable imposition. Ultimately, when they got back from abroad, they had to start all over again with fresh builders.

As an actress, Mary recognized her limitations. If an emotional part came along she would reject it as beyond her range. There was one in their next piece at Wyndham's—peculiarly named *The Mummy and the Hummingbird*—and she disappointed its American author, Isaac Henderson, by saying after he had read the script to them that she could not play Lady Lumley. Instead she suggested that, because more comedy was needed, he could rewrite the ingénue as a 'comedy widow'. Dramatists were used to this sort of thing, and Henderson tried hard without pleasing his exacting management. Lena Ashwell was engaged for the emotional woman, and Mary even looked out an unidentified play by James Albery which had never been acted, and slipped some scenes from it into Henderson's text. The poor man could not get his last act right; one problem was that two characters who ought not to have met had to enter by the same door. Mary decided that after all, as the room was in a hotel and they came in at different times, they might not have met on the stair. Ingenious: but her alterations and additions could not deceive Max Beerbohm, who sensed that the author had begun by writing a melodrama:

> Perhaps an exclusive admiration for the art of Mr Wyndham impelled him to change his tactics. He pitched his scheme in the comedic key, toned it down, and made it 'psychological' and all that. Lord Lumley, instead of being merely a hero became a neglectful husband absorbed in scientific inventions, and this change opened up the way, not only for Mr Wyndham's comedic power, but also for interesting discussions about the proper relations between husbands and wives.

Henderson's troubles did not end there. When he took the obligatory author's call after a cordial reception for the cast the gallery booed him soundly—not that this would have any marked effect on the run.

Once John Drew had bought the American rights, Wyndham and Mary claimed a small percentage. The harassed Henderson, hoping for some justice, at once asserted that his original script, without the Albery additions and 'the comedy widow', would be perfectly acceptable in America; but Drew, having seen the play in London, wanted the Wyndham's text. Henderson, beaten again—a hard life for a dramatist— had to agree. He did have one mild satisfaction, for on Broadway Drew's nephew, Lionel Barrymore, stole the notices in a small part, and his uncle was furious. 'Every night', he said, 'I have to play second fiddle to that preposterous nephew of mine.'

At Wyndham's, in a quick revival of *Mrs Dane's Defence*, they had a new man, A. E. Matthews, whom Charles had seen with Hare at the Criterion. Offering him a year's contract, Wyndham asked him what salary he wanted; and, remembering that Hare had advised him to ask three times what he was getting in *A Pair of Spectacles*, Matthews croaked nervously, 'Twenty—' 'Speak up!' said Wyndham. 'They wouldn't hear you in the stalls.' (A nice reversal of the little boy at the back of the gallery.) Again Matthews struggled to say twenty pounds. Again he could not finish. Impatiently, Wyndham broke in, 'I'll pay you twenty-one pounds a week—go up and sign your contract.' Matthews, who knew Wyndham had thought he was going to say twenty-five, would have signed anything to be in *Mrs Dane*, and here he had his first real West End chance. In one sense it had to be a terrifying engagement because the principals had already appeared two hundred times. Still, it was an actor's play—Henry Arthur Jones, as always, saw to that—and everyone who acted with him learned a great deal from Wyndham.

One night, while they were walking home together after the show, Matthews carried a malacca cane.

WYNDHAM  Never let me see you with a walking stick.

MATTHEWS   [*startled*] Why not?

WYNDHAM   In a drawing-room scene on the stage, would you carry a cane? Very well, then: if you get used to a walking stick and haven't one, you don't know what to do with your hands. You feel awkward with them. You might even put them in your pockets to get them out of the way! Next day you find yourself out of a job because I've given you the sack.

Here the young actor thought he could score. 'In your cross-examination,' he said, 'you placed one foot on the bench and one hand *in your pocket*.' Blandly, the old actor replied, 'I'm so glad you noticed that. I hope you saw that I kept my hand there—I didn't distract the audience's attention by taking it out *during* the speech.' Thereafter Matthews put his hand in his pocket only when buying something. Wyndham, never less than soothing, would be exceedingly kind, reviving *Betsy* and giving him the lead, and also recommending him elsewhere. It was real generosity. Seymour Hicks would recall how, when thoroughly downcast—as he might well have been—by the notices for his Valentine in *Quality Street* (Vaudeville, 1902), Wyndham had reassured him. 'Don't worry . . . I got awful notices for my first performances as David Garrick. I was compared unfavourably with Sothern. I don't play it any better today, but now the Press is eulogistic. There's only one thing to be frightened of, Hicks, and that's when you get good notices. Then—be careful!'

Years later Wyndham received, retrospectively, a bad notice from James Agate. As a young playgoer Agate had seen him sometimes in Manchester and preferred Henry Neville, who played Sir Daniel Carteret and other Wyndham parts out of town. Sydney Blow, juvenile lead in the tour of *Mrs Dane's Defence*, disagreed. Neville, he said, was full of tricks that angered his fellow-actors; as soon as he came on he would bump into Blow with his 'ample stomach' until eventually they were up against the back wall: 'The West End would never have accepted Neville in a Wyndham part.'

While playing Garrick in the summer of 1902—and somehow the play was fitting—Charles Wyndham was knighted in the Coronation honours: the third actor in succession to Irving (1895) and Bancroft (1897). Even this award had its drama. When an expected official letter failed to arrive at either one of the theatres or at the Hyde Park Hotel (where Wyndham was living then), Mary, practical in an emergency, thought of the Garrick Club and insisted that a messenger should go there. She was right (through life an uncomfortable habit). Like Wyndham, she had been especially anxious because, five years earlier, it was rumoured that he would figure in Queen Victoria's Diamond Jubilee list. When no letter came, and friends began to sympathize, he dismissed the subject as if it were quite unimportant, doing it so naturally, with experienced aplomb, that Mary admired him still more. George Rowell has surmised that Wyndham was not knighted because his name at that time meant such *risqué* farces as *Brighton* and *Pink Dominos*. Ironically, after Victorian straitlacing had been relaxed, and there was no longer need to be circumspect, nobody—not even the Queen herself—could have objected to Wyndham's choice of play.

His knighthood was popular with the profession, the public and the critics. That evening he was wildly applauded on his entrance as Garrick; and at Ada Ingot's line, 'A man who is an honour to his country', Mary momentarily stopped the show. (Most plays contrive to be appropriate on these occasions.) A hundred yards or so from Wyndham's, at Daly's by Leicester Square, Rutland Barrington added two verses to a number about the fictitious Rajah of Bhong in a musical comedy, *A Country Girl*:

> When we read in the list that's long as our fist
>     All the titles that mark an occasion,
> It's a sign of the age that a man on the stage
>     Has successfully made an invasion.
> And no matter the roles—far apart as the Poles—
>     There was nothing this actor could frighten.
> He is 'Garrick' today, but he first made his way
>     To our hearts as Bob Sackett in 'Brighton'.

> Piece, piece—many a piece—he's played in his management long,
> And in fact such a lot that a knighthood he's got
> For amusing the natives of Bhong!
> And he'll make a great stir in his new part as 'Sir'
> Will the popular Wyndham of Bhong.

J. T. Grein talked of the refinement of Wyndham's style, the subtlety of his humour, his distinguished speech: 'He is, on the stage and in life, the incarnation of what all the world has accepted as a model—a perfect gentleman.' This from a leader of the New Drama, Ibsen's ardent pioneer, was generous. Grein might easily have dismissed the new knight as commercial, the plays as trivial, but he did not: 'May he continue to flourish, a master of his art, a veteran in his profession, yet a juvenile in power, in spirit, and in fertility.'

## II

Lewis Waller, who acted in the revival of *Still Waters Run Deep*, had gone into management with a season in Liverpool. After travelling up to watch him in a piece of romantic nonsense, *Monsieur Beaucaire* (eighteenth-century Bath, complete with Beau Nash), Wyndham and Mary decided that this would do for the opening of their new theatre, and

Waller agreed. Unluckly, the calendar did not, so *Beaucaire* went instead to a long life at the Comedy while Charles and Mary were involved—with frustrating delays— in planning the décor for the building they spoke of simply as their 'new theatre'. The phrase grew into its name. Coincidentally, the handsome façade in St Martin's Lane looked across to New Row, which had once been New Street.

Sprague's thirtieth theatre, larger than Wyndham's and seating 1,200, was built on the cantilever principle which avoided awkward pillars. It had a three-tiered auditorium, approached through an ample foyer, and its dress-circle bar was one of the most spacious in London. Charles and Mary's friend, Claude Ponsonby, an expert on Louis Seize décor, proposed that seats in stalls and dress circle should be upholstered in tapestry which had to be ordered from Paris: costly but enduring, it lasted for over twenty years. The prevailing colours were gold and white. Medallions of French royalty hung from the walls; curtains and hangings were in brocade and velvet; and the spirits of Peace and Music, with cupids dressed as Summer and Winter—all copied from bronzes in the Ponsonby collection—surveyed the house from above the proscenium arch. The lines of Sprague's auditorium swept gracefully from stalls to gallery. In time Charles and Mary's New Theatre would house the finest English acting of the century, though in 1903 these were excitements beyond the horizon.

The Marquess of Salisbury, who (we remember) would allow a theatre on his land only if it were Charles Wyndham's, died in the year that the New was opened. His link with the sister theatres may be less dignified than the formidable Tory Prime Minister would have wished. It is simply the name of a tavern, the Salisbury, that stands on the corner of St Martin's Court and Lane, a place of glittering glass and gleaming mahogany still loved by the acting profession.

While back in 1903 Charles and Mary waited for their theatre to be ready—'Oh, how tired I got of all the business letters and interviews!' Mary wrote—they gave *David Garrick* at Windsor for a State visit by the King and Queen of Italy. Told that some of the Italians spoke no English, Wyndham was thoughtful enough to have a synopsis of the plot translated and distributed among the guests. King Edward, almost too closely interested in production detail, decided that one property was incongruous and commanded the use of a vase valued at £10,000 from the Royal collection; something that gave Percy Hutchison, the stage manager, an anxious night. After the performance (no breakages) in the Waterloo Chamber, the King said, 'When are you going to get a new play, Wyndham? I have seen this one seven times.' Superficially genial; but for an actor-manager a trifle hollow: new plays were not so easy as all that, especially when the New Theatre's first production had to be settled.

Wyndham had an idea that musical comedies might do well there—as indeed they would, and have—and Mary called on George Edwardes, paternal impresario of Daly's and the Gaiety, who lived near her in Regent's Park. To her surprise, he rejected the proposal: it would be three years, he said dogmatically, before cabmen knew where a new theatre was, so he never took one. When she reminded him that they had played to full houses ever since Wyndham's was opened, less than three years earlier, he replied with charming tact that of course their own audiences would follow wherever they went. Knowing him to be as astute as anyone in the business, Wyndham was somewhat dashed. Maybe, he thought, it would be better if they opened the theatre themselves. On 13 March 1903 they did just that, returning to *Rosemary*, Mary's favourite. In spite of some wistfulness for a new play—and Wyndham may have recalled King Edward—*Rosemary* immediately warmed the new house; the King promptly and properly visited it.

They did not stay there long. Charles decided to move *Rosemary* across the court to Wyndham's, and Forbes-Robertson came to the New with a version of Kipling's novel, *The Light That Failed*. Kipling had been curiously aloof from the stage. Though he must surely have thought of playwriting when he returned from India at the age of twenty-three, and settled in Villiers Street (immediately opposite a music-hall, Gatti's-under-the-Arches), nothing happened, though Irving did hint at a play for the Lyceum. 'I should rather like it', Kipling wrote to a friend, 'but actors are rummy folk.' As it chanced, the one play derived from his work that lasted for any length of time was *The Light That Failed*, a fairly dull and belated effort—the book was published in 1891—by a novelist-dramatist, 'George Fleming'. Staged at the Lyric earlier in 1903, it had gone over to the New; for years it remained in the Forbes-Robertson repertory, with Forbes-Robertson himself as the blind artist, Dick Heldar, and Gertrude Elliott as the heroine, Maisie. Sarah Bernhardt had once written to suggest a version 'from the English', but—actresses being rummy folk—she would not name her part, Maisie or Dick. Not that it mattered, for the version was never completed, if indeed it was ever begun.

For a while Charles and Mary would shift restlessly between their three theatres: as a rule one of these was let. Programmes (twopence) discreetly indicated Wyndham's knighthood; where other members of the company had a Mr or Miss before their names, he had simply a small blank space, just room enough for the invisible 'Sir'. These cast-lists always took the same form—his name at the top, hers at the bottom. No rigid 'order of appearance': neither players nor audiences would have dreamt of it.

# III

Again and again when a play was rehearsed Wyndham would be dubious. More often than not he was wrong; but that never occurred to him at the next dress rehearsal. Certainly not at *Mrs Gorringe's Necklace*. The author of this, Hubert Henry Davies, born and brought up in the North of England, had lived in America, and it was an American agent that sent *Mrs Gorringe* to Wyndham and *Cousin Kate* to Cyril Maude. Both were taken. When Davies read his play to Charles and Mary they thought it very funny, but the company was decidedly not amused, and after a gloomy session in the Wyndham's office Mary and Davies walked in silence through St Martin's Court. On the way to the New they met the permanently brash Percy Hutchison. 'Oh, well,' he exclaimed brightly, 'let's hope it acts better than it reads!' Davies, who had been very low, suddenly caught Mary's eye and they both melted into laughter—the only laughter that afternoon. Though a first-act run-through on the New Theatre stage was as gloomy as the reading, Wyndham need not have bothered. The play lived on its first night, and it went on living through a career that put Davies securely among Edwardian dramatists.

His excessively scatterbrained Mrs Gorringe reveals her character on entering. Having just left a polo match, she confesses that she has no idea how it is going: 'As soon as anyone explains to me how the score stands, they always go and change the board.' In some ways the woman seems to be an extension of Mrs Parbury in *The Tyranny of Tears*; just the part for Mary, who proved now—if anyone had doubted it—that she was an *ingénue* no longer but an accomplished comedienne. We can imagine her in such a scene as this:

JERNIGAN (*the detective*)   And how did you come to discover the diamonds were missing?

MRS GORRINGE   Well, I went up to my room when I came in from the polo match, and suppose the dressing-table to be there—[*points to Vicky*] where Miss Jardine is. And the door where this one is. [*Goes to the door, opens it, goes just outside and comes in again*]. I closed the door. [*Closes the door and goes towards Vicky as she says*] Then I crossed over to the dressing-table in quite an ordinary manner, just as I am doing now. [*When she has nearly arrived at Vicky she stops suddenly*]. Oh, no. I've made a mistake. The dressing-table, of course, would be there. [*Points towards Mrs Jardine*]. I was thinking of the one at home. [*She pauses a moment undecided, then says*] I must come in again. [*She then runs to the door, opens it, goes just outside, closes it, opens it again, and puts her head just inside to say*] Now you are to suppose I didn't come in before.
[*Takes her head back and closes the door*].

MRS JARDINE   [*scarcely able to restrain her impatience*]   I shall scream in a minute.

MRS GORRINGE   I crossed over to the dressing-table—which, of course, is here now. [*Points to a spot near Mrs Jardine, walks towards it, and stands still*]. I opened my jewel-case. I don't know what made me do that then. I suppose I must have had a presentiment. Oh, no. It was to get these rings. [*Bends up her hand to show her rings*]. I thought it looked different somehow, and what was it I said to myself? [*Frowns as she thinks for a moment*]. Oh, yes. I remember saying to myself, 'Well, that's funny!' Then all at once it came across me like a flash of lightning, and I clasped my hands and exclaimed [*clasps her hands dramatically*], 'Great Heavens, my diamond necklace has gone!' [*Drops her dramatic pose and tone*). Just like that.

Just like that: Mary would have missed nothing. Wyndham, with fewer chances, did not much enjoy his own part, but realizing what Mary could do he agreed to present the play. As a Captain Mowbray, staying (like Mrs Gorringe) at a country house where the necklace was stolen, he did little more than play polo off-stage (and save the match) and be in love with the daughter of the house. Wyndham was proud of the fact that in 1867 he had appeared as Kate Terry's lover, and that now, thirty-six years later, he was playing opposite her daughter, Mabel Terry-Lewis.

Davies had yet to write his small masterpiece. J. C. Trewin has wondered whether a play that, as *Mrs Gorringe's Necklace* does, ends in a suicide, can legitimately be termed a comedy without qualification. At the time no one objected—probably because Mrs Gorringe, seldom given to consecutive thought, was herself an entertainment. Davies, a gentle, amusing man—like Jones, of the sterner puritan stock—was a student of feminine psychology. Hugh Walpole, a loyal friend, was conscious of Davies's 'struggle between real life and the life of the theatre'. At the première (13 May 1903) Mary noticed that her own real life got through to friends in the house. They laughed at the mention of Mrs Gorringe's three children—it was known that she had three sons herself—and again when the detective asked if she wore diamonds and she replied, 'Oh, no, I wore turquoise'—another laugh, as Mary herself always wore turquoise on the stage. After the production of this tragi-comedy critics in accustomed form spoke of Davies as a 'promising dramatist'—a promise which he had hardly time to fulfil, for he died at forty-eight. Still, he would give Mary her best part in his best play, and she and Wyndham were fond of the man Walpole called 'a whimsical, laughing knight-errant'.

Sydney Grundy the dramatist, teasiest of men, went to Wyndham's twice. Each time Mary was out of the cast, and he sent her a detailed account of such items as cab-fares, loss of time, and moral and intellectual damage: 'A cheque at Miss Moore's convenience will oblige.' Eventually he did see her performance and wrote to thank her:

I began to think that the play was dead and the theatre done, or that I was too old to enjoy them; but I find that the play still exists, and that I can enjoy it as much as ever. You have a play—a real play—a properly made play—the work of a playwright, not an ex-journalist (though for all I know he may be one).

You were a joy. A real bit of character. I kept saying to myself, 'But this is very familiar—I know this woman—she comes to our house.' That,

I suppose, is the best test. It is not any particular woman, but a type—an essence. . . . Mr Davies is a lucky man to get his work so well cast.

He was. *Mrs Gorringe* succeeded, and in September they transferred it over the way to the New while Charles Frohman, at Wyndham's, put on Barrie's 'uncomfortable' comedy, *Little Mary*, with John Hare, Gerald du Maurier and (chubbily as a schoolboy) A. E. Matthews. It was Barrie at his least tolerably whimsical, a kind of homespun *Doctor's Dilemma*, in which Nina Boucicault—later the first Peter Pan—cured a number of aristocrats of their ills, real or imaginary. Asked how it was done, she replied, 'By little Mary.' And who was 'Little Mary'? The stomach, of course, a phrase here coined by Barrie. The cure, 'Home Rule for the English,' was to get patients to eat less. At the first night people wondered whether the knowledge of Little Mary's identity would affect the run. It did not. But in the end the play would slip irretrievably into the darkness.

# IV

This had been a prosperous year for Charles and Mary. After tiresome delays they had opened their third theatre and they had also resolved a long-standing financial worry going back as far as 1899 when Joseph Pyke had approached them with a proposal. During the 1870s three little houses in New Bond Street—the premises of a wine merchant, a breeches-maker, and a carver and gilder—were rebuilt, and the Grosvenor Gallery (of Gilbert's 'greenery-yallery' line from *Patience*) came into being. Now, Pyke said, the building was for sale; he felt sure that an immediate offer of £100,000 would be accepted on a deposit of only £20,000. Would they come in with him? If they would produce half the deposit he would pay the other half and (he thought) borrow the rest from Coutts. They agreed, and paid their share.

Unhappily, because of the Boer War the banks—Coutts included—had to call in loans. Despairing, Charles and Mary foresaw that they would have to sell Wyndham's Theatre, which, in any event, was mortgaged to Pyke for £40,000, and to Mary's bank for £10,000. As it happened, when the war news improved Coutts did not call in the money, but it took four years to sell the Grosvenor Gallery, and the profit was far lower than Pyke had predicted—about £2,000 each, 'less all the worry and strain for which no money can compensate'. In 1903 Wyndham wrote formally to Mary to the effect that from the Grosvenor sale he would discharge his share of the £10,000 she had originally borrowed from her bank when the theatre was contemplated. (The Grosvenor Gallery site now contains the Aeolian Hall.) By this time the partners would have felt proud of their visible achievements, the 'bricks and mortar'. Their first home, the Criterion, recently renovated, was now leased by Frank Curzon; moreover, in Wyndham's and the New they had a pair of dignified turn-of-the-century theatres which they had watched from the foundations. Some ideas failed, as we have seen: the LCC had banned a winter garden on the flat roof of Wyndham's overlooking Charing Cross Road. Nevertheless, the company did rehearse there, weather permitting. Charles also had an idea which pleased Mary's economical mind: the engagement of an expert permanent staff to change the sets at both theatres:

> Of course these changes would have to be timed, but we did not foresee any difficulties in that. The men engaged being not only experts, but all working together by the year, would probably accomplish their work very quickly.

A good notion; but it did not come off.

By now, after many years in management, they had stockpiled a mountain of scenery, kept in their Jermyn Street store. In order that when needed they might put on a set from stock, Mary conceived the plan of photographing all their sets and binding up albums for reference. If an expensive production needed four changes she would undertake to turn up an old drawing-room in the store; and it pleased her very much when the one scene that had cost them nothing got excellent notices. They must have argued about these things, especially after Wyndham, 'in a panic', had rushed off to Maples and spent £400 in two hours on furniture and ornaments for another set in an elaborate production. With strange prescience, Mary looked to a time when, 'though an interval may be arranged, there will be no need to drop the curtain for scene-changes'. She had never believed in spending large sums on scenery, especially interiors:

> Given the shape of room required and the walls decorated in unison, the real effect can be made as in a house, by the furnishings. All then necessary is the tasteful arrangement of each article, some flowers, and those numerous etceteras that make a room look as though it belonged to a house.

Mary rebelled also against the money they wasted on buying plays she knew they would never do; this although there were times when she had to admit that Charles's extravagance paid off. An unexpected failure would be followed by a desperate search for what to do next. When they did fail—and this was rare—she must have wondered why, out of a vast pile of unacted scripts, they had chosen so unwisely. Wyndham was still drawn to the French theatre. Memories of those long-running Criterion farces stirred him to pay inflated sums—to Mary's frank horror— whenever he went to a Paris theatre and was betrayed by the reception.

Perhaps she felt he paid too much for their next production, *My Lady of Rosedale*, which was Comyns Carr's adaptation of a piece named *La Châtelaine*. Out of sympathy with the play, though recognizing it had a good part for Wyndham, she believed that a straight translation would have been better. Max Beerbohm said that Comyns Carr had eliminated all traces of Frenchness; unless he had known its origin he would have vowed that Carr had written it himself, incorporating the after-dinner speeches for which he was renowned, and which Wyndham's personality could transfigure for the stage. Again Wyndham (at sixty-seven) had to make love to Mabel Terry-Lewis (thirty-two, and about to retire on her marriage: she returned after her husband died). Released from a small part in *My Lady of Rosedale*, Mary organized a popular tour of *Mrs Gorringe* in 'one-night stands', so comfortably devised—a comment on the efficiency of English railways during 1904—that without undue anxiety they could play a matinée in Worcester and an evening performance in Manchester.

*My Lady of Rosedale* pined quickly. Just as quickly they needed a new play, and Mary now suggested a purchase of her own: *The Bride and Bridegroom* by Arthur Law, whose Criterion comedy, *A Country Mouse*, was a winner. Alas, on the New Theatre first night (5 May 1904) an anonymous letter warned Wyndham that there would be a disturbance, apparently because he had not engaged a certain actress for a character quite unsuitable: Mary was tart about this. At the end the gallery protested, according to plan; when he could be heard Wyndham said he had expected the demonstration. Someone shouted 'Liar!' which upset Mary terribly. Pandemonium ensued; two gallery factions—for and against—attacked each other; the stalls championed Wyndham; and for twenty minutes the storm raged foolishly, the only trouble of this kind that Charles and Mary met during twenty-seven years. Charles was reluctant for the facts to be made public. With old-fashioned courtesy he explained, 'It is not possible as they concern a woman.'

The night had a sequel which resembled a scene from *Mrs Dane's Defence* (Wyndham as cross-examiner). It seemed that one of the leaders of the gallery gang was a girl who worked in Herbert Beerbohm Tree's office. Tree, readily romantic, could not believe the story—she was such a nice girl—but he promised to question her and returned with a just-as-I-thought expression; the girl had denied being in the theatre that night. All the same . . . As Tree was incredulous, Wyndham urged him to bring along the girl in the presence of a solicitor. Seeing them arrive, Mary guessed that as the girl was pretty (there Tree was right) they could expect little from the interview. At first she swore that she had been nowhere near the theatre. When Wyndham asked her where she had been, she answered, 'Shopping.'

WYNDHAM  [*à la Sir Daniel Carteret*]  But there are no shops open at that

A dinner at the Argonaut Club, given for Sir Charles on his knighthood (1902):
seated, *l.* to *r*: Mrs Henry Arthur Jones, Mrs Tree, Mary Moore, Winifred Emery,
Lady Wyndham. Standing, *l.* to *r*: Cyril Maude, Henry Arthur Jones, R. Birnbaum,
Charles Wyndham, Lewis Waller, T. P. O'Connor, Max O'Rell

On the roof of Wyndham's (1916), J. M. Barrie reads from *The Admirable Crichton*,
in rehearsal for an all-star charity performance. Bernard Shaw (not in the cast) stands
slightly aloof (*l.*); Ellen Terry, in vast hat, is seated (centre), with Mary Moore standing
behind her. Johnston Forbes-Robertson is sitting centre *r.*, and Gerald du Maurier
extreme *r.*

When Wyndham put on *She Stoops to Conquer* with himself as Young Marlow and Mary Moore as Kate Hardcastle at the Criterion in 1890, he was accused of turning Goldsmith's comedy into a farce.

A photograph taken soon after the aged Sir Charles was married to Mary Moore in 1916. Their acting partnership had begun with *Wild Oats* at the Criterion in 1886

Dramatist, clubman, wit,
James Albery wears Hamlet's suit of
inky black so that the cartoonist,
Alfred Bryan, could quote from
*Hamlet*: 'How pregnant sometimes his
replies are.'

Bronson Albery (1881–1971),
manager, known affectionately as
'Bronnie', put on many plays that
today only the subsidized companies
would dare

Sir Donald Albery (*right*) and Ian B. Albery (*left*), Bronnie's son and grandson, both in
management. Sir Donald retired in 1977; Ian Albery now controls the family theatres

hour. Please be careful what you say, as my solicitor Mr Peckham is taking note of everything.

[*Girl sinks to her knees beside Tree*]

GIRL [*to Tree*] Please forgive me. It is true; I was there that night. I did take part in the row . . .

Apparently she had been with the gang on other noisy occasions. To Tree's chagrin, she admitted that she was a great admirer of a certain 'well-known romantic actor' (presumably Lewis Waller). The drama appealed to Tree and Wyndham, and for Mary's benefit they recreated it with considerable relish. But the play that was in the middle of all this failed, and it was some years before Arthur Law attempted anything else.

# CHAPTER SIXTEEN

# Red Roses for Captain Drew
# 1904–1908

Wyndham, almost too healthy—much too healthy to worry about his own understudies—was never 'off'. Then (as it had to) it happened. While he was in New York at the beginning of an American tour he was knocked down in the street. In great pain, and with his shoulder dislocated, there could be no question of his going on that night at the Lyceum, where they had played *David Garrick* and *Mrs Gorringe's Necklace* for three weeks each, and were in the middle of a similar run of *Rebellious Susan*. The audience had settled; the cast was dressed and ready. But with no good understudy to play Sir Richard Kato, Mary decided to do *Mrs Gorringe* instead, in the same scenery and costumes. The manager went out to tell the waiting audience what had happened, to announce a change of programme, and to promise money back to anyone who wished to leave. (No rush for this.) The understudy began Captain Mowbray shakily, and in the second act gave up altogether and read the part. Furious, Mary called a rehearsal for next morning, when the actor informed her coolly that it was unnecessary to do the last act as he could read it. More and more furious, she insisted that they continued to rehearse until he knew the part from beginning to end, even until it was time for curtain-rise. Though the man went on arguing, he submitted. That evening he did know the part—luckily, for Mary, in her most obstinate mood, would have made him rehearse all night. After a while Wyndham, though still in pain, returned to the cast, and they moved on to Boston, where Mary caught a heavy bronchial cold which kept her from the stage during the first week; it relieved her to hear that because Wyndham was warned he must not act until his shoulder had healed completely the rest of the luckless tour would be cancelled. They sailed instead for Italy, and Wyndham had some helpful treatment from a doctor in Rome.

During their absence Cyril Maude—currently homeless because of Haymarket Theatre repairs—had played at the New in *Beauty and the Barge* by the improbable union of W. W. Jacobs and Louis N. Parker. That Christmas, down St Martin's Lane at the Duke of York's, *Peter Pan* had its première. There has been a legend of an unscripted stage wait during the setting-up of the Home under the Ground; but, though Gerald du Maurier, the Hook, certainly 'improvised' on some of the day's leading actors, this front-cloth scene was apparently in the script submitted to the Lord Chamberlain. Though a long-memoried playgoer said in 1945 that Wyndham was one of the subjects, evidence is now inconclusive, and by the first revival the scene had vanished. Theatrically, the year was historic in St Martin's Lane. At the New the incorrigible Fred Terry and Julia Neilson put on *The Scarlet Pimpernel*, apotheosis of all romantic absurdity. No one knew then about Sir Percy and his Marguérite, and the relentless Citizen Chauvelin; it took some time for word-of-mouth to get about, but 'Golden Fred' nursed the 'demmed elusive' Pimpernel into a recurring costume-classic; and it proved in the end to be even more lucrative than *David Garrick*.

Wyndham himself, who had hoped (with Frohman) to stage at the New C. M. S. McLellan's *Leah Kleschna*, could not get back in time. Lena Ashwell in a vigorous melodrama was a thief's daughter who herself attempts a robbery, and is caught: more emotional exercise for an actress who called herself 'the great criminal' of the stage: 'I have broken all the commandments. I have committed all the crimes. One day I shall write a book—it will be a very small book—and it will be called *Crimes I Have Not Committed.*'

Wyndham and Mary had had a longer absence than usual when at length they got back to the New and *Captain Drew on Leave*: Hubert Henry Davies again, and one of his better plays, if inferior to *The Mollusc*. As Drew RN, 'a breezy, high-spirited man of about 45', Wyndham had to look 'weatherbeaten in appearance and young in manner'—not difficult for him in 1905. When Drew hears that his hostess is 'not the kind of woman even a sailor would think of making love to', he replies cheerfully and chivalrously, 'I know no such kind. I once met a missionary on her way to Japan . . .' and proceeds to flirt with the dull and neglected wife; a scene together when he winds her wool could hardly fail with Wyndham's devotees. A month later (stage time) the pair have a tender farewell which, as Hugh Walpole—who admired *Captain Drew*—had to confess, endangers the play gravely. It is nothing more than the 'old theatrical scene of the woman going to the man's room at night, there to be discovered'. Walpole did note

> a remarkable characteristic of these Davies plays . . . they, more perhaps than any other plays in the English language, do what good novels do—make us speculate on the lives of the characters in them before and after the action we have been shown.

169

(St John Hankin, able to create 'people who lived beyond the action', was a less sympathetic dramatist.) At the end of *Captain Drew*, the insensitive husband, wishing to atone, proposes a visit to their boys at school. Nothing would have been likelier to please his wife: a gentle end, not a full stop, but a comma. The audience, Davies knew, could finish the sentence.

Marion Terry, cast judiciously as the wife, excelled in these 'pure' characters. When she played Mrs Erlynne in *Lady Windermere's Fan* she upset her public, who liked to think of her as respectable on and off the stage. Sir John Gielgud has wondered whether, in admiring Marion's acting more than Ellen's, his parents could have been 'slightly disapproving of the Bohemian life that Ellen lived'. As the house-guest in *Captain Drew*, an altogether more worldly woman, Mary had to say such things as 'One must treat the servants as equals nowadays—to keep them in their place.' After more than seventy years, Ben Travers remembers his delight in this exchange between Wyndham and Mary:

MISS MILLS    I whisper all my secrets to the roses.

CAPTAIN DREW    Is that why they look so red in the face?

When he saw *Captain Drew* he was nineteen and working in the City. Spending all his afternoons in theatre pits (2s.6d.), he was attracted immediately to 'that enchanting comedy actress, Mary Moore, rivalled only among her contemporaries by Ellis Jeffreys, with Marie Tempest a poor third.

At Christmas 1905 Charles and Mary moved the play—one they always hoped to revive—to Wyndham's, where it ran until March. Fred Terry and Julia Neilson were at the New meantime in the second of their annual seasons (costume drama with an infallible sense of style) which would continue until 1913.

# II

By now the Barker-Vedrenne theatre of ideas (which some have called the Thousand Performances) had been set up at the Court in Sloane Square. Wyndham and Mary, deep in the theatre theatrical, went to see *You Never Can Tell* which Shaw had once begged them to do at the Criterion. Mary had hankered after Dolly, the twin, but Wyndham, who did not see himself as the five-shilling dentist, told Shaw that his plays were twenty years ahead of their time. Now, in reply to a letter of congratulation, Shaw replied Shavianly that he was flying from these shores and what he called his success—actually the most troublesome thing that had ever happened to him. Indeed, he had promised his wife to catch Thursday's train for the South of Ireland; before that he had to get through three weeks' business; he would not call because Wyndham would probably get round him and make him promise a play which would 'bind him to write something at least possibly popular'. He had sworn never to write another line that any manager in his senses would look at. 'Better let me break down the palings for a younger man ... I can't begin as a popular playwright at fifty'.

Shaw wondered whether Wyndham had thought of Hilaire Belloc as a possible playwright, as clever as Wilde and with more knowledge of the world and modernity of culture. (It was unlikely that Charles and Mary had, for Belloc, in spite of his protean qualities, was by no means a recognized theatre-man.) The letter ended with the cheerful hope that when they had had enough of popularity and big receipts, Wyndham and Mary Moore might play half a dozen matinées at the Court for 80 per cent of the gross—or, if they preferred a certainty, £5 a week. *'Bon voyage!'* Later that year, when *Major Barbara*, with Annie Russell and Granville Barker, was running at the Court, Mary received a determined Shavian postcard:

> I am afraid I shall have to withdraw it unless you both come and play for me, for nothing less can save that terrible last act. It can be done, but we have not got anywhere near it yet. Kind of you not to mention it; but bless you, I know.

> G.B.S.

# III

During 1905 Wyndham had to serve as both an arbitrator and an expert witness. The first role was in a problem of rival authorship, almost another Vezin-Albery dispute. The play was Henry Arthur Jones's *The Silver King*, a redoubtable melodrama once praised by Matthew Arnold, of all unexpected connoisseurs. Before its flamboyant birth in 1882 with the imperial and imperious Wilson Barrett, a hack dramatist, Henry Herman, had helped Jones with the framework. Apart from a few phrases and the end of the second act, Herman, so Jones insisted in public more than once, 'never wrote a line of it'. For all this, when *The Silver King* ('O God, put back Thy universe and give me yesterday!') had stormed into triumph Herman claimed to be its part-author—a claim Jones refuted in *The Era* during 1885, while acknowledging that Barrett had pulled together 'a very curious and slipshod bit of stagecraft'. Herman died in 1895. Years afterwards Barrett, who had toured the play extensively, chose to describe himself as part-author. This claim Jones countered in a stinging and ironical reply: 'a masterpiece of cruelty', Max Beerbohm wrote to him; 'how the worthy gentleman survived it I cannot imagine.' Deciding that enough was enough, Jones asked three wise men,

171

Squire Bancroft, Wyndham and Ben Greet, to arbitrate; and in January 1905 they found that Wilson Barrett had no title whatsoever to the authorship. Wyndham would soon have a closer tie with Henry Arthur, whose daughter Gertrude (known as Jill) married Mary's eldest son, Irving Albery, in 1906.

As expert witness, Wyndham gave evidence during a hearing when Mr Justice Ridley had to decide when an actress was not an actress. The question was debated in an action against Messrs Gatti for wrongful dismissal. The plaintiff, engaged as a 'Gibson Girl' in *The Catch of the Season* (which ran for two years at the Vaudeville), had two lines to speak. Did this make her an actress, and therefore entitled to employment for the run of the piece, or was she a show-girl subject to a fortnight's notice? Edward Marshall Hall, K.C., appeared for her. Seymour Hicks, the play's part-author, said, 'If one line makes an actress, I don't know where we shall end', at which Marshall Hall raised the customary 'laughter in court' by replying, 'I only want to know where you begin.' Here Mr Justice Ridley complained that he would not have his court turned into a theatre. On the third day Wyndham supported the plaintiff: a chorus girl, he contended, became an actress even though she had only a single line. The jury found for her, with damages of £200.

Henry Irving, one of Wyndham's oldest actor-friends, died in that autumn of 1905, and the coffin was borne through Westminster Abbey under a pall of laurel leaves. Ellen Terry, for so long his leading lady, was very much alive. On 12 June 1906 theatrical London celebrated her jubilee with a shilling fund (which raised £3,000) and a commemorative performance at Drury Lane which raised twice as much. The scenes were extraordinary; crowds waited all night and next morning to greet every leading player, and many secondary players of the West End stage. Twenty-two Terrys were in a programme of over five hours, and the day's heroine herself played Beatrice; Wyndham, at sixty-nine, was Charles in a scene from *The School for Scandal*; Mary, Queen Victoria in a tableau. Duse, Réjane, the Coquelins, and Caruso came to London for the occasion, which ended in an affectionate tumult when Lady Bancroft introduced Ellen Terry, 'born in a merry hour', to an audience that needed no introduction.

Hubert Henry Davies, by now almost a house dramatist (as Jones had been), was writing a new play which eventually grew into *The Mollusc*. His first draft delighted Mary with an enviable part, but a pernickety Charles wanted changes; the play should be in three acts instead of four, and the husband's love for the governess must go. Further, he wanted only four characters, an innovation in the Edwardian theatre, though casts had been shrinking and *Captain Drew* and *The Tyranny of Tears* had six characters each. That was partly because neither of them had country-house settings; their people, belonging to the middle class, dispensed with footmen and ladies' maids. Quartets would become commonplace—Lonsdale's *On Approval* is as neat as any—and the telephone has made them easier to manage. But in 1906 they caused something of a stir. Thus H. M. Walbrook:

> When Mr Haddon Chambers kept us interested in *The Tyranny of Tears* with only six characters he was very properly credited with no mean achievement. Mr Davies has gone two better, and written a play that has not a dull moment, with only four.

While Charles and Mary were on holiday in Egypt they received a revised script. Mary waited while he read it—romantically, they were sitting on the balcony of the Savoy Hotel at Assouan—and to her disappointment he passed it over to her, saying, 'No good.' Unconvinced, she went through the script and saw where things had gone wrong. Charles had told Davies to take out the drama—in other words, the husband's love for the governess. But the play needed it; the wife's discovery of her husband comforting the girl was effectively the second-act curtain. Mary argued for this, and as they had brought the first script with them, they were able to go over the missing scenes and to replan the construction. On their way home Davies met them at Naples and read them a final version which satisfied both.

For Mary the return journey proved to be more dramatic than anything in the play. The train from Naples arrived in Rome at noon; Wyndham, Mary and Davies were in the restaurant car. They had been told that the Berlin portion of the train would leave before the Paris portion, which would wait in Rome for about half an hour, giving Wyndham plenty of time to send a telegram. Mary felt that a walk would do them all good: the day was bright and cold, and she returned to the train to fetch her coat while the two men walked on. The moment she got into the restaurant car it moved; being shunted, she thought. Then the train began to gather speed, and when she asked what was happening she heard to her horror that she was now in the Berlin portion. Her coat, her dressing-case, everything else she needed were in the Paris portion, which was still in Rome. She asked whether the train would stop at the next station if she pulled the communication cord. The conductor said it would, but that it would cost her fifty francs. Though she had no money with her, she pulled the cord, but the train swept on past the first station, and when she asked why they had decided not to stop the conductor told her heartlessly that she was now on her way to Berlin. Nothing else. Sympathetic fellow-passengers offered to lend her money; probably because he had treated her unfairly, even the conductor offered her a hundred francs, and she accepted it. Four hours later the train stopped just long enough for her to get out at a small station: it was bitterly cold, she had no coat, and when she tried to explain her plight to the stationmaster in sign-language (for she had no Italian either), she could merely point at his own coat, which

173

he kindly lent her. She also managed to get a wire sent to the stationmaster in Rome, asking him to tell 'the two Englishmen' that she would return by a train due in at ten that evening. Her wait seemed endless as she walked up and down the platform and used some of the borrowed hundred francs to buy a glass of cognac. She asked the stationmaster to give her a label addressed to himself so that she could send back the coat he had urged her to keep for the journey.

At length the train came; anxious to save some money for emergencies, she travelled third-class. When she got to Rome Wyndham and Davies were not there: the stationmaster said he had done nothing about her telegram because no one had inquired for her. With all the sleepers taken on the night train to Paris, he advised her to go to the Continental Hotel and travel on the next night. Now she had to explain her position to the hotel manager. A boy on a bicycle, whom he sent to buy a nightdress, came back saying he could find nothing because it was too late. Mary, suffering at the time from rheumatism, then asked the hotel clerks to lend her a warm nightdress, and they were most affronted that anyone should believe they wore such a thing. However, a woman produced one, and a brush and comb.

Next morning Mary discovered that all the sleepers from Rome to Paris were taken. Resourcefully, she sent a telegram to Turin, booking one from there. The hotel manager trusted her to pay the bill, and he lent her some more money and his own overcoat, better and newer than the kind stationmaster's (which he duly promised to return). That night, at eleven o'clock, she arrived at Turin, thinking her troubles were over. But no! When she claimed the sleeper she had booked by telegram the conductor—saying he was busy—asked her to wait until the train left the station. While she waited she saw on the platform a man speaking to the conductor and handing him a tip (or, more likely, bribe). The train moved out. Mary again asked for her sleeper; the conductor now told her blandly that they were all gone, but that he would make up a bed for her in a first-class carriage. Unable to get him to understand, she asked a passenger to explain in Italian that she refused to move from the sleeping-car corridor until she got the berth she had booked. Firmly, she declared that she would not move; if she had to stay there all night, and caught a severe cold, her family would bring an action against the railway company. The conductor became temperamental, almost weeping; she told him that his best way out was to send for the man who had her berth. The noise of the argument had disturbed other sleeping-berth passengers, and one of them, an elderly Scot, offered her room in the four-berth cabin which his daughter and her friend were sharing with him. Gladly, she accepted. She had sent several telegrams to Wyndham in Paris, keeping him up to date with her misadventures, and asking him to meet the train. Instead she found her son Irving on the platform; happening to be in Paris, he had met Wyndham and heard the story. But

174

why, Mary asked, were the pair not in Rome when she arrived? They had been assured, apparently, that their train would stop at the little station where she had alighted. In keeping with the mad logic of the whole business, it did not stop (probably had no intention of doing so), and they were whirled on inexorably towards Paris.

Exhausted and unwell, Mary had another unpleasant shock at the hotel. Her luggage had certainly come; when she opened the trunk everything was in place, but all her jewellery had gone. Only the empty boxes remained. The jewellery was never traced.

# IV

In April 1907 Charles and Mary returned to the Criterion for a revival of *The Liars*. Houses were big; profits small; since they had first performed Henry Arthur's comedy, players' salaries had doubled. For some time these had been rising. Over twenty years before, at the Bancrofts' retirement in 1885, a journalist asked them, 'You are, I think, responsible in great measure for the present high salaries paid to actors?' Squire Bancroft agreed that salaries had risen to an extraordinary extent:

> During our career we have paid the same actor, for playing the same part in the same piece, eighteen and sixty pounds a week, with an interval of some ten years only. There are examples, of course, in which an actor improves his position so rapidly as to command a great increase of salary in the same theatre: for instance, we ended by giving a member of our company ten times the salary at which we originally engaged him; and another, who first received nine pounds a week, was last paid fifty. When that great artist, Mrs Stirling, played in *Caste* at the Haymarket Theatre she received seven times the salary of the original representative of the Marquise de St Maur.

The highest salary Bancroft ever paid was a hundred pounds a week with 'other charges and contingencies', for a special engagement. ('No, it was not to Mrs Langtry!'). When they induced Ellen Terry to return to the stage in 1875 she was content with twenty pounds a week, at that period a high figure.

Wyndham and Mary considered that casting for revivals should be even better, if possible, than for the original. *The Liars* had an expensive company of sixteen; they were relieved that their next play had only four. Rehearsing *The Mollusc* during the run of *The Liars*, they opened Davies's play at the Criterion on 7 October 1907, with Mary in the most rewarding part she would have ('It fitted her like one of her own pretty dresses,' said H. M. Walbrook). She played an incurably lazy wife who hardly moves from chair or sofa. Arranging a bowl of flowers is beyond her. When her patient husband shows signs of being in love with the governess she agrees at first that the girl must go. 'I'm not the woman to put up with that sort of thing,' she tells her brother Tom, but then reacts as one would have expected:

MRS BAXTER   It's most inconvenient; everything will be upside down.

TOM   . . . Learn to do without Miss Roberts, and make him forget her.

MRS BAXTER   Very well. She shall leave this house directly—directly I recover.

TOM   Recover from what?

MRS BAXTER   From the shock. Think of the shock I've had; there's sure to be a reaction. I shouldn't wonder if I had a complete collapse. It's beginning already. [*She totters and goes towards the staircase*]. Oh dear, I feel so ill. Please call Miss Roberts.

TOM   You were going to learn to do without Miss Roberts.

MRS BAXTER   That was before I was ill. I can't be ill without Miss Roberts.
[*Puts her hand to her side, turns up her eyes and groans as she totters out*]

TOM   Oh! Oh! You Mollusc!

As Tom, sturdily home on leave from America and resolved to cure the Mollusc of her 'molluscry,' Wyndham (said Walbrook) had a

scene of sheer farce in the first act, which he played with all the gaiety of his Bob Sackett days; in the second and third there is comedy of the richest in his attempts to rouse his sister, and their abject failure; and just towards the end there is a love scene with the governess, a little spun-out, perhaps, in its opening, but . . . beautifully acted. All though the play, in fact, we had this masterly comedian at his best, and London theatregoers know what entertainment that means.

They did know; and the first-night audience, like its successors, went on cheering.

Mary had understood for some time that the young dramatist William Somerset Maugham wanted her to act in his *Mrs Dot*, and she had promised to do so. When *The Mollusc* looked like running he asked if she would return a script that he now had another chance to place. She agreed reluctantly, and elsewhere the metallic Marie Tempest went into *Mrs Dot* with ringing success. Maugham wrote to Mary after seeing her in *The Mollusc*:

I am writing these two or three lines to tell you how extraordinarily good I thought your performance was. I am aware that everyone has told you that, but I want to tell you too. The play would be nothing without you. I have just got back from Paris, where I saw everything that was to be seen; I can assure you there is no actress on the French stage who could equal your impersonation of Mrs. Baxter. It is quite wonderful. I am very sorry that the course of things has made it impossible for me to look forward to seeing you in my little play.

During the run a card reached Mary's dressing-room: 'We are your fellow-passengers on the express from Rome to Paris, and have just recognised you! May we come round?' Obviously they could, and did; it had startled them to find that Mary Moore had taken refuge in their sleeping cabin. These were members of the Scottish Weir family, and a few years later she would meet them again in the South of France.

# V

Regularly, Charles and Mary took a holiday abroad; there was no question of working through the summer months, and as a rule the annual pattern looked like this. On their return from Europe in September a short tour would precede a new London production (in October or November) which might run until April or May; the next play, if successful, could last until July. Runs in pre-coach-party days were shorter; a hundred performances excellent. Wyndham used his vacations as an excuse for hospitality. A natural host, at Homburg he once gave a picnic in the woods (a kind of continental Yacht Room); a long table set among the trees, a band, races afterwards. He invited friends to join his family, and sometimes he prepared a production while away. Dramatists had no objection to coming out to him. He asked Henry Arthur Jones to discuss *The Case of Rebellious Susan* at St Moritz; earlier, when Albery was with him in Switzerland, they had mapped out adaptations together. Travel, an inherited passion, he adored for its own sake. Once, when a boy abroad, he and his father had visited Zurich: an eight hours' ride in a bumpy coach. As soon as they had dined they went down to look at the lake. They saw it. 'And now', said his father, 'we may as well go on. If we stayed a week you wouldn't see any more.' And immediately they started on an arduous night journey.

At first Mary used to join Wyndham, his wife and son and daughter. St Moritz was their favourite; sometimes she would have one of her own sons with her. In later years, when she and Charles were alone, they went to Marienbad, Kissingen, Algeciras, Nice, Monte Carlo, Cimiez, twice to Egypt, and several times to Italy. As she grew older she would take a cure, Charles usually accompanying her. Socially, their *affaire* had been accepted, and in the theatre, where so many actor-managers had actress-wives, it almost seemed that they were married. It was quite natural that Charles should have a permanent leading lady who was also his business partner. People might gossip, but their partnership was never a public scandal. Something about Miss Moore was so eminently discreet: she was such a good hostess; she dressed so beautifully on and off the stage. Not a great actress, she could always make her audience laugh, and never, never with the vulgarity of, say, 'Ma' Wood.

How they arranged matters domestically we can merely hazard. They never shared the same London address; when Mary left Melina Place she lived at 3 Ulster Terrace, Regent's Park; in 1887 Mr and Mrs Wyndham moved into the Manor House, St John's Wood Park, which they left after ten years. When Wyndham went to live at the Hyde Park Hotel his wife, always a dim figure, receded into deeper shadow. Retiring though she was, she did appear in public at a dinner the Argonaut Club gave to her husband on his knighthood. A photograph shows her sitting at one end of the table, with Mrs Henry Arthur Jones at the other end. Between them: Mrs Tree, Mary and Winifred Emery (Mrs Cyril Maude). Behind the table: Cyril Maude, Henry Arthur Jones, R. Birnbaum, Wyndham, Lewis Waller, T. P. O'Connor, and the writer Max O'Rell. Gossips might observe—and doubtless did—that Charles stood immediately behind Mary. When he finally broke with his wife in the late Nineties, he took a suite overlooking the Park, in what was known then as Hyde Park Court, and (thriftily) furnished it from the theatre store. At first a temporary arrangement, he liked it so much that he stayed on even when the Court became the Hyde Park Hotel. Altogether he remained there for seventeen years.

After Mary's health had given way and she believed she would have to retire from the stage, she rented a house in Sunningdale and a small London service flat. Whatever their private arrangements, they never appeared to be living together; but it is plain that alone neither could have done so much for their theatres. Before Mary's arrival Wyndham's place as a talented comedian was already assured; as business partners they turned the Criterion into one of the smartest houses in London, gradually abandoning featherweight frivolity for plays of more substance. Later, without Mary, Charles would not have been able to clear the site on which Wyndham's and the Albery now stand, let alone find the means to build.

They often disagreed—chiefly, we can be certain, about money, which always obsessed her. She must have felt he was over-generous, particularly in response to begging letters. Once an importunate woman, needing a loan to pay dressmaking debts, said that her husband would be very angry if he knew she owed more than £3,000. The amount troubled Charles, so he showed Mary the letter. Long afterwards she admitted her want of sympathy: no woman deserved help who could run up so large a debt without her husband's knowledge, and no self-respecting woman would have approached a stranger. Wyndham, as ever, was sympathetic (though probably all she got was a friendly letter). Mary for her part never lent money 'because it loses me a friend'. She preferred to say right out, 'I will *give* you five pounds.' There were times, following a difference with Wyndham, when she threatened to resign; invariably he coaxed her to change her mind. ('Perhaps I knew in my heart from the first that I should eventually give way.') Yet remembering what she did, it is wrong to regard her as the weaker. To her complaint that he had no one to tell him his faults, he rejoined that, while she was alive, she need not worry about it. He must have appreciated profoundly how much he owed to her. In October 1907 she wrote to Sir Seymour King, the solicitor who had acted for her during the Wyndham's Theatre negotiation. It is a revealing letter, probably written because she looked intuitively to a time 'when you and I and Sir Charles may alas be no longer here'. Ten years earlier Sir Seymour had recorded for her the terms of Charles's proposed agreement. After stating how much each of them was to find, with details of the mortgage and of her percentage should the theatre be sold or let, Sir Seymour added:

> You will see that this practically amounts to making you a present of £10,000, and in addition to this you are to have one-fourth of the profits.

Now, after a decade, Mary returned the letter and wrote to him:

> You did me the greatest kindness. . . . I would like you to know that I never took advantage of what I think was intended by Sir Charles at the interview you had with him. On the contrary, in addition to finding the £10,000 on the terms referred to in your letter—which was . . . repaid to my bank, £5,000 by myself and £5,000 by Sir Charles—I have paid half of every other expense in connection with the building of Wyndham's Theatre. . . . Sir Charles and I entered into an agreement to that effect which, of course, made the one based on your letter null and void. I was only too pleased to find myself in a position to take up this independent attitude and everything is now in legal order. But, as Sir Charles's solicitor does not understand the sentence in your letter . . . it would be most kind of you if you would add to your former service to me and construe it for him.

Sir Seymour answered that the paragraph was obviously no part of any proposed arrangement, but 'a gloss or interpretation placed upon it at the time, so far as my memory serves, by Sir C. Wyndham . . . In any case, the paragraph in question was superfluous.'

# VI

Soon after *The Mollusc* had opened they appeared in a Windsor performance for the visit of the German Emperor and Empress. King Edward chose *Still Waters Run Deep* (not another *David Garrick* this time); Charles and Mary were the Mildmays—he had played the husband at the Royalty over forty years earlier—and Lewis Waller the seducer, Captain Hawksley (Wyndham's part in 1867). Believing Mrs Sternhold should not be the hard creature she usually was, he cast Marion Terry for the part. Marion had her own charm and warmth, though she suffered from the Terry weakness—an indifferent memory which, as Sir John Gielgud has said, the family had several ways of covering. At Windsor Marion had two lapses. First, when warning Mrs Mildmay against Hawksley's advances, she said, 'In a few moments he would have been in this room *on* your feet.' This was fairly mild. But after Mrs Mildmay's father had said, 'Why, it's poor John Mildmay!' she should have interrupted with 'Your daughter's husband and the master of this house!' Instead, Marion Terry substituted 'The father of your child and master of the house!' at which the oddest sound filled the Waterloo Chamber: 'I can only describe it as a checked laugh,' Mary said. She had no trouble herself: that night she added to her collection of 'Royal' jewels an enamelled brooch with 'E.R.' in diamonds on one side and a portrait of Edward on the other.

Still attractive and apparently youthful, she was now a grandmother, for Jessica Mary Albery, Irving's first child, had been born in 1908. Her health started to test her. She had to leave *The Mollusc*, and because the comedy (in spite of full houses) was unthinkable without her, Wyndham took it off while she crossed to Paris for medical advice; he spent the interval looking for plays in Vienna. By early June they were back and *The Mollusc* ran profitably for two further months. Mary's next appearance in a Davies play would be without Charles, and Charles's next play had no part in it for her. Having more than one theatre, they could separate when needed, but they did so rarely. Their public expected to see them together. Wyndham and Moore: their names chimed across the West End years.

# CHAPTER SEVENTEEN

# Half a Loaf for the Public
# 1908–1919

True, their public liked nothing unexpected. That was one reason why *Bellamy the Magnificent* failed at the New. Though his public might allow Charles to flirt—and outrageously, if required—he was not allowed to be, like Roy Horniman's Bellamy, a society roué. In the best scene of Horniman's play (adapted from his own novel), Lord Bellamy is at cards with his guests. One of these, who has lost heavily, accuses Bellamy (on the strength of an anonymous letter) of cheating.' Other guests are indignant, but Bellamy agrees to a search, in which a card is found up his sleeve. Instantly he realizes who put it there—his valet—and he realizes why: he has been making love to the valet's wife. With a glance in the man's direction, Bellamy murmurs, 'Very clever, Smith; very clever, Smith.' *Curtain*. A strong theatrical moment, and the piece had some wit, but Wyndham's admirers could not take the almost stock suicide that followed. (Ironically, Robert Loraine, the valet, would play years later the one important part that defeated Wyndham: Cyrano de Bergerac.) During the run Mrs Patrick Campbell took the New for a series of matinées of Hofmannsthal's *Electra*, and Yeats's *Deirdre*. Unaware that Wyndham and Mary saw a performance from a box, she would hear later that, 'for the first time, they credited me with some good sense'. Her notices were less than kind.

A week after the première of *Bellamy the Magnificent* (without Mary) Mary herself opened at the Criterion (without Charles) in *Lady Epping's Lawsuit*, a satirical farce by Hubert Henry Davies. Instead of four characters it had nineteen, and in the court scene there were optimistic stage directions for 'barristers, solicitors, clerks, pressmen, footmen, and the general public'. This Lady Epping has theatrical ambitions; for every possible reason nothing of hers has been acted, but she takes up a young dramatist who at least has had one play done. (Max Beerbohm, though, could not imagine any manifestation that could possibly win him fame: certainly no cause why a clever woman like Lady Epping could stand a moment's flirtation with him.) They are staying in the Epping house when the dramatist's wife, aware how things are going, warns him, 'You'll go filling your play with dukes and duchesses and you'll get so mixed up you won't know how to make them talk to the servants.' He answers. 'I'm observing all that now: I'll be servant-perfect by to-morrow.'

Little of the rest is comparably plain. A court scene skates off into fantasy. The judge has been a guest of Lady Epping, so we get such exchanges as this:

LADY EPPING   The fourteenth—let me see—oh yes! [*Brightly to judge*] That was the Sunday *you* spent with us!

JUDGE   [*smiling at Lady Epping*] And very much I enjoyed it.

LADY EPPING   I'm so glad. *Do* come and see us again.

A few minutes later she tears up a letter, an important piece of evidence. The whole court rises in excitement, shouting and gesticulating, counsel, judge and usher urging her to stop:

LADY EPPING   Oh look what I've done! [*She scatters the bits of paper*]

The act closes with the judge's advice to her: 'You have told us it is your habit to tear up your letters.'

LADY EPPING   Yes.

JUDGE   Extend it to your plays.

There were theories that Davies had based Lady Epping on one or another society personage with literary ambitions. Eric Lewis, as the judge, injected some extra humour by imitating Mr Justice Darling, before whom during the run Mary appeared in a genuine court. Messrs Shoolbred, of Tottenham Court Road, sought to recover from Wyndham and Mary the sum of £267 6s. 7d., balance of a contract for work at the Criterion in 1907. The defendants claimed that it had not been to their satisfaction and that certain colours did not match. Shoolbreds had contracted to supply a yellow drop-curtain and upholstery for the stalls; carpets; new arm-rests; curtains and pelmets for the boxes and proscenium, and—this was the trouble—blue satin trimmings on the curtains and round the 'family circle'. Mary particularly wanted 'soft artistic Natier blue'; and they had provided 'bright Cambridge blue', a mistake that angered her because (so she said) she had introduced Natier blue to England in a dress she wore during the first act of *The Mollusc*. All

Sean Kenny's set for *'Oliver'!* which opened at the New in June 1960. His aim was 'to give the feel of Dickensian London'. *Oliver!* has broken many records, and has been revived at its old home, now the Albery

LORD CHAMBERLAIN'S OFFICE

*I, the Lord Chamberlain of* **The Queen's** *Household for the time being, do by virtue of my Office and in pursuance of powers given to me by the Act of Parliament for regulating Theatres, 6 & 7 Victoria, Cap 68, Section 12. Allow the Performance of a new Stage Play, of which a copy has been submitted to me by you, being a* play *in 2 Acts entitled* "Man of La Mancha" *with the exception of all Words and Passages which are specified in the endorsement of this Licence and without any further variations whatsoever*

*Given under my hand this* 5ᵗ *day of* March *1968.*

Cobbold

*Lord Chamberlain.*

*To The Manager of the* Piccadilly Theatre London

T 38.

In the year that the censorship of plays came to an end the last licence issued for the Piccadilly Theatre was for *Man of La Mancha* 'given under my hand this 5th day of March 1968' by Lord Cobbold, Lord Chamberlain.

of the bill (£1,398) had been paid except the sum in dispute. The judge, probably thinking, 'Then you'll know what Miss Moore is fussing about', ordered the jury to the Criterion to see for themselves. From the witness-box Mary intervened: 'I hope you'll come too.' (This was rather like Lady Epping, but he replied that it was not in his province.) Having inspected the materials, the jury disagreed unhelpfully both about the colours and the validity of the complaint. Thereupon Mr Justice Darling said that he felt sorry for the plaintiffs because it was difficult to satisfy a lady (Mary Moore) who was so fastidious. But, they *had* failed to satisfy her and she was now entitled to judgment, with costs. *Lady Epping's Lawsuit* gained nothing from the extra publicity. Its run was short, but Mary could remember, at any rate, that the Princess of Wales (later Queen Mary, and an informed playgoer) had come one afternoon to a charity performance of *Mrs Gorringe's Necklace*, and in the evening, tirelessly, to *Lady Epping*.

After both *Lady Epping* (Criterion) and *Bellamy* (New) had failed, Charles admitted the mistake: the public expected Charles Wyndham and Mary Moore and left—as Mary put it prosaically—unsatisfied with only 'half a loaf'. But it was getting wretchedly hard to find plays that would suit the two of them. Charles, at seventy-two, wanted to play younger—far younger—men. He looked fifty at most. Mary, her figure still trim at forty-six, could not go on playing youthful heroines for ever. *Bellamy the Magnificent* would be Wyndham's final performance in a new play; thenceforward they had to rely on old successes.

## II

As usual, Fred Terry and Julia Neilson occupied the New for their winter costume-revels, and in January 1909, when appearing in *Henry of Navarre*, they took an inventory of the theatre's furnishings, a splendid document. The royal box had a crimson pile carpet, two pairs of Rose du Barri silk brocade curtains and valances, two footstools and a retiring-room furnished with a carved gilt suite upholstered in the same silk brocade, three marble console tables, and one fancy four-lamp electrolier. The adjoining lavatory had a crimson pile carpet. The theatre's dressing-rooms, less well equipped, were provided with enamelled 'chambers'. The offices, heated by open fires, had their apparatus of fenders, coal scuttles and pokers; and the gentlemen's cloakroom for the stalls boasted two mahogany rails and sixteen brass hooks (one broken).

Wyndham's, as elaborately furnished (we have no census of hooks) held an extraordinary première on the night of 27 January 1909. In period *An Englishman's Home*, ascribed to 'A Patriot'—and staged by Frank Curzon—was well over three hundred years away from *Henry of Navarre* next door; the gap in manner and matter was illimitable. Outside it was a foggy evening; within, pit and gallery were half-empty. During the first act people on the stage were complaining of fog, a small shared experience that brought stage and audience closer. One character, a Mr Brown (acted by Charles Rock), had joined the Territorials: others laughed at him for 'playing at soldiers'. But in the fog enemy troops had invaded Britain; the Englishman's home was occupied; Brown—seen to be bearing arms—was shot by an enemy firing-squad. The play had arrived in London at a time when stories of swelling German power filled the newspapers; the first audience, thin though it might be, cheered through the night. An anonymous author had quickened something many people hardly knew they possessed—a sense of patriotism.

Daily outside the theatre queues lengthened in Charing Cross Road and St Martin's Court; Lord Roberts ('Your country needs you') and R. B. Haldane, Secretary of State for War, declared the play to be the finest propaganda they had known. They did not exaggerate, for men rushed to join the Territorials. Far off in Natal the author, showered with congratulatory telegrams, was a serving soldier, Major Guy du Maurier. He had left the untitled script for his younger brother Gerald to read; Gerald (who was acting in *What Every Woman Knows*) supplied the title and took the play to Frank Curzon. It was, literally, fame in a night, but Guy wrote nothing else of mark. He was killed in the First World War.

That May, while *An Englishman's Home* was still thriving, as it did until the end of July (the customary date), Charles and Mary travelled to America in search of a play for themselves: they had heard of a Broadway success called *Nobody's Widow*, by Avery Hopwood (it would not reach London for eight years, and then under another management and another title, *Roxana*). While they were in mid-Atlantic Charles Frohman cabled to them, inviting them to act in *The Mollusc* for a month at the Empire, New York, an offer they refused because they had no one else with them. Back came Frohman's reply: hoping they would agree, he had already sent their 'company'—two players, Sam Sothern and Lilias Waldegrave—in another liner. It was a risk. *The Mollusc* had failed when Frohman did it originally in New York, but even summer heat could not affect a month's full houses. Frohman begged them to return during the winter, and they acquiesced.

Coquelin *aîné*, the great French actor, had died early that year. Charles and Mary, who loved him, had visited him whenever they were in Paris; Mary called him Uncle Coquelin and, reciprocally, he called her his niece. In November a company of English actors and writers went over to Paris to present to the Comédie Française a bronze medallion designed by Johnston Forbes-Robertson, who had studied art before going into the theatre. In the party were Wyndham himself, Squire Bancroft, John Hare, Arthur Bourchier, H. W. Massingham (who edited the *Daily Chronicle*), and Max Beerbohm on behalf of his brother Herbert. Max could be trusted to relax any pomp. 'I wish you were I', he wrote to Reggie Turner,

184

'for my mission is one that you would really revel in: to present myself, in ceremonious attire and just a hint of half-mourning . . . at the Théâtre Français. . . .'

## III

In January 1910 Wyndham and Mary were back in New York for another month with *The Mollusc*, to be followed by a tour. Suffering as before from acute rheumatism, Mary could not bear the bitter cold. Advised to give up her part and go to a warmer country, she left Mrs Baxter to her understudy and sailed for Egypt, lonely at first, though such a gregarious person could never be long without companions. In March she moved on to Naples. There Charles, who had completed the American tour, met her; and in London they started a series of Criterion revivals, beginning with *Rebellious Susan*, so affectionately received that they reopened with it after the summer holidays. Next *The Liars*, and more good houses until Christmas.

With Mary's health still worrying, they spent much of 1911 abroad, and while in Madrid saw a play by Martinez Sierra (a writer little known in England) which Mary coveted for herself; Charles obediently bought the English rights, but they were never able to produce it. This was the year of King George V's coronation, and they had to be back in London for two major theatre events: first, on 17 May, a Drury Lane command performance at the visit (not so long after *An Englishman's Home*) of the Kaiser and his Empress. The choice was Bulwer Lytton's comedy of manners from the 1840s, *Money*, produced by Squire Bancroft, who knew more than anyone, in terms of the stage, about these already legendary Victorian dinosaurs. *Money* contains the famous club scene in which Alfred Evelyn—Macready's original part—tests the integrity of his entourage by feigning to lose a vast fortune at cards. George Alexander played Evelyn, and Wyndham, quite unsuited but 'looking a picture' (according to Mary), was Captain Dudley Smooth: 'I never inherited a farthing—I never spent less than £4,000 a year—and I never told a soul how I managed it.'

Within five weeks that stage army, 'leaders of the profession', came round again in a Coronation gala performance at His Majesty's. Wyndham, chairman of the executive committee, had to resolve a last-minute crisis when Lena Ashwell, a vigorous feminist, claimed that the programme neglected women of the theatre. Determined to do something about it, she wrote to the Queen, but fortunately, before sending her letter, showed a copy to Wyndham and suggested Ben Jonson's *A Vision of Delight*, which had an all-woman cast. Unable to read the masque before his committee meeting, Wyndham had to rely on what Mary could tell him, and no one on the committee was noticeably

185

excited; the programme was long enough already. Lena Ashwell's idea appeared to be doomed until Charles remembered something Mary had said about the end of the masque, women throwing roses into the audience. At this Tree murmured: 'Beautiful, beautiful! . . . Shower of roses! . . .' Clearly, the masque was in; he was to direct it; and the Queen did not get Lena Ashwell's letter. After the meeting, Sir John Hare, who was not a Jacobean, took Wyndham aside and said knowingly: 'That was a clever touch, Charles—introducing that shower of roses!'

On the night Wyndham played Garrick (what else?), and Mary, Ada (they may have remembered King Edward years before). Ellen Terry and Mrs Kendal romped through the Letter Scene from *The Merry Wives*, if one could accuse Madge Kendal of anything so indecorous as romping; Herbert Tree, surrounded by every West End actor, delivered Mark Antony's oration, a gala essential; Arthur Bourchier was Puff, and Charles Hawtrey, Sneer, in scenes from *The Critic*; and Mrs Patrick Campbell, in her deepest contralto, spoke a new prologue to the Jonson masque in which a mollified Lena Ashwell appeared as Phantasy. A stage army and, as ever, all-conquering.

# IV

One morning about then a young naval officer, home on leave from the Mediterranean, received a letter from a friend which had got into the wrong envelope. It had been written to a Mrs Bird, and Mrs Bird received the letter that should have been his. Politely, she asked him to lunch and to bring his sister. The sister met another guest, who was sitting next to her. She was Una Rolleston, and he was Bronson Albery. They were married at Marylebone Church on 27 March 1912, with Jessica Albery as a bridesmaid. Bronson, a barrister-at-law, was the second of Mary's sons to marry into a literary family. Una was the daughter of T. W. H. Rolleston, the Irish scholar and poet and friend of W. B. Yeats, whom he met at Ernest Dowson's house in Rathgar, Dublin. He made too a handsome demon in *tableaux vivants* of *The Countess Cathleen* at the Chief Secretary's Lodge. During 1891 Rolleston, Yeats and Ernest Rhys founded the Rhymers' Club in an upper room of the Cheshire Cheese tavern off Fleet Street; and, also with Yeats, Rolleston founded the Irish Literary Society, though they differed about the kind of books to be published.

As a girl in Ireland, Una met Yeats and other such close friends of her father's as Douglas Hyde (one day to be President of Eire) and Alfred Perceval Graves. Her father, an amateur photographer, 'caught' Yeats lounging in a deck-chair in the Rolleston garden. She never thought she would live anywhere else until, when she was twenty-five, her father and his family moved to Hampstead. His connections with *The Times* and other journals had developed, and he stayed in London for the rest of his life, a friend of George Moore whose short stories (in Irish) he had translated back into English: Moore found them 'much improved after their bath in Irish'. He dedicated the 1920 edition of *Esther Waters* to Rolleston, 'an Irish Protestant like myself, who would always love Ireland without hating England'. Rolleston wrote the lovely version of Angus O'Gillan's The Dead at Clonmacnoise' which Yeats used in his anthology *Poems and Ballads of Young Ireland*:

> In a quiet water'd land, a land of roses,
>     Stands Saint Kieran's city fair;
> And the warriors of Erin in their famous generation
>     Slumber there.

## V

Wyndham once told Cyril Maude that he prayed: 'O Lord, keep my memory green.' Did Maude know what he meant? A hope that he would not be forgotten, Maude presumed. 'Oh, no!' said Wyndham. 'It means: "O Lord, keep me young in my ideas."' In another sense, his memory was no longer green. Through his acting career he had suffered from sudden lapses, often losing single words in a sentence, which he would cover up artfully by substituting a word of his own. This was the first warning of the aphasia from which his father had suffered; gradually it worsened, owing maybe to the longer gaps between new parts. Mary thought so: he could have lost his facility because there was no need, as in earlier days, to study continually and under pressure. Whatever the cause, disaster struck on the first night of the revived *Mrs Dane's Defence* in May 1912. During his scene with Mary (Lady Eastney) Charles had to propose, and then to recall a youthful love affair. He lost a word; though Mary prompted him behind her fan, he fluffed the rest of the speech and blamed her for intervening: if she had not, he complained, he would have found the right word or substituted another. In the cross-examination scene he should have said, 'Your father was vicar of Tawhampton?' Instead he said, 'Your father was vicar of Wakefield?'

How did the rest of the cast fare? We know that Lena Ashwell, so concentrated as Mrs Dane, could not handle the situation; for her, Wyndham's gap-filling could be 'excruciatingly funny as well as miserably tragic'. The nervous strain was intolerable, and she had suddenly to leave the cast with an attack of shingles. Mary's health was affected as well; altogether, the revival was disastrous; an alarming experience for the young Mrs Bronson Albery seated in the audience. Soon after the play had opened Mary collapsed and specialists advised her to retire from the stage and to live quietly for the rest of her life—a diagnosis that induced the heaviest gloom until her son Irving called in Eustace Smith, the doctor they had had as children. He was less sombre: if she went to Folkestone and did nothing at all she would probably feel better within a few weeks. That was right: after a fortnight she was able to return to the cast. At the end of the run she was prepared to stay in Sunningdale, but Wyndham begged her to go with him to Kissingen, where his son Howard had found the cure beneficial. They enjoyed an exchange of theatre stories with the American actor William Crane; otherwise the stay hardly helped her, and she spent the autumn at Sunningdale alone. In the spring of 1913, returning from the South of France, Wyndham slipped in a Paris street and was confined to his room for three weeks nursing a badly bruised leg, while Mary negotiated the transfer of *L'Habit Vert* from the Variétés to the New. Appalled by the suggested salaries, she actually beat down the leading comedienne, Jeanne Granier, from £60 a performance to £40. In the event the play drew good houses, but it was too costly to last.

Once more Mary was tempted to linger in Sunningdale. Charles, however, implored her to try another cure, this time at Baden-Baden, a rigorous régime of hot baths, exercises and diet. One day the doctor asked her brusquely why she walked like an old woman. She told him that because she felt weak she moved slowly. 'You would not walk like that on the stage?' he said, and she agreed that she would behave like the character she was playing.

DOCTOR   Very well . . . You are an actress, aren't you?
MARY   I hope so.
DOCTOR   Then when you go out, walk like Miss Mary Moore . . . If not, you would do much better to remain at home.

Miss Mary Moore, unaccustomed to such candour, had to say that the treatment had done some good; she was back in the following summer. What exactly was wrong with her is problematical; her last years were deeply clouded when what is said to have been elephantiasis disfigured the beautiful face. (This, no doubt, was why she always wore hats of unusual size.)

# VI

As President of the Actors' Benevolent Fund, Wyndham had to organize annual matinées. With his memory so hazed, they decided in 1913 to take a production of *David Garrick* on tour and prepare slowly for the Fund performance. Every morning Charles communed with the prompter, and every night the company gave him the lines surreptitiously. He managed his curtain speech fairly well until one evening he began, 'Your kind applause makes me feel like Oliver Smith—' Sensing that something was wrong, he stopped, turned to Mary, and muttered audibly, 'What the devil's the fellow's name?' Mary supplied it, he corrected himself, and resumed (while the audience chuckled at Sir Charles's wit). Finally, at the New on 16 December they acted *Garrick* to a full house, and Wyndham recollected every word—an achievement for a man of seventy-six plagued by aphasia. Mary, now fifty-one, disliked playing Ada; yet she could hardly escape, and there was nothing incongruous in Wyndham's practised gallantry. In the audience young Jessica Albery enjoyed the 'drunk' scene, for so long a legend of the English theatre. She did not know—no one did—that it was Charles Wyndham's last appearance on the stage, an unannounced farewell (after more than half a century) before a cheering house. It could have been arranged far less happily.

Wyndham had not fully ceased to act. At this period the cinema was in its growing pains. The theatrical profession looked wryly at films and film-making (described by someone as 'the rock-steady representations of the present-day advance in animated photography'): and Allan Aynesworth, dignity at war with impudence, retorted when made an inadequate offer: 'My dear man, you'll have to pay me more than that if you want me to jiggle about in front of your magic-lantern.' Even so, the 'magic-lantern' did help Wyndham on what Stephen Phillips called 'the slant of life'—it was silent, and in his only film (it had to be *David Garrick*) words were no problem. Other problems he disposed of with an actor-manager's hauteur. When Jellings Blow, his business manager, mentioned the *Garrick* possibility Wyndham asked how long the business would take. Blow thought about a day. 'A day!' Wyndham exclaimed. 'Why, it only plays two and a half hours. How can they spin it out to a day?' Blow hinted that they liked (as they expressed it) to 'shoot' some scenes twice, with the camera variously placed. Wyndham still hesitated; this process would take much too long. So the cameraman agreed tactfully to make do with a single 'take' of the whole thing and to film it entirely in the theatre. All was smooth until Wyndham had to be asked to play a scene down-stage. He glared angrily: 'Young man, are you trying to teach *me* how to play Garrick?' It was a purely rhetorical question.[1]

Early in 1914 Bronson Albery formed a partnership with the abundantly professional actor Allan Aynesworth. They presented three plays, two of them at the family theatres, an exercise in versatility (and one of the minor entanglements of which stage history is full). First, at the Criterion from 23 February to early May, *A Pair of Silk Stockings* was a light comedy by Cyril Harcourt (whose 'very light comedy', *The Reformer*, had been an odd cuckoo in the nest during Barker's reign at the Court). Transferred to the Prince of Wales's on 11 May, it had its last performance there on 9 June. Two days later Aynesworth and Charles's dear friend, Sam Sothern, who had each acted in it, appeared at the same theatre in an insignificant piece, *An Indian Summer*, which lasted only

[1]See Note on p. 223.

until 20 June. Whereupon (14 July) Aynesworth and Sothern moved to Wyndham's with an intentional, though not very funny, travesty of 'crook' drama, *From Nine to Eleven*, written by an American, Walter Hackett; in more profitable London years he would have the disturbing habit of constructing his plays during rehearsal. This one failed, and when it ended (31 July) Aynesworth and Sothern returned immediately to a Criterion revival of *A Pair of Silk Stockings* which survived—across the declaration of war—to 12 September. Young Mrs Albery, during this dizzying period, had her first experience as 'the management's' wife, a position she took seriously and would enjoy.

Mary at length hit upon a comedy with a sound part for herself, *Sir Richard's Biography*, by Wilfred Coleby, and she arranged to put it on at the Criterion that autumn with a cast that included the almost inevitable Sam Sothern. The cure at Baden-Baden that summer was ineffectual, depression supervened, and without knowing why, she wanted to go home. Realizing (as she did not) that war was imminent, the doctor agreed, and on the Thursday before the declaration she left Germany, though Charles had asked her to wait three days so that they could travel together. Belatedly he saw the danger himself and hurried back, barely in time. A trivial episode proved again how differently they thought about money. He had asked Mary to check his hotel bill; finding several extras wrongly charged, she took him to see the manager—one of many similar occasions—and got the extras deducted and a promise of reduced charges later on. She was wise enough to keep the corrected account. On Charles's return he showed her his final bill; she noticed that all the extras had gone back, and they stopped the cheque. Delightedly, she found she could pay the debt only at the end of the war.

It was an unpropitious hour to open *Sir Richard's Biography*, but her company was engaged and she went ahead. In a first piece, *The Little Stranger*, Sydney Fairbrother appeared with Teddy Garrett, who was fifteen but looked like a tiny child. Wyndham was producer. Mary, in *Sir Richard*, wore an evening gown by Worth. But, for all these incidentals, the night was uninspiring and the business poor; no one in October 1914 felt like theatre-going, and even a short visit to the provinces (Mary took Wyndham with her) lost substantially. He would never act again; her own career was not quite over. During the spring of 1915 Sir Oswald Stoll offered her a month's Coliseum engagement in a potted version of *Mrs Gorringe's Necklace*, her three principal scenes linked by a film. She loved the vast audience—as not every straight actress had done—and hoped one day to do the court scene in *Lady Epping*, with a filmed summary of the earlier acts: an ambition never realized.

Soon the Criterion was to have one of the bonuses of the wartime theatre. James Welch and Ernest Thesiger had been touring in a thoroughly idiotic farce, *A Little Bit of Fluff* (the title spoke for it); Welch had to leave the cast, but his athletic understudy George Desmond deputized for him, and kept the part in London. At the dress rehearsal Charles and Mary were horrified; Mary said that the play was utterly feeble, and that only Welch's genius might save it. They refused to allow it to open; but after long and tedious discussion they relented, and *A Little Bit of Fluff* ran triumphantly for three years. It was still running when the busy melodrama of *The Chinese Puzzle* reached the New Theatre in July 1918. George Alexander, who owned the rights, had died a few months before; now his St James's management lent the scene-models and assembled Chinoiserie to Leon M. Lion, the part-author, for his own production at the New. Arthur Bourchier was to play the subtle mandarin; but when C. B. Cochran, who had Bourchier under contract, demanded 10 per cent of the gross, Lion swiftly changed the character (to suit his own physique), to a small yet dominating figure from the south of China. He was still present after nine months when illness obliged his leading lady, Ethel Irving, to retire. A classical actress from the Old Vic succeeded her. She was called Sybil Thorndike.

# VII

By this time, after nearly thirty years together, Charles and Mary had been married. Lady Wyndham, as unobtrusively as she had lived, died in January 1916; since Charles in his old age needed Mary more than ever, it seemed pointless to put off the ceremony, which took place in March at the Chertsey Register Office with Lady Waterlow and Mary's sister Haidée as witnesses. After a few days in London, they went on to Bournemouth, where they entertained both Irving Albery (on Army leave) and Bronson, with their families. In London Mary resumed her war work for the Star and Garter Home at Richmond; and every Thursday they asked twenty wounded men to a matinée and tea at the Criterion. During 1917 they went to live at 43 York Terrace. Wyndham, who had been fond of the view of Hyde Park from his hotel window, now overlooked Regent's Park; in a large ballroom they hung the pictures they had kept at the Criterion, one of them Pettie's portrait of Charles as Garrick (he bequeathed it to the Garrick Club, where it still hangs), and another Hugh Rivière's portrait, the last to be painted. The rooms were furnished with the chairs from *David Garrick*, and a table and Chippendale chairs from *Rosemary*.

Wyndham's aphasia had intensified. He gave up trying to speak, knowing that if he did the wrong words would come. Once, when he did try, and Mary—seeking to help—prompted him, he cried in distress: 'My God! My God! I can't remember.' Some of the stories about his complaint were apocryphal, but Mary did vouch for this scene at a railway station:

WYNDHAM  I want a first-class ticket for a place a short way from town where I always go, but I can't remember the name.

191

CLERK   I am afraid I am unable to help you, sir. What is it like?

WYNDHAM   Oh, it's a charming place. Everyone knows it—lots of flowers and things.

CLERK   I really don't know what place you can mean, sir. Perhaps you would remember it if I mentioned some. Windsor?

WYNDHAM   No, no! Lots of flowers, and everyone goes there to do something.

CLERK   Perhaps you mean the races at Ascot?

WYNDHAM   No, no! But it's a place near there. Where they do something with sticks.

CLERK   Sunningdale? Bracknell?

WYNDHAM   Yes, yes, that's it! Of course that's it! You might have known I meant Sunningdale. Give me a ticket.

CLERK   But you said, sir, there were a lot of flowers. Sunningdale is for golf. I have never heard there were any flowers.

WYNDHAM   Didn't you? Well—that's not my fault. Give me a ticket.

*[Runs to catch train].*

Mary used to tell Charles's familiar stories for him, but when they invited soldiers from St Dunstan's to tea at York Terrace, Jessica (then aged nine) would insist upon holding the floor herself.

Wyndham had been a great walker. In his last days, if he went out alone he generally made for one of his own theatres, which solved any problem about getting him back. If he hailed a taxi himself he could not tell the driver where to go, and would come home with a fare on the meter that meant he had been driven half over London. (It annoyed Mary.) Jessica was staying at Sunningdale when they discovered early one morning that Sir Charles had vanished. Somebody in the household hurried after him, but he refused to return: he was walking to the theatre, he said, and it was left to Mary to lure him home again.

At eighty years old and in sharp decline, he had to be ordered a complete rest, and for many months during 1918 they lived at Sunningdale. Getting back in the autumn to Regent's Park, he managed to attend a West End dinner for Arthur Collins of Drury Lane, and to acknowledge an ovation when the chairman called on him. No more than that: a man who had been one of the readiest speakers of his age in the English theatre could not now utter a word of thanks.

He would see the end of the war. They arranged a Criterion matinée and a tea for five hundred wounded men; and on Christmas Day 1918 they entertained Irving Albery, home on leave, Sam Sothern, and other of their intimate friends: Bronson was still away, serving in the Royal Naval Reserve. But the end was now very near. On New Year's Day Charles Wyndham was taken ill; and, after a lingering fortnight he died at York Terrace on 12 January 1919, aged eighty-one.

## CHAPTER EIGHTEEN
# 'A Genius Like Wyndham'
# 1837–1919

When Charles Culverwell changed his name by deed-poll to Charles Wyndham it could have seemed that, officially, he shut out much of his previous life. It was odd how seldom he reverted to his early career as a surgeon and to those events in the American Civil War that would have served an extrovert for reminiscence and small-talk during the rest of his days.

Nobody called Wyndham an introvert—it would not have been in an actor's nature. But somehow he chose to hide the detail of the Civil War. It emerged only in occasional speeches—those in America and, at home, during the fighting in South Africa. Old men are assumed to see a distant past more lucidly than the present, but here Wyndham's aphasia damaged any coherent recollection. When he was close on eighty he recounted to an acquaintance, Herbert Swears—the dramatist-friend of the Kendals—a story from the Civil War which he continually confused with the Great War (then in progress). 'He had been an Army surgeon', said Swears, 'and, as far as I could gather, had wandered away one night from the forces of the North and was given a capital evening's entertainment by the enemy. But as he referred to the Americans as Germans and the Germans as Americans, my head was in a whirl before he had finished. Actually, he never did finish.'

Long before this his stories would have a clearer definition. In an American speech he recalled an evening, towards the end of 1862, when as Dr Charles Culverwell he sat with other officers in a Federal mess and talked of a coming emancipation of the slaves. Though this was not the war's main issue it had caught the public imagination most strongly. One by one, the officers asked a coloured slave, whom they called Sam, what he would do in future. He said nothing. On the appointed day, 1 January

193

1863, the questions showered good-naturedly. 'How do you feel now, Sam? Speak up!' Culverwell-Wyndham remembered the pause. Sam was silent; he merely smiled, and he went on smiling. Thousands of wounded men were dying, thousands more would suffer in the next two years, and thousands more would die—all, in effect, for Sam's sake and yet he could express nothing.

Trifling, maybe; but we realize in another age why anyone as naturally responsive as Wyndham should remember this and why it would return to haunt him during other wars. Fundamentally serious, he would have gone beneath his colleagues' light-hearted chaff. Moreover, he was himself infinitely expressive, with an actor's eloquence in glance or gesture.

Though he will live with the expert comedians of English stage history, he could have done much else if his public had let him. A few matters—such as the romantic panache of Cyrano—were outside his range. Still, he was a masterly technician; critics, prepared to mock the plays he chose, rarely grumbled about his acting. Players who appeared with Wyndham learned more from him than from anyone else. Delicate and instinctive, he had a quick sense of detail. We have seen that he warned A. E. Matthews never to use outside the theatre a walking-stick the actor might come to miss on the stage; he assured others that if they let their hands fall limply they could never raise them with a natural grace during the rest of the scene. An intelligent actress, Gertrude Kingston, recorded this: Wyndham taught her more about 'the *business* of acting, of the *mechanics* of representation' than any instructor she knew. And Dame Madge Kendal, not the most generous of women, applauded Wyndham's way with gesture, his trick of using a chair, 'turning it round, leaning on the back, putting his feet on one of the rungs and generally making it subservient to his mind'.

Actors were proud to work with him. Lena Ashwell's experience in his 'lost days', during the pathetic revival of *Mrs Dane's Defence*, did not blur her view of Wyndham in his prime. After two competitive matinées in New York her admiration was fortified. The plan was to discover whether she or Margaret Anglin, who had created Mrs Dane on Broadway, was the better:

> I had very few rehearsals with the company and none of the scene in the
> third act, and during that test I found what having acted with a genius
> like Wyndham really meant. Everything he had prevented me from
> doing, though clearly set down in the stage directions to be done, made
> me the winner.

There were dissenters. In his Manchester youth the critic James Agate remained noticeably unexcited. Ben Travers, grand master of English farce, has described Wyndham to me as 'a stick, like Mr Kendal before him'. Some people considered his voice to be hoarse and disagreeable. Yet at his death W. L. Courtney said in the *Daily Telegraph* that when a woman was asked why she found Wyndham so charming she answered without thought: 'It's his voice.' That, Courtney added, was the inscrutable thing:

> Wyndham's voice would not be put very high in the scale if we followed masculine views ... the fascination remains for most of us an inscrutable mystery.

It does still, for no writer from his own day would leave a really evocative phrase. Vocal quality means more than tone and timbre; so much rests upon inflection. Wyndham's command of this startled a girl, Constance Smedley, who met him early in the century in Mary's dressing-room at the Theatre Royal, Birmingham, and set down rapturously what she heard:

> Delicate, subtle, but governed by inexorable and yet comprehensible laws like music ... As Sir Charles spoke, I beheld a master making inflections ripple, mount, and flash.

Courtney also honoured Wyndham as one of the 'most adorable lovers' on the English stage, an art developed by

> a multitude of little touches which seemed so impromptu and yet were so obviously studied ... there was a diffident humility, an ingratiating manner, a suggestion of great kindness, and rising in and through these, a growing passion, which eventually carried the heroine whom he was addressing, and the audience off their balance.

(This adds to the puzzle of the remarkable voice that Henry Arthur Jones swore had only two notes.) Bernard Shaw, no advocate of Criterion-style French folly, attacked the late nineteenth century's intolerable stereotyping of the lover. In his own comedies, so he claimed, he exploited the manner used by Charles James Mathews—a style continued, and superbly heightened, by Wyndham, who recognized his own characteristics in Bluntschli of *Arms and the Man*.

# II

Surprisingly, the spoilt child Gordon Craig, who could be an erratic judge, asserted that Wyndham 'probably had much more natural talent than Irving'. Of these two men who had acted together in youth, Wyndham did seem, superficially, to have the advantages—health, buoyancy, looks. When seventy he could deal with parts he had known in his twenties; and he failed to look old enough in the last act of *Rosemary* even with the heaviest make-up. His energy astonished. Opening at the Criterion—true, at only thirty-eight—he was on stage more or less throughout a triple bill which covered *Brighton*, and its frenzied Bob Sackett. He could cram a prodigious amount into a single day: Squire Bancroft frequently saw him go into a post-office and scrawl a hurried note or send a telegram to himself as a reminder (perhaps because he was always afraid his memory might fail as his father's had).

Friends knew him affectionately for his off-stage pleasures: for the parties he gave at the Yacht Room; in his splendid St John's Wood house; or on holidays abroad. Whenever he saw a play, and whatever it was like, he had a courteous habit of calling on the manager and thanking him. Craig, at twenty-four, toured as juvenile lead in Sardou's *La Tosca*; Wyndham, having seen this at Eastbourne, sent round a note to compliment the youth on 'a great advance in the profession'. They did not meet then; in fact, they never did; but Craig hoped years afterwards that he had 'answered nicely' and given Wyndham 'the happiness which comes to an elderly man who has said a kind word to encourage a youngster and finds it has been appreciated'.

Wyndham was generous to those in need, as well as to the young: to May Whitty, when she toured as a girl in *The Candidate* ('he was not a bit like a manager'); to James Albery when 'he was down'; and to Wilde in the last sad fading. Jones, whose plays—more than any others—broadened Wyndham's scope, had profounder respect for his acting than for anyone else in the leading parts. Though Jones could be tiresome at rehearsal (Tree once excluded him from Her Majesty's), his daughter Doris gathered that the way Wyndham treated him had intensified his regard. With most managements Henry Arthur had arguments that could smoulder into acrid quarrelling; during his friendship with Charles and Mary nothing 'really unpleasant' disturbed them.

Open-handed to a degree Mary would call impossible, Wyndham (under her guidance) could be careful in business; else he would not have left £197,000, divided equally between his son and daughter and his widow. He used to tell Henry Arthur: 'a good manager must be a cheese-parer'. Now and again they agreed to disagree. Jones detested the adapted foreign play; Wyndham, who had existed on these in his first Criterion decade, was more liberal:

> Against adaptations generally it is not wise to rave. There is no more reason for objection in this respect than there is in the engagement of artists to come to England to play. Art belongs to no country. All or nearly all of the success of England's career is born of appreciation in Art and Science of the achievements of foreign countries and improving them. This habit constituted the first charge made to me against England in my Paris schooldays. I was struck with it then because I knew no better, and did not realise how true it was.

196

Jones, as usual, held out. Approving of literal translation, he condemned hack pieces 'from the French' with an 'impossible hybridity of manners, customs, modes of thought and morality'; the characters were unlike Englishmen, Frenchmen, or even human beings:

> What would the French say if their stage was as dependent upon adaptations from the English as the English stage is dependent upon adaptations from the French? Would they not consider it a national disgrace?

Wyndham said nothing in print. In his dressing-room he would have been quietly urbane.

Every seven years, he believed, fortune would compensate a man for all that had gone wrong meantime. Fortune seldom abandoned him until the end, when aphasia curtailed his acting life and withdrew him from many people who had sustained him in private. Herbert Swears has left a picture of him in old age, at eighty years able 'to run down three flights of stairs and digest a brick. His teeth were his own, white and regular, and his gait was upright, brisk and alert.' True,

> To follow his mental processes was not a little difficult. Looking at the fire he would observe "that's a good dinner," and conversely when dinner was announced he would invite one to go into the fire with him. One afternoon I took him to see Pinero's *His House In Order* at the West Pier Theatre, Brighton. He slept through most of the play, but when the curtain finally fell, he noticed that the scene painted on the drop curtain represented a view of Venice. "Ah," he murmured with his adorable sigh, "I remember driving about there." He did not explain how he had accomplished that remarkable feat in the city of canals.

At Wyndham's age he was bound to lose friends by death. Two, though not in the fighting forces, were casualties of the war. Charles Frohman went down in the liner *Lusitania*, torpedoed in 1915 off the south coast of Ireland (the Old Head of Kinsale). Charles and Mary had loved his enthusiasm and humour, and his courage in reviving *The Mollusc* in New York against fearful odds. Then in 1917 Hubert Henry Davies died; after serving in France as a hospital orderly he had a mental breakdown and never recovered: 'as truly a willing victim in the cause of his country', said Hugh Walpole, 'as any soldier in France'.

We know how women admired Wyndham's voice. Herbert Swears said that he survived a rare test of popularity, getting on equally well with both women and men. 'Intensely of the theatre and never theatrical', he was unconscious of his good looks, exquisitely mannered and a brilliant talker. Undoubtedly his gift for friendship made Criterion playgoers want to lean over the edge of the stage and shake hands with him. An intimate theatre, but how many actors have had this hypnotic friendliness? Charles Brookfield said wittily that Wyndham had one foot in the grave

197

and one in the Criterion. His initials still decorate the walls, though today few who see the repeated CWs have any idea what they mean. That is a pity. They should never be obliterated.

# CHAPTER NINETEEN
# 'Arrangin' the Chairs'
# 1919–1938

As soon as Bronson came out of the Navy he joined his mother and Charles Wyndham's son Howard in managing the family theatres. Bronson's legal experience was important, especially in framing contracts: he had no need to bring in a solicitor.

A few months after Charles's death Mary herself gave her final performances. The transient choice (1919) was Gladys Unger's *Our Mr Hepplewhite*, set in a furniture emporium with Arthur Wontner at its centre, Mary as a personage who was called the Dowager Lady Bagley and behaved like it, and—as her son—Leslie Howard in only his third London part. (The King and Queen visited the Criterion.) This was followed by Cyril Maude in *Lord Richard in the Pantry*, a snobbish upstairs-and-downstairs farce, with crowded servants' hall, which filled the theatre for five hundred performances. Over at the New a minor version of *Little Women* is remembered chiefly because Katharine Cornell (Jo, the tomboy sister), made her sole English appearance. Gerald du Maurier, out of the Army and debonair as ever, returned to Wyndham's with the easy naturalism too many actors between the wars would try vainly to imitate. Before he joined up, du Maurier—who like Wyndham would be the unofficial leader of the profession—had had the triumph of a baffling career: baffling because he could waste on the most mediocre material an often uncanny imaginative gift. Barrie's *Dear Brutus* (Wyndham's, 1917) had tested him. As Dearth, the artist in the enchanted wood who chooses, as his 'second chance', obscurity with a daughter he never had in real life, du Maurier used incomparably what an elegiac poem would call 'his quick and seeming unconsidered art'. Daphne du Maurier (at ten she had to be led sobbing from a stage-box) said that no one was out of step or out of tune:

It was as if they were in reality bewitched by the spirit of the wood, and trod softly because of it, bathed in magic ... The wood is gone, but somewhere in the silence of Wyndham's the trees form like shadows and the branches stir, and Lob stands in the centre of the dusky stage, his finger to his lips.

Two years later, his war service a parenthesis, du Maurier would be back in the 'haunted' theatre where he never did anything more touching.

Behind, at the New, the nineteen-twenties had begun with A. A. Milne's early flutter of thistledown, *Mr. Pim Passes By*, all (as Mary Moore would have recognized ruefully) depending upon the amiable Carraway Pim's form of aphasia: he has muddled two names (Jacob Telworthy and Ernest Polwittle) that for him are curiously similar. Irene Vanbrugh and her husband 'Dot' Boucicault were in this, but it had to be transferred because Mary had let the theatre, from February 1920, to an actor-manager, Matheson Lang, whose forthright cape-and-sword attack was totally different from du Maurier's next door. He opened in a melodrama, *Carnival*, as an Italian tragedian playing Othello to his wife's Desdemona and repeating the jealousy theme in private life. It was powerfully actable: Lang, under-prized as a classical tragedian, seized the time to give several matinées of *Othello*, a grand temperamental performance largely ignored. (The West End suspected Shakespeare, who had no share in post-war euphoria.) Without official need to consult his proprietress, Lang found her so helpful that he did ask her advice—always (he said) of the greatest value. Their arrangement worked hand-in-glove; but as a leading actor who—at night, anyway— was drawing the town to one of her theatres, Mary believed Lang should have a suitably visible social life. In the end, accepting that (his professional work apart) he was shy and unambitious, she left him to his own domestic routine.

He and his actress-wife Hutin Britton had a holiday during the summer of 1920, and Mary put on the first-produced piece by a young actor, Noël Coward. Though *I'll Leave it to You* was as flimsy as its title, the audience loved it, the author made a curtain-speech (which he also loved), next day most of the critics approved, and it ran less than a month. During a last sad week Mary increased the gloom when she cautiously cut the stage lighting by half. Lang returned (on a fully lit stage); and on the night before his première with the grease-paint heroics of *The Wandering Jew*, he looked in on Gerald du Maurier next door at Wyndham's. 'How about the new play?' du Maurier asked. 'All I can tell you', said Lang, 'is that it has a different leading lady in every act, and I have to wear a different beard in every act.' 'Good Lord', said Gerald, 'looking for trouble, aren't you? I'd rather you than me!' Neither of them had any sort of box-office trouble: du Maurier's current comedy, *The Prude's Fall*, in which he was an amorous Frenchman, ran until March 1921, and in *The Wandering Jew* Lang was burnt nightly at the stake until the following August.

Coward, resilient after the failure of his comedy, was with the family next as an actor. Towards the end of 1920 Bronson presented at the small Kingsway Theatre Beaumont and Fletcher's Jacobean romp, *The Knight of the Burning Pestle*, about a chivalrously romantic grocer's apprentice. Though his manager would keep faith with the classical theatre, Coward, who played the apprentice, was all too rapidly bored. The production, unveiled at Birmingham Repertory Theatre, was by Nigel Playfair, who had acted in the comedy during his youth and retained a sentimental attachment. To help the Jacobean atmosphere (so he thought), he abandoned curtain and footlights and lined the stage with uneasy gallants sitting on stools and sucking clay pipes. Coward, still only nineteen, played Ralph with a lock of hair in a careful crescent at the side of his face. When the revival reached London a year later he was still (and unexpectedly) playing the poor apprentice 'with a stubborn Mayfair distinction which threw the whole thing out of key'. One night the company—it included the very young Hermione Baddeley—was excited to hear that Mrs Patrick Campbell had entered a stage-box. She meant a lot to the profession, however capricious she was (and she rarely ceased to be). Excitement waned when she slept almost throughout the evening; Coward sent her an outraged message, and next night she turned up in the same box, kept awake, and, with hands swathed in long white gloves, applauded everything he said. Just before Christmas he developed a temperature, insisted on 'going on', and gave sixteen members of the company mumps. Playfair took over as Ralph. All considered, ninety-seven performances (mumps included) was a good record.

Mary had settled into a routine. Twice or thrice a week she drove to the New, where she had an office on the top floor. Wyndham, an ardent walker, had never owned a car, but her son Irving, who was an early motoring enthusiast—he once bought a steam-car by mistake at an auction—persuaded her to have a Rolls-Royce; in the long run (he assured her) no more expensive. Though she warned her chauffeur to drive slowly, the car moved so smoothly she never knew when he was driving fast. Jessica, her eldest grand-daughter, welcomed the car; she was old enough to be most embarrassed when Mary failed to tip taxi-drivers adequately. On the journey from Sunningdale they wore motoring veils; and when they had a puncture the wheel had to be taken off, a tedious ceremonial. In her York Terrace ballroom Mary began to give Sunday *thé-dansants*, inviting the lions of the moment to roar together. Cyril Maude, who had brought the Paul Jones dance from America, blew the M.C.'s whistle; male guests might find themselves dancing with Marie Tempest, Adeline Genée, or Evelyn Laye. To her horror—she was not a good dancer—Jessica was expected to attend. Having (like Dearth) always wanted a daughter, Mary could now be extremely trying: not only did she dominate Jessica, she even suggested adopting her, a plan Jessica's parents sternly resisted. ('Thank goodness they would have none of that!')

201

Mary had views on Jessica's clothes, and insisted at one point that she should wear a velvet coat with an ermine collar—far too showy for a child of thirteen who prayed, as they went about London, that they would meet none of her friends.

Gossips enjoyed stories of Lady Wyndham's thrift, many of them exaggerated, or even invented. Sixty years on it is hard to sift true from false. At one theatre she was said to have inked in the worn treads of the stair-carpet; again, 'they are taking up the pavement outside the Criterion because Lady Wyndham dropped a threepenny bit'; again, a theatre cat was banished because its kittens needed more milk. When Mary took her young grandson, Donald Albery, to the Coliseum she had a crowd of other children with her for whom she demanded free seats as a matter of course.

Like most people excessively careful, she could also be generous, and she gave a good deal of money to a brother who was often in trouble. Very near to her eldest son Irving, a stockbroker (this too was a bond), she let him have the Manor House at Farningham—with invariable disputes when she came down to the room she kept for herself. Politically, mother and son did agree; Irving in 1935 became Conservative Member for Gravesend. In 1922 her youngest son, Wyndham, whom she described as 'a rebel but a very charming one', had stood for Labour in South Hammersmith—an adventure that need not have fretted her, for the Tory Sir William Bull had held the seat for twenty-nine years. (One day Sir William's son Peter would appear resignedly at the Criterion in *Waiting for Godot*.) Bronson was still active outside the family enclaves; in 1922, stirred perhaps by family history, he put on at the Queen's an operatic version of *David Garrick*, staged originally by the Carl Rosa at Covent Garden; among the operatic cast one straight actor was Miles Malleson (Squire Chivy), who would be one of the few great classical comedians of his era.

# II

At Wyndham's, when Gerald du Maurier longed for a Cornish holiday, he asked if for a month A. E. Matthews would take over Bulldog Drummond in the resounding 'thick-ear play', and as a reward go with another production of it to America. While he was away (du Maurier elaborated) 'Matty' could engage a fresh cast and give each of the players in turn a week's run. This would ensure a fully rehearsed company for New York, and all Matty would need for his own performance would be a week's rehearsal with the stage manager. It seemed cut and dried: 'The lines aren't important. Just get the situation and the fights in the right place.' After five days du Maurier was curious to know how the new Bulldog was getting on.

MATTY   All right. Except for the last act.

DU MAURIER   Don't worry about it. I seldom say the same thing two nights running. Have a go at a matinée.

So Matty had the ordeal of playing a part he did not know, with its creator and part-author watching in the stage-box. At the end of the first act du Maurier, less airy than usual, rushed into the dressing-room: 'I've never seen the play from the front before—it's all wrong! Alfred Drayton's part should be played by Jack Dempsey and Bulldog by Georges Carpentier. I'm entirely wrong for it, and as for you, Matty, you don't even look like one of Bulldog's puppies!' All the same, du Maurier dashed off to Cornwall that night, leaving Matty to get on with it. Box-office takings were steady (and du Maurier would not have been an actor-manager if this had failed to annoy him). Later, Matty and his company appeared at the huge Knickerbocker Theatre in New York. Though this was as different from Wyndham's as anywhere one could find, *Bulldog*, its brisk pugilism, and its acid-bath, more than repeated the Charing Cross Road furore.

Mary said once that in all her years as a manager she had turned down only one major success—*Tons of Money*, which elsewhere ran for over four hundred performances. (Tactfully, she omitted her original resistance to *A Little Bit of Fluff*.) She added, 'You can't judge farce. You must see it acted. *Tons of Money* might have been as great a failure in London as it was in New York. With farces no one can tell . . . Besides, the Criterion got *Ambrose Applejohn's Adventure* instead.' And after Hawtrey's piratical skirmish at the Criterion (did anyone realize that Wyndham, thirty years before, invented the term 'farcical comedy'?), then came the first play of the century's best farce-writer, Ben Travers. It happened like this. Travers had designed *The Dippers* with Charles Hawtrey in mind, basing it on the rage of the moment: speciality ballroom dancing, for which Vernon and Irene Castle were renowned (Vernon died in the war). In the farce Travers's Hawtrey character is called in at the twelfth hour to act as partner to the Irene Castle character at a war-profiteer's ball. Without knowing his fate, he agrees. Hawtrey bought an option on the play, got caught up in the long run of *Ambrose Applejohn's Adventure* and sold the option, whereupon Cyril Maude had the part when *The Dippers* followed *Ambrose Applejohn* at the Criterion. Binnie Hale, effervescing as 'Irene Castle', sang a number called 'Dusky Nipper' (words by Travers; music by Ivor Novello). Hermione Gingold walked on and understudied. 'Her only marked contribution to the play', said Travers, 'was an occasional caustic estimate of it backstage.' Hawtrey, who did at least direct, was less caustic. 'My dear fellow', he said, 'your name as a dramatist will be remembered long after this little trouble has been forgotten.' He was right, though at the time no one was more astonished than Ben Travers himself.

# III

Maybe the best-known tale of Bronson Albery—one that got into his *Times* obituary—is of an inconspicuous New Theatre rehearsal. James Bernard Fagan, running a repertory season at Oxford, had hired the bar for rehearsals of *Heartbreak House*; Tyrone Guthrie, six foot six and utterly inexperienced, had been told on the morning of his first job as assistant stage manager to 'arrange the chairs'. While he pondered hopelessly, a stranger appeared and inquired what he was doin'? Guthrie explained. The stranger asked him what the set was like, nodded, got the chairs in order, and went on hands and knees with a tape-measure: 'They'll want the dimensions acc'rate, yer know.' That was in 1923; nearly twenty years afterwards Guthrie met and recognized the helpful stranger who had even disguised his voice so that the ASM might not recognize him. Bronnie, in more vital matters, became Guthrie's 'valued adviser and staunch friend'.

At a charity matinée Mary had seen Sybil Thorndike in Katharine's death scene from *Henry VIII*. Immensely impressed, she told the Cassons (Lewis and Sybil) that if they could find a good New Theatre play she would underwrite possible losses. Joy in the Casson household; a long search; the suggestion of Henri Bataille's *Scandal* in an English text. Mary agreed; but presently this was changed to St John Ervine's *Jane Clegg*, with the uncompromising study of a betrayed wife that Sybil had created long ago at the Gaiety, Manchester. *Scandal* next, and a scene at a French rose harvest for which Lewis Casson had the set sprayed with attar-of-roses. Indefatigably, Sybil Thorndike fitted in some *Medea* matinées. More important, she went on to a full-scale production of the once-banned dark tragedy of *The Cenci*, its first public performances in England a hundred years after Shelley's death. Sybil, near her meridian as a tragic actress, played Beatrice: Bernard Shaw, seeing her one afternoon, knew that he had found his Saint Joan, pillar of faith and fire, and told his wife so when he returned to Adelphi Terrace.

Ready as ever to swerve from mood to mood, Sybil Thorndike came across to the Criterion during the New Year of 1923 in one of her high-holiday parts, April Mawne, 'The Girl who made the Sunshine Jealous', in *Advertising April*, Herbert Farjeon and Horace Horsnell's satire on the cinema. Bronson Albery, Farjeon's childhood friend, put it on, and it angered many of Sybil's admirers: 'You are very funny, Miss Thorndike, but do remember that Tragedy is your realm. You cannot rule in both.' Horsnell, one of the wittiest and most gentle of men, wrote in a verse autobiography:

> The Tragic Muse (who ne'er leaves things half done),
> Ingenious Sybil! finds their play good fun;

And (Hecuba persuaded from her woes),
She takes the stage in frills and furbelows.

For the Cassons at this stage in their development, no one was more
comforting than their manager. Sybil liked Bronson at first meeting—he
reminded her of du Maurier, whom she adored. They complemented each
other; he knew almost always what the public wanted, something of
which Lewis and Sybil, with embracing enthusiasm, had very little idea.
The main thing was that the three of them united in unqualified love of
the theatre. When *April* ended after five months' hilarity they took it on
tour with *Scandal*, *Jane Clegg* and *Medea*, a gloriously diverse quartet. At
the New, meanwhile, Bronson had realized the uncharted possibilities of
theatre management. As he sat in his office he saw a couple of strange
objects hoisted past the window: a six-armed image and a Chinese coffin.
The play in rehearsal was a thriller of the period, *The Eye of Siva*, and
Bronson hastened to tell its author, Sax Rohmer, that no properties like
these had ever gone into his theatre. Returning glumly to his desk, he
heard a ferocious growl and saw his window darkened by a caged and
snarling leopard on its way up. The play duly ran, but Bronson could
hardly have been more relieved when it was transferred; the Strand
Theatre inherited the problem of accommodating a jungle-creature
scarcely house-trained. It was a relief to have only human actors when the
Cassons came back in *Cymbeline*, though almost at once the magical
fantasy failed (London would have nothing to do with its union of Snow
White and the Renaissance). Mary Moore and Bronson were more
confident about its successor: undoubtedly Sybil was, because, as her
brother Russell said, she had to do 'a bit of throttling'. The play,
performed some years earlier in New York, was *The Lie* by Charles
Wyndham's friend from the Nineties, the now aged Henry Arthur Jones
living out his last years in Hampstead. At a fiercely melodramatic crisis
Sybil Thorndike had to bring down the curtain on her cry of 'Judas sister!'
which for more than two hundred performances had every audience
applauding. Dedicating *The Lie* to her, Jones wrote in gratitude: 'What
words can I choose to describe the patient tenderness of your quiet early
scenes, swelling into stronger but still reserved and self-contained
emotion, startled at last into the poignant and terrific fury of your great
tragic abandonment?'

Una Albery, theatre-minded as anyone in the family had to be, read
scripts for her husband, and kept a notebook with plot-summaries and
notes on casting. When Shaw's *Saint Joan* arrived Casson excitement was
not altogether matched by Albery response. 'Costume plays' were no
longer modish; Shaw was not invariably popular. 'Everybody thought it
would fail', Una Albery told me. 'But if you listen to everybody, you would
never do anything.' (For 'everybody' here, read 'everybody except the
Cassons'.) Shaw read the play to them in his house in Hertfordshire, and

205

Sybil Thorndike wrote to her naval-cadet son that they were going to do it 'as soon as the silly old *Lie* is finished'. (That was not for Jones's hearing.) Bronson was at the Ayot St Lawrence meeting, and Sybil could tell that he was 'not too keen'. It took courage to put on *Saint Joan*, courage that, artistically and commercially, would be rewarded.

The cast's excitement rose when, as he generally did, Shaw read the script at the first rehearsal; he acted every part, and 'at tense moments', said the actor O. B. Clarence, 'I expected he would rise and tramp up and down the stage.' Clarence, who had been a down-at-heel father in *The Lie*, was now the Inquisitor with a speech in the Trial scene, 'composed so wonderfully, with such light and shade, such subtle changes, so gentle and temperate and yet decisive in intention, that as long as it could be heard it almost spoke itself'. Joan, in Sybil Thorndike's rendering, 'had a timeless quality. No one has forgotten the radiance of her belief; it was again a part played from within.' At length the production, in its illuminated-missal décor by Charles Ricketts, opened at the New on 26 March 1924, with Lewis as the English chaplain; Ernest Thesiger wryly truthful as the Dauphin; and the fourteen-year-old Jack Hawkins as the page at the wind-changing by the Loire: Shaw had read the part in 'a ridiculous falsetto—I thought he was quite mad but nevertheless tried to mimic him'. It is sometimes overlooked that critics received *Saint Joan* less gratefully than the public did. West End playgoers queued and queued again. On 25 October, thirty-first week of the run, weekly gross takings had reached £2,533 14s. 6d., and the weekly attendance 9,268—both records for the New.

Raymond Massey, writing to me from Beverly Hills, California, has described the manager of *Saint Joan* and other productions in which he appeared during three decades:

> In the years between the wars Bronnie was one of the three or four outstanding theatrical managers in London. He was essentially a "front-of-the-house" man although he was much concerned with the productions housed in his three theatres, regardless of whether or not the plays were directly under his managerial control or tenant productions. Like many good managers I have known, Bronnie Albery kept in touch with backstage affairs by remote control, observing theatre conventions and responsibilities meticulously. He never approached players personally but always worked through producers. I was in ten productions at the Wyndham Theatres, most of them at the New Theatre (now the Albery) as an actor, director, and once as an author, and I never knew Bronnie to go through the pass-door. Yet he knew about the mood and temper of his companies and nothing transpired backstage of which he was not aware.
>
> Once, in 1952 or thereabouts, when Bronnie Albery was dissatisfied with what he considered an identification with the Garrick Club of a fictitious club (which I had made the locale of a melodrama I had written and produced at the New Theatre), he wrote a well-reasoned statement to me which resulted in adjustments satisfactory to both of us.
>
> This independent production had nothing to do with Albery; we were

tenants and he was the landlord, but we were in his theatre and in his opinion deserved his help. That help came in writing, for Bronnie distrusted verbal confrontations. His Balliol logic and his experience at the Bar, short though it was, stood Bronson Albery in good stead in a long and distinguished career in the theatre where such qualities are sometimes in short supply.

(The melodrama, adapted from Bruce Hamilton's novel, was *The Hanging Judge*, in which Godfrey Tearle had his last West End part.)

The Thorndike story must grow confused because, as if *Saint Joan* were not enough, the marathon-actress managed to smuggle in various special performances. When she and Lewis had to leave the New—let again to Matheson Lang—they took *The Lie* on tour, returned to *Joan* at the Regent, King's Cross, and became involved with Lennox Robinson's *The Round Table*, which Sybil insisted on doing at Wyndham's. She insisted against Bronson's advice; the part, he warned her, was not big enough. He was right. After this failure, another regal tour of *Saint Joan*; next, an Albery–Casson *Henry VIII* at the Empire, Leicester Square, of all improbable theatres. James Agate wrote of Sybil's Katharine (emerging from the opulent Ricketts décor): 'In suffering she moves you to shattering depths of spiritual pity.' While *Henry* was being prepared, Bronson Albery offered an eighteen-year-old Laurence Olivier £5 a week to walk on, understudy if required and share the assistant stage management (for Olivier the last job was the trickiest; on a doubtless agonizing occasion the ASM rang down the curtain at the wrong moment). Carol Reed was another novice in the cast, fittingly at the Empire's final production before the theatre went over to films.

# IV

Mary had hoped that after his death someone would write a book about Charles Wyndham. When nobody did she attempted her own memoirs. Her family resisted the publication—during the mid-Twenties there was still some feeling against a mistress—so she had to compromise by issuing the book privately in 1925. It is now a collector's piece, presenting Wyndham as a man loved by all, and especially by the author herself. This is what she had intended; her book, by implication—as a rule unintentionally—is an almost comparably full self-portrait. By 1926 she had delegated much responsibility to Bronson; but she still kept an eye on the way things were going; if not an all-seeing eye, certainly wide-open. When Basil Dean said that he was dramatizing the intricacy of a best-selling novel, Margaret Kennedy's *The Constant Nymph*, both mother and son encouraged him; within forty-eight hours of reading the script they had bought the play for the New, and it moved serenely (and elaborately) forward. Edna Best, the 'nymph', was perfectly cast. Though

Noël Coward, who opened as Lewis Dodd, the composer (fifty years on, we would call him 'beat'), loathed the man and collapsed after three weeks, John Gielgud, his understudy, proceeded to play Lewis for a year—a valuable engagement, as Sir John's letter to me shows:

I only heard of Charles Wyndham, who had retired and was supposed to be distinctly gaga in his last years, but I did see Lady Wyndham on several occasions, at first nights etc. She had been very pretty as Mary Moore, but in old age suffered from some disease—elephantiasis I believe my Mother told me—and was ungainly with a swollen, disfigured face. However, I fancy she was a shrewd and clever business woman, though the chief gossip about her was her stinginess!

However, she still entertained, and to my great surprise she invited me to a *thé-dansant* at her house in York Terrace one Sunday afternoon—a strange occasion. There must have been, I think, a small orchestra (perhaps the same quartet which always obliged between the acts at the New Theatre, when the leader, Philip Christie, used to pop up through the hole in the imitation palm leaves over the orchestra pit and favour us with a solo on his violin). Lady Wyndham presided and danced with all the young men including me, with a pekinese tucked under her arm which made steering a bit difficult, and Lady Alexander rivalled her in energy, got up to kill in a white wig and *mouches à la Marquise*, very overdressed and corsetted in steel to show off her figure. There was a buffet with a disdainful butler who looked down his nose at one as he poured out a reluctant and minute whisky and soda.

All this must have been in the middle Twenties, when I followed Coward in *The Constant Nymph* for a year's run, and I fancy Lady W. must have decided then that I was a promising bet. Anyway, at the end of my two seasons at the Old Vic when I went into Julian Wylie's *Good Companions* Albery and Wyndham offered me a three-play contract which they afterwards extended for three more, so I worked for them from 1931–1936 when I went in *Hamlet* to America with McClintic.

Howard Wyndham was a silent and mysterious figure whom I never knew except on nodding terms. (The only time he seemed to emerge as a personality was when Lucie Mannheim arrived from Germany—with a huge sheaf of photographs in many roles—and fascinated both Wyndham and Albery to an astonishing degree. They tried to involve me in starring with her but I ducked out after I had studied the play they wanted, which at first I had rather liked, and was severely reprimanded for doing so—but I held my ground.)

Irving I knew very slightly but he never seemed to be around. I was devoted to Bronnie, who gave me a wonderfully free hand in casting and, though careful, never went on about expense in the big productions I did. He engaged Komisarjevsky both for *Musical Chairs* and *The Seagull*, though the Russian treated him rather contemptuously: "Albery is just a tradesman!" When *Bordeaux* was such a sudden and tremendous success, he immediately raised my salary to £100 a week, so of course I was over the moon.

Unfortunately he knew I had no great interest in the money side of the theatre. Of course I should have bought the rights both of *Musical Chairs* and *Bordeaux*, both of which I brought him. I did feel a bit annoyed when, soon after *Richard* opened, he sold it to Dennis King for New York and King removed my three principal supporting players to appear with him in it there, as Bronnie had failed to confirm their London contracts from "fortnight's notice" to "run of the play."

The production, copied from mine, only ran a few weeks, which mollified me slightly, but still ruined my chances of doing it in America. Probably he was shrewd enough to realise this would eventually happen—as it did three years later with *Hamlet*—and his one interest was in London. I don't think he ever sent a production to the States.

But he was splendidly helpful over casting and criticised my work very kindly and encouragingly. He jumped at the idea of Olivier for the *Romeo and Juliet* of 1935, and we were always on the best of terms in rather a schoolmaster–head boy sort of relationship.

When I was coming back from New York after *Hamlet* we planned to do a new play of Emlyn Williams about the Lost Dauphin, and Bronnie suddenly decided he would not do it. I never really knew his reasons, but Emlyn and I went into management and did it ourselves—with disastrous results. It ran only just over a week!—so Bronnie was proved right. We had no quarrel but I was sorry to leave his management, of course, after so many successes. After that, we became much more intimate and I was always delighted to meet him. He was oddly shy in some ways, and guarded, like most entrepreneurs, but I think he had real taste and a deep love of the theatre and, of course, all his work for the Arts Council and the Old Vic was invaluable, throughout the second war and after.

Bronson added to his commitments by helping to establish the Arts Theatre Club which opened in 1927—a hundred yards around the corner from the New—'to provide the amenities of a London club and a congenial place for those interested in both sides of the curtain.' This intimate theatre (339 seats), in the basement of a Great Newport Street building between Charing Cross Road and St Martin's Lane, was excellent for 'try-outs' and, as a club, it had no fear of the Lord Chamberlain. Bronson showed again his care for the profession when in 1930 he lent the New Theatre for the inaugural meeting of Actors' Equity. Looking across the 'platform', he would have seen Dame May Whitty, who had acted as a girl with Wyndham; Sybil Thorndike, now a Dame herself; and that eternally formidable matron, Dame Madge Kendal.

# V

On 6 April 1931 Mary Moore, Lady Wyndham, died, aged sixty-nine. Jessica, now grown up, knew that her grandmother had mellowed; at her death they had reached a closer relationship. Jessica divined that beneath the business-woman's efficiency and the hostess with a wide circle of friends—she was always writing letters—Mary had been unhappy. It was not very easy to come to terms with the fact that she had been Wyndham's mistress: tragic, too, for a beautiful woman to have been so disfigured for so long. Before her death she lost the power of speech and, though Jessica's visit obviously pleased her, she could not put it into words.

Mary Moore left a personal estate of £178,428; her three sons were appointed trustees. Souvenirs of Wyndham's career went to her son Irving in trust for Jessica, 'believing that she will value them and take care of them'; she bequeathed to each of her sons one of her 'Royal' jewels—those given to her after Command Performances—and her library and other jewels were divided between her grandchildren, Jessica, Moira, Sheila, Michael, Peter, Donald and Allan. Her daughters-in-law, Gertrude, Una and Ruby, could choose any furs, cloaks or evening gowns 'other than costumes'. She asked for burial in the same grave as Sir Charles in Hampstead Cemetery, and set aside £500 for a better and more lasting granite memorial. (She had paid £87 for a granite stone over the grave of her first husband, James Albery, and always kept the grave in order.) To stage history she had bequeathed 'bricks and mortar' (literally so at Wyndham's and the New), and as a comedienne, her notable performances in *The Case of Rebellious Susan, The Liars* and *The Mollusc*. She is permanently in the honours list of the late-Victorian and Edwardian theatre.

# VI

During November 1931 Ronald Mackenzie's *Musical Chairs* had a promising trial at the Arts. When it moved to the Criterion, Gielgud noticed that what he called 'a fatal habit of being too much aware of the audience' became increasingly destructive to his concentration. On-stage he had to play the piano, a chore not helped by the presence one night of Arthur Rubinstein in the second row of the stalls. Finally, he was cured of looking into the audience when, having spotted Noël Coward, he saw after the interval that the seat was empty. Coward told him later that he could bear it no longer because (a) Gielgud overacted, and (b) he could see the join in Frank Vosper's wig. Mary had once used the Criterion's intimacy to get a better performance from an actor in *London Assurance*. On matinée days, he explained, he was never able to act so well in the evening. What a pity! she said; a charming friend was coming especially to see him. When, delighted, he kept asking her to indicate this friend, she merely said 'Dressed in pink' and tantalized the poor man until she admitted that the guest existed only in her imagination.

While *Musical Chairs* was running, Gielgud persuaded Bronson to let him do two Sunday night performances of Gordon Daviot's *Richard of Bordeaux*, at the New Theatre but presented by the Arts Theatre Club. Gwen Ffrangcon-Davies takes up the story in a letter to me:

> I remember we tried out *Richard* on a very "if-it" basis, and the clever Motleys did the costumes and decor on a shoe string. We none of us thought it was commercial, but that it was charming and well worth

210

doing. After the two trial performances—the notices were polite, I remember—I certainly thought that would be the end of it. But Bronnie always had faith and urged John to make some suggestions to Gordon Daviot which she adopted, strengthening the play with the results that everyone knows. But it was Bronnie who had faith and stood by his opinion when some managers might not have been willing to take the risk. I had a long wait after Anne's death in Act II and he often would drop in for a chat and a cup of tea. One charming thing he did for me was a bit of "spoiling." In Act II Anne came on in a lovely pink dress smelling a pink rose. I said I could not get the feel of things if I had to smell a property rose so I was given a real one at every performance. The play ran a year and the cost in the winter months must have been considerable—even in those days. Dear Bronnie. I was very happy and so were many others to be with him.

Wyndham and Albery staged two other plays by the quietly civilized Scottish dramatist who called herself Gordon Daviot. One (April 1934) was *The Laughing Woman* (with Stephen Haggard), and the other (in June) *Queen of Scots* with Gwen Ffrangcon-Davies as Mary Stuart. Ralph Richardson, cast for Bothwell, asked to be released, and Bronson invited Laurence Olivier to learn and rehearse the part in eight days. (He did.) *Queen of Scots* was followed that November by Gielgud in *Hamlet* ('the courtier's, soldier's, scholar's, eye, tongue, sword'), key performance of a generation and a period, and in André Obey's stylized fable, *Noah*. Bronson had brought the original French *Noë* first to the Arts (1931), and then to the Ambassadors. With his family in Paris he had seen one of the formal miracles of the Compagnie des Quinze at the Vieux-Colombier on a night when the play started late and an impatient French audience smashed the glass doors. W. A. Darlington said:

He brought the troupe to London with a repertory of startlingly unusual plays, knowing perfectly well that the general public would not be interested, and that the venture must lose heavily, but he gave connoisseurs of acting an unforgettable treat.

Similarly, Bronson had no qualms about the much-bruited casting of *Romeo and Juliet* at the New during the autumn of 1935. Gielgud and Laurence Olivier would alternate Romeo and Mercutio, Peggy Ashcroft was Juliet and Edith Evans the Nurse. Meeting Bronson at the Garrick Club (where he was always a prominent figure—the New, the Arts, and the Garrick were the vertices of a triangle), Darlington asked, a shade dubiously, if the revival could run. Bronson did not pause: 'It will run six months.' For *Romeo and Juliet* this would have been a sensation. As it was, 186 performances of a Shakespearian tragedy in an unsubsidized West End theatre during the 1930s was startling enough (though far less startling than it would have been before the 155 for *Hamlet*). Houses were enlarged by persistent devotees who went again and again to argue and compare: 'O Romeo, Romeo! wherefore art thou Romeo?' To which

211

Bronson would have replied, on behalf of his actors and his balance-sheet, that there was all the reason in the world.

# VII

While the New had become for a time John Gielgud's theatre, and, it followed, mainly classical, Wyndham's and the Criterion traced the old West End pattern, an unpredictable mosaic. Wyndham's, du Maurier's professional home in the early 1920s (and also handy for the Garrick Club), was given after the middle of the decade to Edgar Wallace, an instant playwright who if needed could run up a vigorously competent drama over the week-end. *The Ringer* (1926) was more than competent; Charles Laughton oiled a path through *On the Spot* (1930) as a doomed Chicago gang-leader; tickets for the rapidly thrown-together *Smoky Cell* (1930) reproduced cards admitting American journalists to an electro-cution; and *The Green Pack* (du Maurier again at Wyndham's and strangely cast) opened on the night before Wallace's death in Hollywood during February 1932. When, later that year, a play (far from the Wallace idiom) about a big furniture shop began its run at Wyndham's, Basil Dean (who directed *Service*) told the author, Dodie Smith, not to take a call. It was an unrealistic prohibition. Obediently at the première she kept to her box while the curtains multiplied. There were nineteen of them. Then the box door was flung open by an elderly, soldierly-looking man accompanied by his pretty, white-haired wife. Both urged her to hurry down to the stage:

> When I told them of my instructions from Basil the man said: "Never mind that. You don't refuse a call like that, not in our theatre." It dawned on me then that this was Howard Wyndham, joint owner of Wyndham's Theatre. He and his wife then, literally, pulled me out of the box, down the short flight of stairs, through the pass-door and into the prompt corner, then they gave me a fairly hard push, and I found myself walking on the stage.

Edgar Wallace would have needed no encouragement.

Over in Piccadilly Circus, Lilian Braithwaite and Ellis Jeffreys were a pair of dowagers in Ivor Novello's comedy *Fresh Fields* (1933): Ellis Jeffreys must have had a wistful memory of the Criterion stage forty years before, and her music-hall number in *The Bauble Shop*. 'I'm a maiden up-to-date, I'm a pal for any mate.' The line fits exactly the man-eating girl in another Criterion comedy (1936) which survives, in its modest fashion, as a historical monument while *Fresh Fields* has vanished into the mist of West End record. The new comedy had reached the director, Harold French, as a script by Terence Rattigan, labelled *Gone Away*. Bronson engaged for it the languidly bewitching Kay Hammond and one or two others. He proposed that French should go to see a young man called—er—here he had to look up the name—ah! Rex Harrison—in his current play, *Heroes Don't Care*: 'I'm told he's quite good.' True; and they engaged him. They could not think of anyone for the naval officer until French saw Roland Culver at cards in the Green Room Club (christened by that popular clubman of long ago, James Albery). Culver was just the man, so they put him under contract as well. Rehearsals started. The author, lurking shyly in the shadows, had two inspirations: *Gone Away*, the original title which suggested the hunting-field, was wrong for a comedy about a cramming establishment for potential diplomatists on the west coast of France, so he came up with *French Without Tears*: ideal, though neither an international compliment to the director nor a glance back at the Criterion of the 1880s. The second inspiration altered the last few seconds of the play, which had to be a surprise: instead of a walk-on character, Lord Heybrook—previously unseen—Rattigan substituted a schoolboy, a winning theatrical stroke at just the right time.

For all this, the dress rehearsal of the freshly titled play was dire: so bad that Bronson cannily arranged for a replacement within ten days, and Alban Limpus, who had money in the play, withdrew his stake. 'If I'd a hundred pounds,' Rex Harrison has said, 'I could have bought a third share; one of the partners wanted to unload his, and because he couldn't, he made a fortune.' In the depressing small hours at the Criterion, French told his cast to 'do it all over again'. He persuaded 'Holly' Hollingshead, the theatre manager, to watch with him—by this time Albery and Limpus had gone wearily home—and 'Holly's' reaction as the curtain fell was direct: 'Bronson Albery must be potty; I'm going to tell him so in the morning.' Stage history 'does it all over again'. That daybreak the ghosts of Mary Moore and Charles Wyndham must have relived the Criterion dress-rehearsal of *A Little Bit of Fluff*. Both plays had over a thousand performances.

During *French Without Tears* Rex Harrison made several films. If the studio asked for him by day, he did not act at matinées. But once, with a seasonal hangover from New Year's Eve, he assumed—though not called to the studio—that they would not want him at the theatre. He had a Turkish bath and turned up for the evening performance at the Criterion to find Bronson had ordered that he was not to be admitted. It was a fearful shock. Convinced that he was sacked, he telephoned Bronson and asked for an interview. Next day he drove out to Hertfordshire, to The Grove, at Harpenden, where Bronson saw him in his study, gave him a headmasterly dressing-down, reinstated him, and invited him to tea with the family. A very near thing.

# VIII

In Komisarjevsky's production of *The Seagull* (May 1936), last of the Albery–Gielgud plays at the New, Gielgud himself, who would be leaving

213

soon for his New York Hamlet, bequeathed Trigorin after four weeks to a respected and much under-valued actor, Ion Swinley. Edith Evans was the flamboyant actress Arkadina, and Peggy Ashcroft the girl Nina. Dame Peggy has confirmed to me much of what John Gielgud and Gwen Ffrangcon-Davies felt about Bronson: 'He was affectionate and unobtrusive; the great thing was that he let John have a free rein. There was nothing of the "Big Brother" quality of a later and dominant West End manager, Hugh (Binkie) Beaumont.'

Bronson during 1938 became concerned with Michel Saint-Denis's scheme for a London Theatre Studio. Two productions (each with Peggy Ashcroft and Michael Redgrave) were hopeful that autumn at the Phoenix in Charing Cross Road: Rodney Ackland's version of *The White Guard*, a play by Bulgakov about Revolution-torn Russia, and a *Twelfth Night* of disciplined imagination. But money ran out, probably because in the brooding days of Munich and its aftermath people wanted something as light as possible. In the event, London would not have its Vieux-Colombier.

It was then just a hundred years since Charles Wyndham and James Albery were born. Both of them had known—and in their time none better—what a light touch meant.

# CHAPTER TWENTY

# The Fourth Theatre
# 1939–1980

War in September 1939 inevitably darkened the London theatre, though managers soon took heart and began again, not always with the same productions. Life was glum in the West End black-out. Provincial playgoers seemed less inhibited, so when Bronson Albery did present at the New, early in December, a little comedy he had bought before the war began it remained only a few weeks in London before going on tour. Albery found it harder to get plays for the New than for Wyndham's, enveloped in the broad good humour of Frank Harvey junior's *Saloon Bar*, or the Criterion, where *French for Love*, with the glitter of Delysia, was in effect a modern version of much recognized in Charles Wyndham's time. During the spring of 1940 the war intensified, yet theatres held on until the sustained air-raids of late summer. Just before these a revival of Sutton Vane's *Outward Bound* reached the New in the ebb of August, and its famous line, 'Yes, sir, we are all dead—quite dead,' had an impact more than commonly macabre.

Stunned into renewed silence, the West End was very gradually recovering after a gap between 9 September and 3 October: the sole new production had been Robert Atkins's choice (at the Vaudeville) of a seldom-produced Shakespeare comedy, *All's Well That Ends Well*, its name a challenge. Until the war ended the underground Criterion would be out of the lists; leased by the BBC, who saw the value of what had once seemed a disadvantage. (For a while the healing nonsense of *Itma* was among programmes broadcast beneath Piccadilly Circus.)

In late October Bronson staged for matinées at Wyndham's a revue ('a mixture') by his old friend, Herbert Farjeon: *Diversion* was the only revue Edith Evans acted in; her sentimental Kentish hop-picker monologue appealed to current emotion. Bronson drew up a contract, 'necessarily rather harsh-looking', on Wyndham's Theatre writing-paper. Her salary was, curiously, '£10.1s. a week of six, seven, or eight performances, or *pro rata* for any part thereof, plus 12½ per cent of the excess of gross receipts (less library discounts and Entertainment Tax) over £450 in any week.' In the event, there would be a second edition of the revue. Nobody in his day wrote more sharply and economically than Farjeon: Bronson (so his nephew Peter Albery told me) is clearly recognizable in a semi-classic sketch of 1939 about a game of bridge. At the Garrick Club bridge was his passion.

Ultimately, Wyndham's had nearly three years of brisk domesticity in Esther McCracken's *Quiet Week-End*. Next door, Bronson, who for some years had been a Governor of the Old Vic, gradually turned the New into the wartime semblance of a National Theatre. A direct hit in May 1941 disabled the Vic, but its work and tradition lived on in Lancashire headquarters at Burnley, in tours through Britain, and occasional London visits. Thus *Othello* appeared at the New with the powerful German-born naturalized Czech, Frederick Valk—who lacked only a sure command of English—and Bernard Miles as his Iago, earthily malign. By now the Government's new CEMA, shorthand for a clumsily named Council for the Encouragement of Music and the Arts, was moving towards the Arts Council of Great Britain. It had needed war to bring Treasury subsidies to the stage—a development to startle Bronson Albery. For years he had put on personally plays no one would dream of risking without a grant.

In 1942 he became, briefly, joint administrator of the Vic–Wells with Tyrone Guthrie (who still recalled that morning as an unpractised ASM). When Guthrie decided in 1944 that the Vic must return to London both he and Lewis Casson—then Arts Council drama director—looked to Bronson. He let his theatre to the Vic, with Laurence Olivier, Ralph Richardson and John Burrell as directors; and, during a few historic seasons, acting reached a twentieth-century meridian: Laurence Olivier's Richard the Third, superlative in mind and mask; Ralph Richardson's Falstaff, 'apprehensive, quick, forgetive, full of nimble, fiery and delectable shapes'; Olivier as Oedipus, Richardson as Cyrano. We may ask if Olivier ever thought of the too premature *Henry VIII* curtain-fall twenty years before; or whether the shade of an older, slightly puzzled, Cyrano drifted from Wyndham's to watch Richardson; or whether, on a stage so long familiar, Sybil Thorndike (Queen Margaret and Jocasta) sometimes heard the bell-voices of Saint Joan.

Those evenings aided thousands of weary playgoers. Probably they were too good to last: in Guthrie's words, 'the period of glory was brilliant but brief', and as often success ricocheted. Olivier and Richardson were in demand elsewhere, and even if the company could renew itself season by season, at length—after rumour and counter-rumour, affirmation and contradiction—the triumvirate was superseded, and the Vic years in St

Martin's Lane ended (1949–50) with eight months under Hugh Hunt, prefacing a return to Waterloo Road. The light of the final season was *Love's Labour's Lost*, Michael Redgrave in romantic drive as Berowne (and, extraordinary in a small part, only twenty speeches or so, Miles Malleson's Nathaniel 'carrying his little rush-light through the flare of intellectual argument'). Bronson Albery was knighted in 1949. As chairman of the Old Vic Trust (1951 to 1959), he was with the company when, after further internal alarums, it began and completed a five-year plan to stage every play of Shakespeare's except *Pericles*.

# II

*Quiet Week-End* had closed quietly after 1,059 performances that broke the Wyndham's record (though not for long). Daphne du Maurier's *The Years Between* came fittingly to the theatre her father had made affectionately his own. Down at the Criterion, returned intact by the BBC in 1945, Edith Evans in scarcely one of her major creations fluted through Mrs Malaprop's nice derangement of epitaphs in an unambitious production of *The Rivals*. Four years later, and after some intervening performances (Ranevsky, Lady Wishfort), at the New, she was back at Wyndham's (1948)—completing the circuit of the Albery theatres—as the lonely and unhappy woman at the core of James Bridie's tantalizing *Daphne Laureola*. It had almost finished its run when T. S. Eliot's anxiously debated *The Cocktail Party* was its neighbour at the New. This was a complicated story. The play, directed by E. Martin Browne, framed as a fashionable comedy of manners but concerned with personal guardianship and self-sacrifice, had opened to high argument at the Edinburgh Festival of 1949. Its impresario, Henry Sherek, seeking a West End house, approached Bronson Albery, who at least did not tell Sherek (as other managers had) that he was mad to persevere. In fact, Bronson agreed to take the play when a New York run with the Edinburgh cast, led by Alec Guinness, had ended. He made one proviso: if required, the New Theatre opening must be early in May.

Contemplating the Old Vic company still at the New, Sherek gambled on a reprieve until 1 June, the earliest date for leaving New York. He was wrong. Bronson cabled that because houses at the New had dropped alarmingly, *The Cocktail Party* must open not later than 3 May. Sherek, who had arranged for the New York cast to come to London, was in a dilemma; but he engaged other players on the understanding that they might be replaced by the New York 'originals'. As it happened, Guinness—committed to a film—gave way to Rex Harrison, and Margaret Leighton filled in for Irene Worth (Bronson said charmingly: 'To think I shall have my two favourite actresses, one after the other, in my theatre!')

217

A triumphant Wyndham's play (1954), as unlike *The Cocktail Party* as imagination could conceive, was *The Boy Friend*, amiable pastiche of a 1920s musical comedy. When its author and composer, the young Sandy Wilson, had first hunted for a theatre job Bronson had been the only influential person with practical advice: 'Take a course at the Old Vic School.' Being a Governor, he had pulled a useful string or two. Even so, when some time later Brian Oulton and Peggy Thorpe-Bates got him to see *The Boy Friend* he did not offer an immediate contract. A certain amount of caution, a feeling that the piece (originally at the Players') was a club show, preceded an offer of the Criterion. Gervase Farjeon of the Players', Herbert Farjeon's son, held out for Wyndham's, where in the end the run exceeded two thousand performances.

# III

Donald Albery, Bronson's son, was himself an impresario. During the war he had managed the progressively thriving Sadler's Wells Ballet. In 1953, with his own company, Donmar, he put on at Wyndham's the personal favourite among all his productions, Graham Greene's earliest play, *The Living Room*, with Dorothy Tutin. Next year at the New, *I am a Camera* (John van Druten from Christopher Isherwood, and again with Tutin) gave Donald Albery 'enormous pleasure', and active, adventurous years ensued in both London and New York. From W. A. Darlington's daughter Anne, who saw it in Paris where Samuel Beckett lived and worked, he heard of the strange *Waiting for Godot*—'just the sort of thing Donald is looking for', she reported. He bought the English rights of this not immediately lucid allegory of the nature of existence, and for two years tried vainly to cast it. Every leading actor, Olivier and Richardson included, said no.

Finally, the play—which became a minor question-mark of its period—had an Arts Theatre Club trial (1955). Notices next morning were tepid and perplexed. 'It's a bit hard', said Donald Albery to Anne Darlington: 'You find me a play and then your frightful father turns it down.' But, according to form, two Sunday critics duly raved, and Donald transferred *Godot* to the Criterion, where it ran on a high tide of fashion for nearly three hundred performances, though often with an undertow of exasperated comment or more positive disapproval. Una Albery recalls an evening when an old, white-bearded man walked down to his seat in the front row, and the house, believing this must be the Godot it had been waiting for, cheered expectantly. One of the less orthodox authorities on what is now a near-classic is the actor Peter Bull; hardly in love with the play ('the oddest theatrical experience of my life, a nightmarish quality difficult to recapture in words'), he survived in it, through its London life and on tour, as the bullying Pozzo. A frank autobiographical chapter in his book *I Know the Face, But*—would lighten any academic anthology.

Donald Albery, with his almost prophetic instinct for what makes theatre history, also admired Joan Littlewood's individual, frequently anarchic, Theatre Workshop career on an East End stage, the Theatre Royal at Chaucerian Stratford-atte-Bowe. In consequence, *A Taste of Honey* (Shelagh Delaney), more of a 'fringe' play then than it would be considered now, came West to Wyndham's. So in time did Brendan Behan's *The Hostage* and the impressionist *Oh! What a Lovely War!*; and (at the Garrick) *Fings Ain't Wot They Used T'Be*. The Littlewood method grew a trifle predictable, but she did introduce the composer Lionel Bart. Today a handsome chandelier Donald Albery gave to Stratford still hangs above a cheerfully shabby auditorium.

In 1960—a year specially important—Donald, against fierce competition from Bernard Delfont, bought the Piccadilly Theatre tucked away in Denman Street behind the north-west corner of the Circus: not far from the Criterion, but an unlikely address in Charles Wyndham's time. With Donald's son Ian as manager of the Piccadilly, there would be three generations of Alberys to run four West End theatres (total capacity, 3,360). Ian's mother, the singer Rubina Gilchrist, who had been severely injured in an air-raid, died tragically young: her son, who spent his early years with his grandparents in The Grove at Harpenden, acted as stage manager for school plays at Stowe, and it was as stage and production manager and technical director that he worked his way up, taking charge when the Piccadilly, front of house and back-stage, was reconstructed during the 1960s. Since then he has become an expert consultant on technical problems in this country and abroad, as well as a leader in the professional councils of the West End stage.

The other excitement of 1960 was Lionel Bart's musical version of *Oliver Twist*, entitled simply *Oliver!* (exclamation mark important). Three managements already had turned it down, and it opened disastrously at Wimbledon after rehearsals of almost unexampled gloom (memories of *French Without Tears*). The musical director had to be changed over the week-end. Advance bookings before the New Theatre première (30 June 1960) were just £145. Since then all relevant records have been shattered. Everyone that first night talked of Sean Kenny's designs. He had resolved that, because the play had to run like a film,

The sets must help the flow ... and give the feel of Dickensian London ... I think probably most important of all, they must not get in the way ... I began by reading the book again, and as I read I tried to sketch out here and there different parts of the scenes which Dickens himself described. Some were obviously not included in the musical, but I just did it anyway as an exercise and to try to steep myself in some way in old London. Eventually, after about 150 sketches or so, I had the feeling in my head of how Dickensian London felt and smelt, and could almost walk there. The people too—I thought I could understand a bit more. Then I

219

went back to the script and looked at the scenes required . . . I began with the thieves' kitchen. It had not to be just that, a thieves' kitchen; it had also to be the poor, underfed, poverty-stricken, dilapidated, wooden, musty, smoky, cobwebby place. . . .

Kenny thought of it less as a set than as an abstract building in which Dickens's people could live, work and play. What moved him most while he was moulding his structure on the revolve was 'the boy Oliver Twist himself and how he felt'. Sent along at a strenuous pace, *Oliver!* ran for 2,618 performances, toured the United States, and went to Japan, where, done in English, it ran eleven weeks. Under the rules English children could not be used, and even Bill Sikes's dog had to be Japanese.

The traditional see-saw worked overtime in St Martin's Lane when the first run of *Oliver!* ended and another musical, *Jorrocks*, which replaced it promptly lost £70,000. At that period the Albery theatres did a number of musicals. For *Man of La Mancha* (1968), among the last plays where the Lord Chamberlain issued a licence before these became unnecessary, the Piccadilly stage, fore-stage and proscenium wall had to be removed at a cost of £14,000, the safety curtain could not be lowered, and (for the first time in sixty years) this requirement lapsed. An American rock musical, *Godspell*, with its permeating number, 'Day by day', ran at Wyndham's for three years from February 1972.

Bronson Albery died on 21 July 1971, at the age of ninety during a period when the National Theatre company was acting at the New. The *Times* obituarist recorded, as one sign of his professional standing, that Bernard Shaw—to whom he was known then simply by reputation—had waived any written agreement for *Saint Joan*. Writing more personally in the *Daily Telegraph*, W. A. Darlington, a fellow-member of the Garrick Club, said he would never have quarrelled with a man whose integrity and judgement he so much admired:

> There must have been times when, as a critic, I gave cool or derogatory notices of plays he put on. There was certainly a time when, as manager, he failed to see the merits of a play I had written. Yet never a cross word.

The last phrase spoke for a theatre life which had begun, if not quite in the cradle, at least when Bronson's father was still a prolific dramatist. His mother had yet to rescue the family fortunes as a £4 a week understudy. In 1954 he had summarized a manager's view:

> Managers, like actors, follow a hazardous occupation, and they cannot, unless they are Cochrans, expect to participate in the limelight which surrounds the artist. They can, and must, however, share his successes and his disappointments. And they, like the actor, will be wise to remember that, if one day proves to be a choking gall, the next day may well provide a preserving sweet.

Less than two years after Bronson's death the New Theatre became officially the Albery. Irving Wardle began a *Times* notice on 19 February 1973 with the words 'Nothing is going to cure the British stage of its ingratitude and short memory, but the change at least erects a living memorial to Bronson Albery, whose work in the 1930s did more to release the major acting and directing talents of the period and to prepare the way for today's subsidized companies, than that of any other manager of the century.'

# IV

Wyndham Albery, youngest of James's three sons, had been eager to write. Though his profession, accountancy, had little to do with either the theatre or literature, he did publish a few poems. Then, at the death of an Edinburgh University don, Edward P. Brown, who had been editing James Albery's plays, he took on the task himself; in ill-health it occupied him for five years, and the two volumes published during 1939 were a lasting memorial to his father. Wyndham Albery died in 1940, and his brother Irving in 1967; Howard Wyndham had died twenty years earlier. During the 1960s and 1970s another Albery—Peter, Irving's younger son, wounded while leading his company into action near the end of the war—organized from a wheel-chair 2,000 performances by a specialized group called Theatre Roundabout: work, concerned often with spiritual problems, that could be staged in either a theatre or a church. Peter Albery died in 1979.

Through the 1970s Donald (swift to realize the value of the tourist trade) and Ian Albery had fought for many theatre causes, general or particular—one of these the safeguarding of the Criterion when a Piccadilly Circus development endangered the building. Its stage in 1970 had been lifted by six inches to improve the sight-lines, especially from the stalls: this was probably the first British stage set to metric dimensions, a nicety that might have mildly puzzled Wyndham and Mary Moore. In 1978 Donald Albery was knighted, as both his father and Charles Wyndham had been, for services to the theatre; he retired to live in the South of France with his Japanese wife Nobuko, who had studied dramatic art and speech at New York University, acted in the Spoleto Festival, and written a delicately atmospheric novel, *Balloon Top*. Ian Albery, who succeeded his father, became president of the West End Theatre Managers at an hour of almost continuous change. Subjects and styles had widened and loosened; there was no longer the steady London assurance of Charles Wyndham's day, and a manager in the Albery tradition had to be alive to every change (thus Ian in the spring of 1980 welcomed to Wyndham's two companies from the 'fringe' or Alternative Theatre).

Some tastes did remain stable. In the autumn of 1978 *Oliver!* was at the Albery again, and it was still there after two years. That would have pleased James Albery, who, more than a century before, had grown up in Dickensian Southwark. He loved Dickens—his most permanent character, Digby Grant, Esq., would have been at ease in one of the novels—and he twice adapted *Pickwick* (under that name at first, and then as *Jingle*). During Irving's centenary year (1938) Digby Grant returned to the West End at a Sunday-night society's revival of *Two Roses*. Alfred Jingle (acted by Laurence Olivier) slipped back momentarily at the Lyceum matinée of Irving's richest non-Shakespearian parts.

'You shall not be thwarted in your good design', says Jingle in an Albery pastiche. Certainly no one has thwarted the designs of a family that in its generations, its attachments, its complexities, its vigour and its professional wisdom, has spoken full-voiced for the London stage through well over a hundred years.

# Note
WYNDHAM'S ONLY FILM

Six minutes of the little-known film made by Wyndham (see p. 189) exist in the National Film Archive. In the fragment—a remaining 534 feet out of a possible 3,000—Wyndham, looking remarkably younger than seventy-seven, comforts Ada with gestures long familiar in the English theatre. Sydney Blow is wrong when he says in his autobiography that the entire film was made at the Criterion. For the duel they went into the open air; Wyndham's stance again is that of a man half his age. Mary Moore, unrecognizable in a small part, relinquished Ada to a leading actress of the early silent screen, Chrissie White. In her most telling scene Ada writes to her father (played by Louis Calvert): 'The man you made me love I despise, the man you would have me despise I love. I have gone to him.' Produced by Ruffell's Imperial Bioscope Syndicate in 1914, the film was distributed by Jury's Imperial Pictures.

# Wyndham's Crystal Palace Matinées

Among the plays Charles Wyndham put on at the Crystal Palace, starting with *Wild Oats* on 8 September 1874, were the following (his parts are given in brackets);

*Wild Oats* by John O'Keeffe   (Rover).
*The Honey Moon*   by John Tobin   (Count Montalban, with Ellen Terry as Volante).
*The Merchant of Venice* by William Shakespeare   (Bassanio).
*The School for Intrigue* from the French, by James Mortimer   (Figaro).
*The Love Chase* by J. Sheridan Knowles   (Wildrake).
*The Jealous Wife* by George Colman   (Lord Trinket).
*The Ladies' Battle*, from the French, by Charles Reade   (Gustave de Grignon).
*The Marble Heart*, from the French, by Charles Selby   (Volage).
*Henry Dunbar* by Tom Taylor   (The Major).
*Arrah-na-Pogue* by Dion Boucicault   (Shaun the Post).
*Faust and Marguerite*, from the French, by Dion Boucicault (Mephistopheles).
*A Happy Pair* by S. Theyre Smith   (Honeyton).
*Progress* by T. W. Robertson   (John Ferne).
*An American Lady* by H. J. Byron   (Harold Trivass).
*The Road to Ruin* by T. Holcroft   (Goldfinch).
*Love's Sacrifice* by G. W. Lovell   (St Lo).

He also produced Sophocles' *Antigone* and *Oedipus at Colonos* with Hermann Vezin as Oedipus and Genevieve Ward as Antigone, and many other plays at the Crystal Palace.

224

# Bibliography

Principal Sources
Albery Family Papers
MARY MOORE, Lady Wyndham: *Charles Wyndham and Mary Moore.* Printed for private circulation, 1925.
Interviews and letters.


**Adam, Eve** (ed.): *Mrs J. Comyns Carr's Reminiscences.* Hutchinson, 1926.
**Adams, W. Davenport:** *A Dictionary of the Drama, A-G.* Chatto and Windus, 1904.
**Agate, James:** *Ego.* Hamish Hamilton, 1935.
  *Ego 4.* Harrap, 1940.
**Albery, Wyndham** (ed.): *The Dramatic Works of James Albery.* Peter Davies, 1939.
**Allen, Percy:** *The Stage Life of Mrs Stirling.* Fisher Unwin, 1922.
**Anonymous** [H. A. Saintsbury]: *Letters of an Unsuccessful Actor.* Cecil Palmer, 1923.
**Archer, C.:** *William Archer.* Allen and Unwin, 1931.
**Archer, Frank:** *An Actor's Notebooks.* Stanley Paul, 1912.
**Archer, William:** *English Dramatists of Today.* Sampson Low, 1882.
  *The Theatrical 'World' of 1894.* Walter Scott, 1895.
  (Also the volumes for 1895 and 1897.)
**Aria, Mrs Elizabeth:** *My Sentimental Self.* Chapman and Hall, 1922.
**Arthur, (Sir) George:** *From Phelps to Gielgud.* Chapman and Hall, 1936.
**Ashwell, Lena:** *Myself a Player.* Michael Joseph, 1936.
**Atkinson, Brooks:** *Broadway.* Cassell, 1971.


**Baker, H. Barton:** *History of the London Stage, 1576–1903.* Routledge, 1904.
**Bancroft, (Sir) Squire and Marie:** *Mr and Mrs Bancroft: On and Off the Stage* (2 vols). Bentley, 1888.
**Bancroft, (Sir) Squire:** *Empty Chairs.* Murray, 1925.
**Barker, Felix:** *The Oliviers.* Hamish Hamilton, 1953.
**Barnes, J. H.:** *Forty Years on the Stage.* Chapman and Hall, 1914.
**Barrie, (Sir) J. M.:** *The Greenwood Hat.* Peter Davies, 1937.

**Beerbohm, (Sir) Max**: *Around Theatres*. Reissued by Rupert Hart-Davis, 1953.

*More Theatres, 1898–1903*. Collected by Rupert Hart-Davis. Hart-Davis, 1969.

*Last Theatres, 1904–1910*. Collected by Rupert Hart-Davis. Hart-Davis, 1970.

*Letters to Reggie Turner*. Ed. Rupert Hart-Davis. Hart-Davis, 1964.

**Bevan, Ian**: *Royal Performance*. Hutchinson, 1954.

**Blakelock, Denys**: *Round the Next Corner*. Gollancz, 1967.

**Blow, Sydney**: *The Ghost Walks on Fridays*. Heath Cranton, 1935.

**Bradshaw, Percy V.**: *'Brother Savages and Guests': A History of the Savage Club, 1857–1957*. W. H. Allen, 1958.

**Brereton, Austin**: *The Lyceum and Henry Irving*. Lawrence and Bullen, 1903.

**Bull, Peter**: *Bulls in the Meadows*. Peter Davies, 1957.

*I Know the Face But—*. Peter Davies, 1959.


**Casson, John**: *Lewis and Sybil: A Memoir*. Collins, 1972.

**Clarence, O. B.**: *No Complaints*. Cape, 1943.

**Cole, Marion**: *Fogie: Elsie Fogerty (1865–1945)*. Peter Davies, 1967.

**Courtney, W. L.**: *The Passing Hour*. Hutchinson, *n.d.*

**Coward, Noël**: *Present Indicative*. Heinemann, 1937.

**Craig, Edward Gordon**: *Index to the Story of My Days, 1872–1907*. Hulton, 1957.

**Curtis, Anthony** (ed.): *The Rise and Fall of the Matinée Idol*. Weidenfeld and Nicolson, 1974.


**Darbyshire, Alfred**: *The Art of the Victorian Stage*. Sherratt and Hughes, Manchester, 1907.

**Darlington, W. A.**: *6001 Nights; Forty Years a Dramatic Critic*. Harrap, 1960.

**Daubeny, Peter**: *My World of Theatre*. Cape, 1971.

**Davies, Hubert Henry**: *The Plays*. Introduced by Hugh Walpole (2 vols), Chatto and Windus, 1921.

**Dean Basil**: *Seven Ages*. Hutchinson, 1970.

*The Theatre at War*. Harrap, 1956.

**Denham, Reginald**: *Stars in My Hair*. Werner Laurie, 1958.

**Disher, M. Willson**: *The Last Romantic: The Authorised Biography of Sir John Martin Harvey*. Hutchinson, 1948.

**Du Maurier, Daphne**: *Gerald: A Portrait*. Gollancz, 1934.

**Duncan, Barry**: *The St James's Theatre, 1835–1957*. Barrie and Rockliff, 1964


**Elliott, W. H.**: *Undiscovered Ends*. Peter Davies, 1951.


**Farjeon, Eleanor**: *A Nursery in the Nineties*. Gollancz, 1935.

**Fawkes, Richard**: *Dion Boucicault*. Quartet, 1979.

Fordham, Hallam (ed.): *John Gielgud: an Actor's Biography in Pictures.* John Lehmann, 1952.

French, Harold: *I Thought I Never Could.* Secker and Warburg, 1973.


Gielgud, (Sir) John: *Early Stages.* Macmillan, 1939.
*An Actor and His Time.* Sidgwick and Jackson, 1979.

Gielgud, Kate Terry: *An Autobiography.* Reinhardt, 1953.

Glasstone, Victor: *Victorian and Edwardian Theatres.* Thames and Hudson, 1975.

Granville-Barker, H. (ed.): *The Eighteen-Seventies: Essays by Fellows of the Royal Society of Literature.* Cambridge University Press, 1979.

Green, Roger Lancelyn: *Fifty Years of Peter Pan.* Peter Davies, 1954.

Grein, J. T.: *Dramatic Criticism, 1902–1903.* Eveleigh Nash, 1904.

Grossmith, George (junior): *G.G.* Hutchinson, 1933.

Grossmith, Weedon: *From Studio to Stage.* John Lane, 1913.

Guthrie, (Sir) Tyrone: *A Life in the Theatre.* Hamish Hamilton, 1960.


Haddon, Archibald: *Green Room Gossip.* Stanley Paul, 1922.

Hartnoll, Phyllis (ed.): *The Oxford Companion to the Theatre* (3rd edn). Oxford, 1967.

Harwood, Ronald: *Sir Donald Wolfit, CBE.* Secker and Warburg, 1971.

Hatton, Joseph: *Reminiscences of J. L. Toole.* Hurst and Blackett, 1889.

Hawkins, Jack: *Anything for a Quiet Life.* Elm Tree Books; Hamish Hamilton, 1973.

Hawtrey, Charles (ed. W. Somerset Maugham): *The Truth at Last.* Thornton Butterworth, 1924.

Hibbert, H. G.: *A Playgoer's Memories.* Grant Richards, 1920.

Hicks, (Sir) Seymour: *Seymour Hicks: Twenty-Four Years of an Actor's Life.* Alston Rivers, 1910.

Hogan, Robert: *Dion Boucicault.* Twayne, New York, 1969.

Hone, Joseph: *The Life of George Moore.* Gollancz, 1936.
*W. B. Yeats, 1865–1939.* Macmillan, 1942.

Howard, Diana: *London Theatres and Music-Halls, 1850–1950.* Library Association, 1970.

Howard, J. Bannister: *Fifty Years a Showman.* Hutchinson, 1938.

Hutchison, Percy: *Masquerade.* Harrap, 1936.


Irving, Laurence: *Henry Irving: The Actor and His World.* 1951.
*The Successors.* Rupert Hart-Davis, 1967.


James, Henry: *The Scenic Art.* Rupert Hart-Davis, 1949.

Jerome, Jerome K.: *My Life and Times.* Hodder and Stoughton, 1926.

Johnson, Edgar and Eleanor (ed.): *The Dickens Theatrical Reader.* Gollancz, 1964.

Jones, Doris Arthur: *The Life and Letters of Henry Arthur Jones.* Gollancz, 1930.
*What A Life!* Jarrolds, 1932.

Kane, Whitford: *Are We All Met?* Elkin Mathews and Marrot, 1931.

Kendal (Dame) Madge: *Madge Kendal.* Murray, 1933.

Kent, William (ed.): *An Encyclopaedia of London.* Dent (1937 edn).

Kerr, Fred: *Recollections of a Defective Memory.* Thornton Butterworth, 1930.

Kingston, Gertrude: *Curtsey While You're Thinking.* Williams and Norgate, 1937.

Knight, Joseph: *Theatrical Notes.* Lawrence and Bullen, 1893.

Landstone, Charles: *Off-Stage.* Elek, 1949.

Lang, Matheson: *Mr Wu Looks Back.* Stanley Paul, 1940.

Laurence, Dan H. (ed.): *Collected Letters of Bernard Shaw, 1874–1897.* Reinhardt, 1965.
  *Collected Letters of Bernard Shaw, 1898–1910.* Reinhardt, 1972.

Lesley, Cole: *The Life of Noël Coward.* Cape, 1976.

Lion, Leon M.: *The Surprise of My Life.* Hutchinson, 1948.

Loraine, Winifred: *Robert Loraine: Soldier, Actor, Airman.* Collins, 1938.

MacCarthy, (Sir) Desmond: *The Court Theatre: 1904–1907.* Bullen, 1907.

Mackail, Denis: *The Story of J.M.B.* [Barrie] Davies, 1941.

Macqueen-Pope, W. J.: *Carriages at Eleven.* Hutchinson, 1947.
  *Ghosts and Greasepaint,* Hale, 1951.
  *Shirtfronts and Sables.* Hale, 1953.

Mander, Raymond and Mitchenson, Joe: *The Theatres of London.* Rupert Hart-Davis (2nd edn), 1963.
  *The Lost Theatres of London.* New English Library (2nd edn), 1976.

Manvell, Roger: *Ellen Terry.* Heinemann, 1968.

Marjoribanks, Edward: *The Life of Sir Edward Marshall Hall.* Gollancz, 1929.

Marston, Westland: *Our Recent Actors.* Sampson Low, 1888.

Mason, A. E. W.: *Sir George Alexander and the St James's Theatre.* Macmillan, 1935.

Massey, Raymond: *A Hundred Different Lives.* Robson, 1979.

Matthews, A. E.: *'Matty'.* Hutchinson, 1952.

Maugham, W. Somerset: *A Writer's Notebook.* Heinemann, 1949.

Meisel, Martin: *Shaw and the Nineteenth-Century Theater.* Princeton University Press; Oxford University Press, 1963.

Moody, Richard: *Edwin Forrest.* Knopf, New York, 1960.

Moore, Eva: *Exits and Entrances.* Chapman and Hall, 1923.

Morley, Henry: *The Journal of a London Playgoer, 1851–1866.* Routledge, 1891.

Newton, H. Chance: *Cues and Curtain Calls.* Lane, 1927.

Nicoll, Allardyce: *A History of Late Nineteenth Century Drama 1850–1900* (2 vols). Cambridge University Press, 1946.
  *English Drama 1900–1930: The Beginnings of the Modern Period.* Cambridge University Press, 1973.
  *British Drama* (6th edn, 1978; ed. and revised by J. C. Trewin). Harrap, 1978.

O'Casey, Eileen: *Sean* ed. J. C. Trewin Macmillan, 1971.

'Orme, Michael': *J. T. Grein: The Story of a Pioneer, 1862–1935. By His Wife (M. Orme). Foreword by Conal O' Riordan. Censored and Revised by George Bernard Shaw*. Murray, 1936.

Parker, John (ed.)): *The Green Room Book, 1908*. Sealey Clarke.
*Who's Who in the Theatre*, 1st–12th edns, 1912–57.
Parker, Louis N.: *Several of My Lives*. Chapman and Hall, 1928.
Paxton, Sydney: *Stage See-Saws; Or, The Ups and Downs of an Actor's Life*. Mills and Boon, 1917.
Pearson, Hesketh: *Gilbert and Sullivan*. Hamish Hamilton, 1935.
*Beerbohm Tree: His Life and Laughter*. Methuen, 1956.
Pemberton, T. Edgar: *A Memoir of Edward Askew Sothern*. Bentley, 1890.
*The Kendals*. Arthur Pearson, 1900.
*The Criterion Theatre, 1876–1903*. Privately printed, 1903.
*Sir Charles Wyndham*. Hutchinson, 1904.
Purdom, C. B.: *Harley Granville Barker*. Rockliff, 1955.

Robins, Elizabeth: *Both Sides of the Curtain*. Heinemann, 1940.
Rowell, George: (ed.): *Late Victorian Plays, 1890–1914*. Oxford, 1968.
*The Victorian Theatre: A Survey*. Oxford, 1956.
(ed.) *Victorian Dramatic Criticism*. Methuen, 1971.
*Queen Victoria Goes to the Theatre*. Elek, 1978.

Saintsbury, H. A. and Palmer, Cecil: *We Saw Him Act: A Symposium on the Art of Sir Henry Irving*. Hurst and Blackett, 1939.
Sandburg, Carl: *Storm Over the Land*. Cape, 1943.
Scott, Clement: *From 'The Bells' to 'King Arthur'*. Macqueen, 1897.
Shaw, Bernard: *Our Theatres in the 'Nineties* (3 vols). Constable, 1932.
Sherek, Henry: *Not in Front of the Children*. Heinemann, 1959.
Shore, Florence Teignmouth: *Sir Charles Wyndham*. John Lane, 1908.
Short, Ernest: *Sixty Years of Theatre*. Eyre and Spottiswoode, 1951.
Smedley, Constance: *Crusaders*. Duckworth, 1929.
Smith, Dodie: *Look Back With Astonishment*. W. H. Allen, 1979.
Steen, Marguerite: *A Pride of Terrys*. Longmans, 1962.
Sutro, Alfred: *Celebrities and Simple Souls*. Duckworth, 1933.
Swears, Herbert: *When All's Said and Done*. Bles, 1937.

Taubman, Howard: *The Making of the American Theatre*. Coward-McCann, New York (1967 edn).
Terriss, Ellaline: *Just A Little Bit of String*. Hutchinson, 1955.
Terry, Ellen: *Memoirs*, ed. by Edith Craig, Christopher St John. Gollancz, 1933.
Thesiger, Ernest: *Practically True*. Heinemann, 1927.
Thorndike, Russell: *Sybil Thorndike*. Thornton Butterworth, 1929.
Travers, Ben: *A-Sitting on a Gate*. W. H. Allen, 1978.
Trewin, J. C.: *The Theatre Since 1900*. Dakers, 1951.
*Sybil Thorndike*. Rockliff, 1955.
*The Birmingham Repertory Theatre 1913–63*. Barrie and Rockliff, 1963.
*The Edwardian Theatre*. Blackwell, 1976.

**Van Ash, Cay and Rohmer, Elizabeth Sax**: *Master of Villainy*. Stacey, 1972.
**Vanbrugh, (Dame) Irene**: *To Tell My Story*. Hutchinson, 1948.

**Walbrook, H. M.**: *Nights at the Play*. Ham-Smith, 1911.
**Walkley, A. B.**: *Playhouse Impressions*. Fisher Unwin, 1892.
**Ward, Genevieve and Whiteing, Richard**: *Both Sides of the Curtain*. Cassell, 1918.
**Wardle, Irving**: *The Theatres of George Devine*. Cape, 1978.
**Webster, Margaret**: *The Same Only Different*. Gollancz, 1969.
**Wilde, Oscar**: *The Letters of Oscar Wilde*. (Ed.) Rupert Hart-Davis. Hart-Davis, 1962.
**Williams, Harcourt**: *Four Years at the Old Vic 1929–1933*. Putnam, 1935.
**Wilson, A. E.**: *Edwardian Theatre*. Arthur Barker, 1951.

*Dictionary of National Biography; The Daily Telegraph; The Era; The Playgoer; The Stage; The Stage Cyclopaedia; The Stage Year Book* (various years); 'Tabs' (article by Sean Kenny); *The Times: The Theatre; Theatre World; Who's Who in the Theatre* (vols 1–16).

# Index

*(Plays and parts in which Charles Wyndham appeared are indexed under his name, while there is a general entry 'Theatres').*

ACTORS' BENEVOLENT FUND, 135, 188
*Adam Bede* (G. Eliot), 4
Addison, Carlotta, 53
Adey, More, 138
*Admirable Crichton, The* (Barrie), 147
Aeolian Hall, 164
Agate, James, 137, 158, 194, 207
Albert, Prince, 23, 61
Albery, (Sir) Bronson (1881–1971), 2, 123; marries Una Rolleston (1912), 186; in partnership with Allan Aynesworth, 189–90; in Royal Naval Reserve, 192; in management with Mary Moore and Howard Wyndham, 199; presents *The Knight of the Burning Pestle* at Kingsway, 201; puts on operatic *David Garrick* at Queen's (1922), 202; 'arrangin' the chairs', 204; puts on *Advertising April*, 204–5; with coffin and leopard, 205; hears Shaw read *Saint Joan*, 205–6; Raymond Massey's tribute, 206–7; distrusts *The Round Table*, 207; engages Laurence Olivier (£5 a week), 207; encouragement of John Gielgud begins, 208; Sir John Gielgud's gratitude, 208–9; establishment of Arts Theatre Club, 209; lends New Theatre to inaugurate Equity, 209; remembered by Gwen Ffrangcon-Davies, 210–11; brings over the Compagnie des Quinze, 211; loses faith at dress rehearsal of *French Without Tears*, 211; disciplines Rex Harrison, 213; and London

Theatre Studio, 214; in wartime, 215–17; governor of Old Vic, 216; Joint Administrator, Vic-Wells, 216; knighted (1949), 217; Chairman, Old Vic Trust, 217; and *The Cocktail Party*, 217; and *The Boy Friend*, 218; dies (21 July 1971), 220; his view as a manager, 220; critics' tributes, 220–1
Albery (Sir) Donald, 2, 202; manages Sadler's Wells Ballet, 218; Donmar Productions, 218–20; *The Living Room, I am a Camera, Waiting for Godot*, 218; work from Stratford, E., 219; buys Piccadilly Theatre (1960), 219; *Oliver!* at New (1960), 219–20; knighted (1978), 221; retires, 221
Albery, Ian: and Wyndham's Theatre, 147; mother's death, 219; at Stowe, 219; in charge of Piccadilly, 219; President of West End Theatre Managers, 221; welcomes 'fringe' companies, 221
Albery, (Sir) Irving, 78–9, 87, 119, 122–3; dangerous illness of, 154–5; 172, 174–5, 191–2
Albery, James (1838–89), 1–5; birth in Southwark, 13; in Fenchurch Street architect's office, 14; beginnings as a dramatist, 14–20; meets Samuel Phelps, 15; offers Digby Grant, Esq., to Henry Irving, 29; *Two Roses* accepted, 30–3; leaves family business, 35; prolific period from 1871, 38–70; his Cornish comedy, 43–5; adapts *Pickwick Papers*

for Irving, 46–8; quarrel with Vezin, 51–3; and Gilbert, 54; his 'fairy' year (1873), 54–6; moves from Putney to Southampton Street, Strand, 59; adapts *Pink Dominos* for Wyndham, 68; and the Margate barber, 69–70; disagreement with Wyndham, 72–3; and another Vezin dispute, 73–4; 'He revelled 'neath the moon', 76; marriage to Mary Moore, 76; Bronson Howard, 81–2; adapts *Frou-Frou* for Wyndham (unproduced), 79; last original play, *Jacks and Jills*, poorly received, 83–4; adapts *Where's the Cat?* (from *Sodom and Gomorrah*) for Wyndham, 84; noisy house at *Where's the Cat?* 84–5; letters to Mary, 85–6; teaching son to swim, 87; Irving revives *Two Roses* (1881), 88; Wyndham's letter about *The Lancers*, 94, 107; ill health, 99; repolishes *David Garrick* for Wyndham, 107, 108, 112; gives Mary interest in certain adaptations, 113; dies (15 August, 1889), 116; assessment, 118–20, 222

PLAYS: *Alexander the Great* (with J. J. Dilley), 5, 16–17, 41; *Apple Blossoms*, 40, 42–3, 44–5, 118; *Beaten Track, The* (from the German), 96–7, 102, 113; *Chiselling*, 38, 107; *Coquettes*, 30, 35–6; *Crisis, The* (from the French of Augier), 77 (renamed *The Denhams*), 102; *Duty* (adapted from Sardou), 78–9; *Fearns (Genevieve)*, 68; *Featherbrain* (from the French), 97–8, 115; *Femme à Papa* (adaptation), 85–6; *Forgiven*, 42, 49–53, 54, 59, 119; *Fortune* (renamed *Judy Morris*), 57, 102; *Golden Wreath, The* (ballet), 75–6; *How to Act: a Lesson Taught by Garrick* (revision), 16–18; *Ideals* (from the German), 95–6; *Jacks and Jills*, 83–4; *Jesuits, The*, 18, 34–5; *Man in Possession, The*, 68–9; *Married*, 42, 57–8; 97; *Mate of the Mountjoy, The* (with Dilley), 19–20; *Old Love and the New, The* (adapted from Bronson Howard), 81–3; *Oriana*, 54–5; *Pickwick/Jingle* (adaptation), 46–8, 49, 69, 118, 222; *Pride*, 64; *Reinhard and Leonora* (translation), 16, 51–2; *Spectre Knight, The*, 74–6, 85; *Spendthrift, The*, 65; *Starchbacks, The*, 15, 39, 53; *Tweedie's Rights*, 41, 42–3, 44–5, 118; *Two Roses*, 14, 29–36, 38–42, 45, 53–4, 65, 76, 79, 84–5, 88, 90, 102, 112–13, 114–15, 118–19, 145, 222; *Two Thorns*, 15–16, 36, 39–41;

*Victim of Intemperance, A*, 5, 14; *Welcome, Little Stranger* (adaptation of *Le Petit Ludovic*, 122; *Wig and Gown*, 62–3; *Will of Wise King Kino, The*, 56

Albery, Jessica, 180, 186, 189, 192, 201, 202, 209–10

Albery, Mary — see Moore, Mary

Albery, (Lady) Nobuko, 221

Albery, Peter, 216, 221

Albery, (Lady) Una (*née* Rolleston), 186, 190; reads plays, 205; hears Shaw read *Saint Joan*, 206; at *Waiting for Godot*, 218

Albery, Wyndham, 4, 202; edits James Albery's plays, 221

Alexander, (Sir) George, 88, 132, 134, 146–7, 185, 191

Alexander, Lady, 208

*Amber Heart, The* (Calmour), 108

*Ambrose Applejohn's Adventure* (Hackett), 203

American Civil War, 1, 10–12, 193–4

*American Lady, An* (H. J. Byron), 65

Anglin, Margaret, 194

Ansell, Mary, 126

Archer, Frank, 61

Archer, William, 135, 140, 149–50

Argonaut Club, 178

*Arms and the Man* (Shaw), 195

Arnold, Matthew, 171

Arthur, (Sir) George, 150

Arts Council of Great Britain, 2, 209

Arundel Club, 65, 74

*As in a Looking Glass* (novel by F. C. Phillips), 114

Ashcroft, (Dame) Peggy, 211, 214

Ashwell, Lena, 153–4, 156, 169, 185–7, 194

Astley, Hamilton, 94–5

Atkins, Robert: directs *All's Well That Ends Well* (1940), 215

Augier, Emile, 77

Aynesworth, Allan, 189–90

BACK, USHER, 99, 102

Baddeley, Hermione, 201

Baden-Baden, 188, 190

Baker, Barton, 106, 119

Baltimore, 39, 92, 121

Bancroft, Sir Squire and Lady, 14, 30, 37, 56, 78–9, 83, 135, 147, 158, 172, 175, 184, 196

Banks, General Nathaniel, 11, 12

Barker, Harley Granville, 155, 170–1, 189

Barnes, J. H., 137

Barnum, P. T., 11

Barrett, Wilson, 35, 82–3, 136, 171–2

Barrie, (Sir) James, 126, 147, 164, 199

Barrington, Rutland, 159

Barrymore, Lionel, 157

Bateman, H. L., 39, 45–7, 48

Bateman, Mrs, 76

Beatrice, Princess, 135
Beaumont, Hugh ('Binkie'), 214
*Beauty and the Barge* (Parker and Jacobs), 169
Beckett, Samuel, 218
Beere, Mrs Bernard, 114, 124, 126
Beerbohm, (Sir) Max, 129, 133, 143–4, 145, 151, 154, 157, 166, 171, 182, 184–5
Behan, Brendan, 219
Belloc, Hilaire, 171
*Bells, The* (adapted by Leopold Lewis), 47–8, 49
Berlin, 109–11, 173
Bernhardt, Sarah, 161
Bernstein, Herr, 109
Best, Edna, 207
*Betsy* (adapted by Burnand), 78, 84, 158
Bigg, Edith Heather, 115
Birmingham, 54
Birnbaum, R., 178
Bishop, Alfred, 145, 153
Bishop, Kate, 79
Bisson, Alexandre, 98
*Black Ey'd Susan:* by Jerrold, 19, 22; by Burnand, 22–3
Blakeley, William, 8, 94, 146
Blanchard, E. L., 30, 33, 41, 46, 55, 57, 65, 70, 77, 85
Blow, Jellings, 189
Blow, Sydney, 158, 223
Boer War, 11, 148, 151
*Bohemian Girl, The* (Bunn and Balfe), 72
Booth, Edwin, 120
Booth, John Wilkes, 12
Boston, 36
Boucicault, Dion, 21, 123–5
Boucicault, Dion ('Dot'), 140, 200
Boucicault, Nina, 164
Bourchier, Arthur, 123, 147, 149, 184, 186, 191
*Boy Friend, The* (Wilson), 219
Braithwaite, Lilian, 212
Bridie, James, 217
Brighton, 65, 127
Bristol, 10, 41
Britton, Hutin, 200
Broadstairs, 87
Brooks and Dickson, 92
Brough, Lionel, 27
Brough, William, 120
Brown, Edward P., 221
Browne, E. Martin, 217
Bruce, Edgar, 36
Buckstone, J. B., 3, 15
Buckstone, Lucy, 77
*Building News, The*, 60–7
Bull, Peter, 202, 218–19
Bull (Sir) William, 202
*Bulldog Drummond* ('Sapper'), 202–3
Burnand, F. C., 22, 78–9, 115

Burrell, John, 216
Byron, H. J., 27, 41, 65, 72, 74, 88
Byron, Lord, 56

CAINE, HALL, 113
Calmour, Alfred C., 108
Calvert, Louis, 223
Campbell, Mrs Patrick, 135, 181, 186, 201
*Captain Brassbound's Conversion* (Shaw), 45
*Captain Swift* (Chambers), 144, 146
*Carnival* (Hardinge and Lang), 200
Carr, Comyns, 166
Carson, Murray, 136–7, 143
Carton, R. C., 133–4
Cassel, (Sir) Ernest, 142
Casson, (Sir) Lewis, 2, 204, 205–7, 216
*Caste* (Robertson), 14, 20, 37
*Catch of the Season, The* (Hicks and Hamilton; Haines and Baker), 172
*Catherine and Petruchio* (Garrick), 26
*Cenci, The* (Shelley), 204
Chambers, C. Haddon, 144–5, 173
Chicago, 7–8, 36, 37–8, 91–2, 95–7, 121
*Chicago Times, The*, 95–6
*Chicago Tribune, The*, 95–6, 120
Chichester Festival, 150
*Chinese Puzzle, The* (Bower and Lion), 191
Chippendale, W. H., 15
*Christopher of Carnation Cottage* (Anon.), 9–10
Cincinnati, 92
*Circassian, The* (not produced), 104
*Circle, The* (Maugham), 139
Clarence, Duke of, 108
Clarence, O. B., 206
Clay, Frederic, 54–5
Cleveland, 91
Cochran, C. B. (Sir Charles), 191
*Cocktail Party* (Eliot), 218
Coghlan, Charles, 107–8
Coleby, Wilfred, 190
Collins, Arthur, 192
Collins, Wilkie, 4, 56
Comédie Française, 184–5
Compton, Edward, 107–8
Connaught, Duke and Duchess of, 150
*Constant Nymph, The* (Kennedy and Dean), 207
Cooke, T. P. ('Tippy'), 19–20, 22
Coquelin *aîné*, 77, 149, 150, 184–5
*Country Girl, A* (Tanner and Monckton), 159
Courtney, W. L., 195
Coward, (Sir) Noël, 200; in *The Knight of the Burning Pestle*, 201
Craig, Gordon, 47–8, 195–6
Crane, William H., 109, 188
Craven, H. T., 22
Creswick, William, 4, 5, 61
*Critic, The* (Sheridan), 135, 186

Culver, Roland, 213
Culverwell, Alice: marries Bronson Howard, 83; helps Mary Moore, 99. *See also* Howard, Alice
Culverwell family, 6
Culverwell, M. R., 3, 6; instals private theatre, 7; medical baths, 7; hotel-owner, 7; in New York, 12
Culverwell, Dr Robert James, 6
*Cupid in Camp* (G. C. Vernon; from the French), 102
Curzon, Frank, 165, 183–4
Curzon, Lord, 111*n*.
*Cymbeline* (Shakespeare), 205

*Daily News, The*, 118
*Daily Reporter* (San Francisco), 93
*Daily Telegraph, The*, 22, 33, 41, 45, 49–50, 55, 64, 195
Daly, Augustin, 28, 57, 120
*Dandy Dick* (Pinero), 149
Danvers, Edwin, 23
*Daphne Laureola* (Bridie), 217
Darling, Mr Justice, 182–3
Darlington, Anne, 218
Darlington, W. A., 211, 218, 220
Davies, Hubert Henry: *Mrs Gorringe's Necklace*, 162–4, 166, 190; *Cousin Kate*, 162; *Captain Drew on Leave*, 169–70, 172; *The Mollusc*, 169, 175–7, 179–80, 182, 184–5, 210; *Lady Epping's Lawsuit*, 181–3, 197; mentioned, 168, 172–4, 180; dies (1917), 197
'Daviot, Gordon' (Elizabeth Mackintosh), 210–11
Davis, Eliza (Mrs Aria), 71
De Melesville, 23
De Rothschild, Alfred and Leopold, 142
Dean, Basil, 207, 212
*Dear Brutus* (Barrie), 199–200
*Deirdre* (Yeats), 181
Delaney, Shelagh, 219
Denver, 94; *Denver Republican, The*, 94
Desmond, George, 190–1
Detroit, 92
Dickens, Charles, 19, 101, 219–20, 222; *Sketches By Boz*, 8; *Little Dorrit*, 13; *Cricket on the Hearth*, 18; *Oliver Twist*, 27; *Pickwick Papers (Jingle)*, adapted by Albery, 46–8, 49, 69, 76
Dickson, John, 92
Dilley, J. J., 5, 16–17
*Dippers, The* (Travers), 203
Disher, Willson, 108
*Diversion* (Farjeon), 215–16
*Doctor Davy* (Vezin and Albery), 17–18, 41, 52–3, 74
*Doctor Robin* (Vezin's translation), 16–17
Dowson, Ernest, 186
*Dr Johnson* (Leo Trevor), 148

D'Oyly Carte, Richard, 75
Drayton, Alfred, 203
Drew, John, 187
Dublin, 9, 21, 41, 53, 71, 186
Duck, William, 114
Du Maurier, Daphne, 199–200, 217
Du Maurier, Gerald, 147, 164, 184, 169, 199–200, 202–3, 205, 212
Du Maurier, Guy, 184
Duncannon, Viscount (later Lord Bessborough), 130
Duse, Eleonora, 172
Dyas, Ada, 56

EDINBURGH, 45, 53
Edwardes, George, 160–1
*Electra* (Hofmannsthal), 181
Eliot, T. S., 217
Elliott, Gertrude, 161
Elliston, R. W., 106
Emery, Winifred, 178
*Englishman's Home, An* (Guy du Maurier), 183–5
*Era, The*, 72–3, 86, 171
Ervine, St John, 204
Evans, (Dame) Edith, 211, 214, 215–16
Eveson, Isabel, 99–100
*Eye of Siva, The* (Sax Rohmer), 205

FAIRBROTHER, SYDNEY, 190
*Fanchette* (adapted by Bateman), 45, 47
Farjeon children, 115
Farjeon, Ben, 115, 117, 122
Farjeon, Eleanor, 117, 122–3
Farjeon, Gervase, 218
Farjeon, Herbert, 204, 215–16, 218
Farren, Nellie, 72
Farren, William, 39, 112, 124, 126, 135
Faucit, Helen, 3
Fawsitt, Amy, 41, 114
Ffrangcon-Davies, Gwen, 210–11, 214
*Fings Ain't Wot They Used T'Be* (Norman and Bart), 219
Fisher, Charles, 36
'Fleming, George', 161
*Flower Girl; or The Convict Marquis, The*, 4
Fogerty, Elsie, 61
Forbes-Robertson, Johnston, 65, 161, 184
Frankfurt-on-Oder, 110
*French for Love* (Steen and Patmore), 215
French, Harold, 212–13
*French Without Tears* (Rattigan), 213
*Fresh Fields* (Novello), 212
Frith, W. P., 101
Frohman, Charles, 148, 169, 184, 197
*From Nine to Eleven* (Hackett), 190
Fry, Christopher, 150

GARRICK CLUB, 108, 120, 158, 191, 206, 211, 212, 216, 220

Garrick, David, 25
Garrick Médecin, 16
Garrick; or Only an Actor (Muskerry), 108
Genée, Adeline, 201
Germany, Emperor Wilhelm II and Empress of, 179, 185
Giddens, George, 2, 218
Gielgud, (Sir) John, 2, 170, 180; in The Constant Nymph, 208; tribute to Bronson Albery, 208; as Hamlet, 211; as Noah, 211; as Romeo and Mercutio, 211; 212; as Trigorin, 214
Gielgud, Kate Terry, 134, 151
Gilbert, W. S., 54–5, 56–7, 65, 74–5, 79, 87, 119, 127, 164
Gilchrist, Rubina, 219
Gingold, Hermione, 203
Girls of the Period, The (Linton), 60
Glasgow, 88
Glyn, Isabel, 3
Godspell (Tebelak and Schwartz); runs for three years, 220
Goldsmith, Oliver, 121–2, 126, 138, 148
Good Companions, The (Priestley and Knoblock), 208
Gould, Bernard (later Sir Bernard Partridge), 126
Granier, Jeanne, 188
Gravelet, Jean ('Blondin'), 101
Green Room Club (christened by James Albery), 213
Greene, Graham, 2, 218
Greet, (Sir) Philip Ben, 172
Grein, J. T., 131, 153–4, 159
Greville, Lady Violet, 131
Grossmith, George junior, 127–8
Grosvenor Gallery, 164
Grundy, Sydney, 163–4
Guillemand, Mary, 150
Guinness, (Sir) Alec, 217
Guthrie, (Sir) Tyrone, 204, 216
Guy Domville (Henry James), 134

HACKETT, WALTER, 190
Haddon, Archibald, 122
Haggard, Stephen, 211
Haldane, R. B. (Lord), 184
Hale, Binnie, 203
Hall, (Sir) Edward Marshall, 172
Hamilton, Bruce, 207
Hamlet (Shakespeare), 208, 209, 211
Hammond, Kay, 212
Hammond, Surgeon-General, 11
Hanging Judge, The (Massey), 207
Hankin, St John, 170
Happy Land, The (Gilbert), 57
Harcourt, Cyril, 189
Hare, (Sir) John, 14, 57, 68, 144, 157, 184, 186
Harris, Augustus, 62
Harrison, Rex, 212–13, 217

Haste to the Wedding (adapted by Gilbert), 127
Hatton, Joseph, 77
Hawkins, Jack, 206
Hawtrey, (Sir) Charles, 134, 203
Heartbreak House (Shaw), 104
Heath, Caroline, 35
Henderson, Alexander, 65, 85
Henderson, Isaac (The Mummy and the Hummingbird), 156–7
Henley, W. E., 126
Hennequin and Delacour, 68, 78
Hennequin and De Najac, 78
Henrietta, The (Howard), 109
Henry of Battenberg, Prince, 135
Henry of Navarre (Devereux), 183
Henry IV, Part II (Shakespeare), 32
Henry VIII (Shakespeare), 204, 207
Heraud, Edith, 3
Herbert, Louisa, 23
Herman, Henry, 171
Heroes Don't Care (Margot Neville), 213
He's a Lunatic (Dale), 25
Hicks, (Sir) Seymour, 148–9, 158, 172
Hodson, Henrietta (Mrs Labouchere), 25, 56, 58, 105, 107
Hollingshead, John, 69
Holmes, Oliver Wendell, 57
Honey, George, 41
Honey Moon, The (Tobin), 57, 61
Hooker, Brian, 150
Hopwood, Avery, 184
Horniman, Miss A. E. F., 61
Horniman, Roy, 181
Horsnell, Horace, 204–5
Hostage, The (Behan), 219
Howard, Alice (née Culverwell), 115, 120
Howard, Bronson, 38, 60, 77–8, 81–3, 99
Howard, J. Bannister, 61
Howard, Leslie, 199
Hughes, Annie, 137
Hutchison, Percy, 148, 150, 162
Hyde, Dr Douglas, 186
Hyde Park Hotel, 178

I am a Camera (van Druten), 218
I Know the Face, But — (Bull), 219
I'll Leave It To You (Coward), 200
Importance of Being Earnest, The (Wilde), 83, 134
Inchbald, Mrs, 105–6
Independent Theatre, 131
Indian Summer, An (Horlick), 189–90
Indianapolis, 92
Irish Literary Society, 186
Irving, Ethel, 191
Irving, (Lady) Florence, 48
Irving, (Sir) Henry, 14, 23–7, 29, 32, 33–5, 39, 41, 45, 47–9, 71, 76; as godfather to Irving Albery, 78–9; revives Two Roses,

78; 95, 118–19, 135, 149, 154, 158;
Westminster Abbey funeral (1905), 172,
195
Irving, Laurence, 88

JACOBS, W. W., 169
James, David, 10, 30, 38, 41–2, 64, 79, 83, 88,
107, 112
James, Henry, 12, 89–90
Janauschek, Francesca, 93
*Jane Clegg* (St John Ervine), 204–5
Jeffreys, Ellis, 130–1, 170, 212
Jerrold, Douglas, 19, 22
Johnson, Dr Samuel, 121
Jones, Gertrude Arthur (Jill), 172
Jones, Henry Arthur, 22, 128–31, 157, 163,
171–2, 178, 195–7; *The Bauble Shop*,
129–31, 212; *The Case of Rebellious
Susan*, 132–4, 139, 144–5, 147, 155,
177, 185, 210; *The Liars*, 138–41, 168,
175, 185, 210; *The Physician*, 137–8, 140;
*Mrs Dane's Defence*, 145, 152–5, 157,
187, 194; *The Lie*, 205–7. See also *Silver
King, The*
Jones, Mrs Henry Arthur, 178
Jonson, Ben, 185
*Jorrocks* (Cross and Heneker), 220
Josephs, Fanny, 99
Junior Garrick Club, 46, 65, 74

KAHN, 'DR', and anatomical museums, 7
Kean, Mr and Mrs Charles, 3, 19
Keene, Laura, 60
Kendal (Dame), Madge, 10, 109, 112, 186,
209, 194
Kendal, W. H., 10, 155, 194
Kennedy, Margaret, 207
Kenny, Sean, 219–20
Kerr, Frederick, 144–45, 155
King George's Pension Fund, 147
King's College, London, 2
King's Lynn, 108
King, Sir Seymour, 179
King, Dennis, 208–9
Kingston, Gertrude, 194
Kipling, Rudyard, 161
Komisarjevsky, Theodore, 208, 213
Korda, Alexander, 150

LABOUCHERE, HENRY, 25
Lacy, Walter, 72–3
*Lady of Lyons, The* (Bulwer Lytton), 10
*Lady Windermere's Fan* (Wilde), 170
*Lancashire Lass, A* (Byron, H. J.), 27
Lang, Matheson, 200, 207
Langtry, Lillie, 91, 102, 127, 175
*Laughing Woman, The* ('Gordon Daviot'),
211
Laughton, Charles, 150
Lautenberg, Herr, 110

Law, Arthur: *The Bride and Bridegroom*,
166; *A Country Mouse*, 166, 167
Law, Major Edward FitzGerald, 111n.
Laye, Evelyn, 201
*Leah Kleschna* (McLellan), 169
Lee, Robert E., 11
Leigh, H. S., 19, 76
Leighton, Margaret, 217
Levy, J. M., 70
Lewis and Lewis, 143
Lewis, Eric, 182
Lewis, William, 106
*L'Habit Vert* (de Flers and de Caillavet), 188
Liegnitz, 110
*Liegnitzer Tageblatt*, 110
*Liegnitzer Zeitung*, 110
*Light That Failed, The* ('George Fleming'),
161
Limpus, Alban, 213
Lincoln, Abraham, 12
Linton, Lynn, Mrs, 60
Lion, Leon M., 191
*Little Bit of Fluff, A* (Ellis), 190, 203, 213
*Little Doctor Faust* (Byron, H. J.), 72
*Little Mary* (Barrie), 164
Littlewood, Joan, 219
Liverpool, 6, 36, 99–101
*Living Room, The* (Greene), 2, 218
*London Assurance* (Boucicault), 3. *See also*
Wyndham, Charles (parts)
*London Figaro, The*, 54, 79
Longfellow, H. W., 123
Loraine, Robert, 150, 181
*Lord and Lady Algy* (Carton), 133
*Lord Richard in the Pantry* (Blow and
Hoare), 199
Lorne, Marquess of, 94
Louise, Princess, 94
*Luke the Labourer; or, The Sailor's Return*
(Buckstone), 19
*Lusitania* (liner), 197
Lytton, Edward Bulwer (Lord Lytton), 4, 10,
20, 185

MCCARTHY, JUSTIN HUNTLY, 98, 131
McCarthy, Lillah, 147
McClintic, Guthrie, 208
Mackaye, J. Steele, 61
McLellan, C. M. S., 169
Macready, W. C., 3, 14, 185
Maddern (Fiske), Minnie, 115
*Major Barbara* (Shaw), 171
Malleson, Miles, 202
*Man of La Mancha* (Wasserman and Leigh),
220
*Man with Three Wives!, The* (C. M. Rae,
from French), 102, 104
Manchester, 21, 24, 61, 158, 166; Gaiety
Theatre, 204
*Manfred* (Byron), 56

Mannheim, Lucie, 208
Marriott, Miss, 4
Marshall, Frank, 59
Marston, Westland, 4, 20
*Masks and Faces* (Taylor and Reade), 3
*Masqueraders, The* (Jones), 132
Massey, Raymond, 206–7
Massingham, H. W., 184
Mathews, Charles, the elder, 106, 123, 125
Mathews, Charles James, 3, 115, 195
Matthews, A. E., 157–8, 164, 194, 202–3
Matthison, Arthur, 68
Maude, Cyril, 126, 162, 168–9, 178, 187, 199, 201, 203
Maugham, W. Somerset, 139, 145–6
May, Princess (later Queen Mary), 122; as Princess of Wales, 183
*Medea* (Euripides), 205
Meilhac and Halévy, 79
Miles, Bernard (Lord Miles), 216
Millett, Maude, 145
Milne, A. A., 200
Milwaukee, 89, 92
Minneapolis, 92
*Mirth*, 74
Modjeska, Helena, 93
*Money* (Lytton), 83, 135, 185
*Monsieur Beaucaire* (Booth Tarkington and Mrs E. G. Sutherland), 159–60
Montague, H. J., 30, 33, 35, 41–2, 49, 50–1, 53–4
Monte Carlo, 114, 177
Montreal, 92
Moore, Charles, 48; collapse of Victoria theatre company, 59
Moore, Fanny, 117, 155
Moore, George, 187
Moore, Haidée, 71–2
Moore, Louisa, 37, 92
Moore, Mary: (1862–1931), 1, 2, 6, 11, 17, 22, 25, 38; playgoing as a child, 48, 59; sees *Pink Dominos*, 70; collects rents, 71; at school, 71; first theatre engagement (1877 at Gaiety), 71–2; in Gaiety pantomime, 74; meets James Albery, 74; marriage, 76; meets Charles Wyndham, 76–7; lives in Southampton Street, Strand, 78; birth of first son, Irving (1879), 78; family moves to Stone, 78; second son, Bronson, born (1881), 83; writes to Wyndham for Albery, 85; Albery's letters to 'Middlie', 85–6; family moves back to London, 86; Mary's assessment of Albery, 86–7; birth of third son, Wyndham (1882), 89; interview with Charles Wyndham, 99–100; *The Candidate* tour, 99–100; at Wyndham's party, 101; appears in *Truth!*, 102; acts at Criterion, 102; lodging in Mornington Crescent, 102,

104; has first leading part, Lady Amaranth, in *Wild Oats*, 104–6; plays Ada Ingot in *David Garrick*, 107–8; performs at Sandringham, 108; coached by Mrs Kendal, 109; visit to Berlin, proposed, 109; a success, 110; plays *David Garrick* in St Petersburg; loses three sovereigns, 112; reappears at the Criterion theatre (decorated with tour souvenirs), 112; presents from the Tsar, 113; Mrs Wyndham's attachment to her, 114; plays Mrs Mildmay in *Still Waters Run Deep*, and Lottie in *Two Roses*; Albery's letter about Lottie, 114; sails to America for health, 115; news of husband's death, 115; newspaper defamation, 117; first American tour with Wyndham, 120; appears as Pauline in *Delicate Ground*, 120; plays Kate in *She Stoops to Conquer*, 122; plays Grace Harkaway in *London Assurance*, 124, 126; in *The Bauble Shop*, 130; Susan in *The Case of Rebellious Susan*, 132–4; Lady Jessica, in *The Liars*, 140–1; and Prince of Wales, 134, 135; and a hot supper, 136; her favourite part, Dorothy Cruickshank in *Rosemary*, 136–7; as Mrs Parbury (*The Tyranny of Tears*), 144–5; on Wyndham's roof, 147; opening of Wyndham's (10 November 1899), 148; 151; as Lady Eastney in *Mrs Dane's Defence*, 153–5; leaves cast temporarily when Irving Albery is dangerously ill in South Africa, 154–5; contemplates new theatre behind Wyndham's, 156; frustrating delays with new theatre, 160; 'an accomplished comedienne' as Mrs Gorringe, 162–4; Grosvenor Gallery speculation, 164; ideas for scenery, 165; 'enchanting comedy actress' (Travers), 170; adventure with Continental trains, 173–5; her most rewarding part (*The Mollusc*), 175–7; Maugham writes to her about *The Mollusc*, 176–7; takes house in Sunningdale, 178; and Wyndham's excessive generosity, 178–9; involved in law suit, 182–3; acts *The Mollusc* in America (1909), 184; in New York, Egypt and Naples, 185; appears in potted version of *Mrs Gorringe's Necklace* at Coliseum, 190; marries Sir Charles, Chertsey Register Office (1916), 191; moves to 43 York Terrace, Regent's Park (1917), 191; and Wyndham's death, 192; last stage appearance (1919) in *Our Mr Hepplewhite*, 199; and Matheson Lang, 200; and Noël Coward, 200; buys a car,

201; gives thé-dansants at York
Terrace, 201; stories of her thrift, 202;
underwrites the Cassons, 204; 205; her
book about Wyndham, 207; John
Gielgud's memories, 208; dies, aged
sixty-nine, 6 April 1931, 209; her will,
210
Moore, Nellie, 27, 37
Moore, Tom, 60
Mortimer, James, 85
Moscow, 111
Motley, 210
Mr Pim Passes By (Milne), 200
Music and Drama (San Francisco), 93
Musical Chairs (Mackenzie), 208, 210
Muskerry, William, 107
My Daughter-in-Law (from the French),
148

NARES, OWEN, 101
National Film Archive, 223
Neilson, Julia, 135, 169–70, 183
Neville, Henry, 65, 158
New Orleans, 12, 97
New York, 11–12, 28, 35–6, 37, 39, 57,
64–5, 69, 90–3, 95–6, 115, 120, 121, 144,
168, 184, 197, 202–3, 205, 208–209, 217,
221
New York Clipper, The (journal), 92
New York Mirror, 95
New York Times, The, 35–6, 57
Newcastle upon Tyne, 53
Newton, Amelia, 85, 91
Nicoll, Allardyce, 138
Noah (Obey), 211
Nobody's Widow, later Roxana
(Hopwood), 184
No. 10; or, The Bastille of Calvados, 77

OBEY, ANDRÉ, 211
O'Connor, T. P., 178
O'Gillan, Angus, 187
Ogilvie, G. Stuart, 150
Oh! What a lovely War! (Chilton and
others), 219
O'Keeffe, John, 58, 105, 120
Old Love and the New, The (Howard),
60
Old Vic Company, 150; at New Theatre
(1944–50), 216–18
Oliver! (Bart), 219–20, 222
Oliver, 'Patty', 22
Oliver Twist, 27
Olivier, Laurence (Lord Olivier), 207, 209,
211, 216; as Richard III (1944) and
Oedipus (1945), 216, 218
On Approval (Lonsdale), 173
On Guard (Gilbert), 54
O'Rell, Max, 178
Osborne House, 135

Othello (Shakespeare): Lang, 200; Valk,
216
Ouida, 23
Oulton, Brian, 218
Our American Cousin (Taylor), 35
Our Boys (Byron, H. J.), 69
Our Mr Hepplewhite (Unger), 199
Ours (Robertson), 121
Outward Bound, (Sutton Vane), 215
Oxenford, John, 33, 41

Pair of Silk Stockings, A (Harcourt),
189–90
Pair of Spectacles, A (Grundy), 157
Paris, 7, 11, 67, 90, 95, 98, 145, 154, 165–6,
173–5, 177, 180, 188, 211
Parker, Louis N., 136–7, 143, 150, 169
Partridge, Ralph, 101
Passion Flowers (adaptation from de
Musset by Robertson), 109
Patience (Gilbert and Sullivan), 56, 164
Paul, Howard, 92
Pemberton, Edgar, 42, 87
Peter Pan (Barrie), 164, 169
Pettie, John, 108
Phelps, Samuel, 3, 15, 58, 106, 137
Philadelphia, 36, 39, 121
Philanderer, The (Shaw), 131–2, 134
Phillips, F. C., 114
Phillips, Stephen, 189
Pinafore, H.M.S. (Gilbert and Sullivan), 75
Pinero, (Sir) Arthur, 20, 30, 35, 40, 46, 59,
87, 118, 128, 134, 197
Players' Club, New York, 120
Playfair family, 7
Playfair, Nigel, 201
Ponsonby, Claude, 160
Prude's Fall, The (Besier and Edginton),
200
Punch, 126
Pyke, Joseph, 142, 164

QUAIN, (SIR) RICHARD, 115
Quality Street (Barrie), 158
Quebec, 93–5
Queen of Scots ('Gordon Daviot'), 211
Queen's Shilling, The (Godfrey), 37
Quiet Week-end (McCracken), 216–17

RACHEL, 23
Ramsgate, 99, 102
Rattigan, (Sir) Terence, 212–13
Rayne, Lin, 35
Reade, Charles, 25
Realm of Joy, The (Gilbert), 57
Redgrave, (Sir) Michael, 214, 217
Reed, Carol, 207
Reformer, The (Harcourt), 189
Regent Circus, 65. See also Piccadilly Circus
Regent's Park, 76, 78, 86, 161, 178, 191–2

*Rehearsal, The* (Buckingham), 105
Reicher, Edmund, 110
Réjane, 172
Rhona, Madame de, 10, 22, 30
Rhymers' Club, 186
Rhys, Ernest, 186
*Richard Savage* (Barrie and Marriott
 Watson), 126
*Richard of Bordeaux* ('Gordon Daviot'),
 208–9, 210–11
Richardson, (Sir) Ralph, 211; as Falstaff
 (1945) and Cyrano (1946), 216, 218
*Richelieu* (Lytton), 4
Ricketts, Charles, 206
Ridley, Mr Justice, 172
Ristori, Adelaide, 23
*Rivals, The* (Sheridan), 20, 217
Rivière, Hugh, 191
*Road to Ruin, The* (Holcroft), 116
Roberts, Lord, 184
Robertson, Tom (T.W.), 3, 14, 17, 20, 30–1,
 33, 35, 37, 40, 42, 56, 64,
 107–9, 119, 121
Robson, Stuart, 109
Rock, Charles, 184
Rolleston, T. W. H., 186–7; in *Countess
 Cathleen* (Yeats), 186; founds Rhymers'
 Club with Yeats and Rhys, 186; and
 with Yeats, the Irish Literary Society,
 186; moves to Hampstead, 186;
 connection with *The Times*, 186; friend
 of George Moore, 187; Moore dedicates
 *Esther Waters* (1920 edition) to him,
 187; writes version of O'Gillan's 'The
 Dead at Clonmacnoise', 187
Rome, 168, 173–4, 177
*Romeo and Juliet* (Shakespeare), 88, 209,
 211–12
Rorke, Mary, 94–5
Rossetti, Dante Gabriel, 23
Rostand, Edmond (*Cyrano de Bergerac*),
 150
*Round Table, The* (Lennox Robinson), 207
Rowell, George, 30, 119, 158–9
Royal Dramatic College, 19–20
Royal Shakespeare Company, 56, 106
Royce, E. W., 72
Russell, Annie, 171
Russell of Killowen, Lord, 136

ST ANDREW'S, 7
Saint-Denis, Michel, 214
St Dunstan's, 192
*Saint Joan* (Shaw), 2; (New Theatre),
 205–7, 220
St Louis, 37–8, 92
St Moritz, 85, 116, 122, 132, 177
St Petersburg, 111
Saintsbury, H. A., 129, 137
Saker, Rose, 85

Salisbury, Marquess of, 1, 142, 160
Salisbury tavern, 160
*Saloon Bar* (Harvey), 215
Salt Lake City, 94
Salvini, Tomasso, 120–1
San Francisco, 36
Sandringham House, 108
*Saratoga* (Howard), 38, 56–60. *See also
 Brighton* under Wyndham's parts)
Saratoga Springs, New York State, 60
Sardou, Victorien, 78–9, 131, 196
Sartoris, Mrs (*née* Adelaide Kemble), 24
Saturday Half Holiday Movement, 4
*Saturday Review, The*, 136, 140, 143
Savage Club, 55, 65, 74, 76, 118
Savannah, 38
*Scandal* (Henri Bataille), 204–5
*Scarlet Pimpernel, The* (Orczy and
 Barstow), 169
*School for Scandal, The* (Sheridan), 11, 20.
 *See also* Wyndham as Charles Surface
Scott, Clement, 30, 64, 68, 70, 88, 125, 134
Scribe, Eugène, 138
*Seagull, The* (Chekhov), 208, 213–14
*Service* (Dodie Smith), 212
Shaw, Bernard, 2, 41, 45, 131–2, 134, 136,
 140, 143, 147, 151, 170–1, 195, 205–7,
 220
*Shenandoah* (Howard), 120
Shepherd, Richard, 4
Sherek, Henry, 217
Sheridan, R. B., 18, 20, 80, 118, 126, 135, 138,
 148
Sherman, General W. T., 12
Sierra, Martinez, 185
*Silver King, The* (Jones), 129, 171
*Sir Richard's Biography* (Coleby), 190
Smedley, Constance, 195
Smith, Dodie, 212
*Sorcerer, The* (Gilbert and Sullivan), 14
Sothern, E. A., 17, 35, 42, 87, 97, 102, 107,
 115, 120–1, 158
Sothern, Lytton, 102
Sothern, Sam, 184, 189–90, 192
Southwark, 13–15
Southwark Literary Institution, 5
Spiers and Pond, 66
*Spirit of the Times, The* (journal), 91
Sprague, W. G. R., architect of Wyndham's,
 143, 146, 148; designs New Theatre, 160
Star and Garter Home, Richmond, 191
Stephens, W. H., 41
*Still Waters Run Deep* (Taylor), 4, 9. *See
 also* Wyndham's parts
Stirling, Mrs, 3, 175
Stobitzer, Heinrich, 97
Stoll, (Sir) Oswald, 190
Stone, Kent, 78
Studholme, Marie, 127
Sullivan, (Sir) Arthur, 54, 74–5, 127

Sullivan, comédien de Drury Lane (De Melesville), 23
Sunday Times, The, 17, 73
Sunningdale, 178, 188, 192, 201
Swaine, Colonel, 111
Swears, Herbert, 193, 197
Swinley, Ion, 214

TABOR, HORACE, 94
Taste of Honey, A (Delaney), 219
Taylor, Tom, 4, 61, 79
Tearle, (Sir) Godfrey, 207
Telbin, William, 25
Tempest, (Dame) Marie, 170, 176, 201
Tempter, The, (Jones), 132
Terriss, Ellaline, 112–13, 126
Terriss, William ('Breezy Bill'), 77, 88, 112
Terry, Edward, 72
Terry, (Dame) Ellen, 3, 8, 10; with Wyndham at opening of Queen's, Long Acre, 24–6; 39, 57, 61, 76, 88, 95, 138, 147, 170, 172, 175, 186
Terry, Fred, 169–70, 183
Terry, Kate, 4, 8, 24, 25
Terry, Marion, 137–8, 170, 180
Terry-Lewis, Mabel, 163, 166
Thackeray, W. M., 19
Theatre Roundabout, 221
Theatres (in London, unless otherwise noted):
ADELPHI, 24, 118; Albery (formerly New), 1, 160, 165; description of, 160; opens with Rosemary 13 March 1903, 161; Mrs Gorringe transferred to, 164; pandemonium at première of The Bride and Bridegroom, 166; Scarlet Pimpernel at, 169; 178, 181, 188; long run of The Chinese Puzzle, 191, 199; the Cassons at, 204–7; Saint Joan breaks theatre records, 206; The Constant Nymph, 207–8; plays with John Gielgud, 208–14; Old Vic seasons (1944–50), 216–17; The Cocktail Party, 218; National Theatre Company at (1971), 220; Oliver! breaks records, 219; renamed the Albery (1973), 221; Alexandra Palace, 85; Alhambra, 75–6; Arts Theatre Club, 209–11; 218
BALDWIN, San Francisco, 93; Bijou, Boston, 95; Birmingham Repertory, 201; Bush, San Francisco, 93
CABINET, King's Cross, 2, 8; Coliseum, 190, 202; Colosseum, Regent's Park, 8; Comedy, 160; Covent Garden, (Theatre Royal), 125; (Opera House), 202; Criterion: see Chapters 7–13; 2, 8–10, 12, 65; described, 66–67; 144–9, 157, 165–6; Wyndham and Mary return in The Liars, 175; 178; Lady

Epping's Lawsuit, 181–3; 185, 189–90; long run of A Little Bit of Fluff, 191; 192, 195–6; 197; initials on walls, 198; five hundred performances of Lord Richard in the Pantry, 199; 202; Hawtrey in Ambrose Applejohn's Adventure, 203; 204–5, Waiting for Godot (Beckett), 202, 210, 218–19; French Without Tears (Rattigan), 212–13; leased by BBC during war, 215; ITMA, 215; safeguarding of, 221; lifting of stage, 221; Crosby's Opera House, Chicago, 38; Crystal Palace, 57, 61, 66, 69, 102, 104, 113
DALY'S, 159, Dearborn Street Theatre, Chicago, 38; Drury Lane, Theatre Royal, 62, 185, 192; Duke of York's, 169; Empire, 207; Empire, New York, 184
FIFTH AVENUE, New York, 57, 59
GAIETY, Manchester, 61; Gaiety (first theatre), 68–9, 71–2, 107; Garrick, 219; Gatti's-under-the-Arches, 161; Globe (Newcastle Street), 42, 48–9, 51, 54–5; Grand, Cincinnati, 121
HAVERLEY'S OPERA HOUSE, Salt Lake City, 94; Haymarket, 3, 15, 17, 54, 65, 77, 83, 144, 175; Her (His) Majesty's, 185; Hooley's, Chicago, 92, 95
KINGSWAY, 201; Knickerbocker, New York, 203
LONDON OPERA HOUSE, 147; London Palladium, 101; Lyceum, 17, 39, 45–8, 76, 84, 88, 90, 135, 149, 222; Lyceum, New York, 168; Lyric, 161
NEW (see Albery); New, Greenwich, 17
OLD VIC, 2; as New Victoria Palace, 48, 208; Olympic (Wych Street), 28, 65; Olympic, New York, 12; Opéra Comique, Paris, 74
PALACE, 147; Palais Royal, Paris, 70, 121–2; Paradise, Moscow, 111; Park, New York, 91; Palmer's, New York, 121; Phoenix, 214; Piccadilly, 2, 219–20; Prince of Wales's (Tottenham Street), 14, 30, 56, 79; Prince's (later Prince of Wales's, Coventry Street), 102; Prince of Wales's, Liverpool, 36, 99–100; Prince's, Manchester, 24; Princess's, 27–8; 56, 83
QUEEN'S, Dublin, 21; Queen's, Long Acre, 25–8; salary list, 26; Queen's, Shaftesbury Avenue, 202
REGENT, King's Cross, 207; Residenz, Berlin, 109; Royalty (Soho), 4, 9–10, 22, 30, 56–9, 97, 104–5
SADLER'S WELLS, 15; St James's, 23–4; 39–41, 134, 191; Soho, see Royalty;

Strand, 58, 107–8; Surrey, 4, 13–15, 20

TABOR GRAND OPERA HOUSE, Denver, 94; Theatres Royal: Birmingham, 195; Dublin, 41; Stratford, E., 2, 219. Toole's, 89, 126; Tremont, Boston, 120

UNION SQUARE, New York, 92

VARIÉTÉS, Paris, 188; Vaudeville, 29–30; 34, 38, 41–2, 45, 48, 64–5, 69; *Jacks and Jills* poorly received, 83–4; 88, 158, 172, 215; Vieux Colombier, Paris, 211

WALLACK'S, New York, 11, 28, 35–6, 64; Walnut Street, Philadelphia, 92; Wyndham's, 142–3; description of, 146–8; *Cyrano de Bergerac* at, 149–51; triumph of *Mrs Dane's Defence* (1901), 152–5; 157, 160–1; 164, 170, 178; *An Englishman's Home*, 183–5, 190; *Dear Brutus* (1917), 199–200; *Bulldog Drummond*, 202–3; 207, 210; Wallace plays, 212; three years of *Quiet Week-end*, 216–17; more than 2,000 performances of *The Boy Friend*, 218; *Godspell* runs for three years, 220; companies from the 'Fringe' (1980), 221

*Theatre, The* (magazine), 125–6

Thesiger, Ernest, 190, 206

Thomas, Gladys, 150

Thorndike, (Dame) Sybil, 2, 191; as Jane Clegg, as Medea, as Beatrice Cenci, 204; in *Advertising April*, 204–5; in *Cymbeline*, and *The Lie*, 205; as Joan, 206–7; in *The Round Table*, 207; as Katharine (*Henry VIII*) at Empire, 207, 209; as Queen Margaret and Jocasta, 216

Thorne, Thomas, 30, 42, 64–5, 79, 83, 88

Thorpe-Bates, Peggy, 218

*Three Sisters* (Chekhov), 82

*Times, The*, 33, 41, 45, 50, 55, 64–5, 68, 82–3, 126, 186, 221

Tobin, John, 56–7

*Tons of Money* (Evans and 'Valentine'), 203

Toole, J. L., 4, 26–7, 62, 64, 68–9, 89

*Topsyturveydom* (Gilbert), 65

Travers, Ben, 170, 194, 203

Tree, (Sir) Herbert Beerbohm, 84, 144, 166–7, 186

Tree, Mrs (Lady), 137, 178

*Trelawny of the 'Wells'* (Pinero), 30

Trevor, Leo, 148

Trewin, J. C., 163

*Trial By Jury* (Gilbert and Sullivan), 75

*True to the Core* (Slous), 20

Tsar Alexander III and Tsarina of Russia, 111

Turner, Reggie, 184

Tutin, Dorothy, 218

*Twelfth Night* (Shakespeare), 214

Twentieth Century Club, 121

*Uncle Dick's Darling* (Byron, H. J.), 29

*Unequal Match, An* (Taylor), 92

Unger, Gladys, 199

VALK, FREDERICK, 216

Vanbrugh, (Dame) Irene, 140, 200

Vaughan, Kate, 72

Vedrenne, J. E., 170

Venne, Lottie, 78

Verity, Thomas, 66–7, 89

Vestris, Madame, 120

Vezin, Hermann, 4, 15–18, 41; quarrel with Albery, 51–3; 119, 171

Victoria, Queen, 2, 19, 23, 135, 158–9

Victoria and Albert Museum, 66

*Virginius* (Knowles), 4

*Vision of Delight, A* (Jonson), 185–6

Vosper, Frank, 210

Walbrook, H. M., 173, 175–6

Waldegrave, Lilias, 184

Wales, Prince of (later Edward VII), 108, 134–5, 146, 148

*Walker, London* (Barrie), 126

Walkley, A. B., 121

Wallace, Edgar: *The Ringer, On the Spot, Smoky Cell, The Green Pack*, 212

Wallack, Lester, 11

Waller, Lewis, 135, 159, 167

Walpole, (Sir) Hugh, 163, 169, 197

Walworth Literary Institute, 5, 26

*Wandering Jew, The* (Thurston), 200

Wardle, Irving, 221

Ward, (Dame) Genevieve, 61–2

Warner, Charles, 49

Washington, D.C., 11–12, 37, 92, 121

Watts, G. F., 25

Webster, Ben, 3, 19, 118

Webster, Margaret, 101

Welch, James, 137, 190

Wheatley, Dennis, 101

White, Chrissie, 223

Whitty, (Dame) May, 101, 196, 209

*Wicked World, The* (Gilbert), 54

Widdicomb, H., 4

*Widowers' Houses* (Shaw), 131

Wigan, Alfred, 25

Wigan, Mrs, 25, 39

Wilde, Oscar, 23, 83, 134, 138, 142, 146, 154, 196

Wills, W. G., 17, 73

Wilson, Sandy, 218

Wilton, Marie (Lady Bancroft), 4, 14

Windsor Castle, 160, 179–80

Wolfe, Humbert, 150

Wolfit, (Sir) Donald, 17

*Woman in White, The* (Collins), 4

Wontner, Arthur, 199

Wood, Mrs Henry, 101

Wood, Mrs John, 12, 39–40, 57, 65, 77, 84, 97, 178

Worth, Irene, 217

Wyndham, (Sir) Charles (1837–1919): 1; studies medicine, 2–4; beginnings, 5–6; family origins and birth, 6; education, 6–9; as amateur actor, 8; as doctor and married man, 9; in American Civil War, 10–12, 193–4; acts with Mrs John Wood, New York, 12; sails for England, 12; 17, 21–23; shares a dressing-room with Henry Irving, 23; takes part in Kate Terry's farewell, 24; acts with Ellen Terry at opening of Queen's, Long Acre, 25–7; goes into management, 27; appears at Wallack's, New York, 28; touring America, 36–8; returns to London, 56–9; plays Bob Sackett in *Brighton*, 59–60; first of Crystal Palace matinees, 61–2; arrives at Criterion (Boxing Day, 1875), 66; becomes manager (April 1876), 68; appears in *Pink Dominos*, (1877), 69–70; difference with Albery, 72–3; meets Mary Moore, 76–7; in complete control of Criterion, 77; noisy house at *Where's the Cat?*, 84–5; arrested, 85; American tour (1882–3), 91–7; trouble in San Francisco, 93–4; writes to Albery about *The Lancers*, 94; continuing to help Albery, 97; unexpected success of *The Candidate*, 98–9, 102; interviews Mary Moore, 99–100; invites her to party, 101; talks to pit and gallery about late start of *Wild Oats*, 105; Wyndham's Rover compared with his predecessors, 106; changes his name by deed poll, 106–7; command performance of *David Garrick* at Sandringham, 108; visit to Berlin proposed, 109; success, 110; commanded by the Tsar of Russia to play in St Petersburg, 111–12; reappears at Criterion in *David Garrick*, 112; presents from the Tsar, 113; raises social scale of *Still Waters Run Deep*, 114; Wyndham's dog star, 115; his Yacht Room, 116, 137, 196; first American tour with Mary, 120; speaks at Chicago, 121; and Criterion stage hands' strike, 122; Wilde on *London Assurance* costumes, 123; kissed by Lillie Langtry, 127; a sovereign for the manager, 127; in the Jones plays, 129–41; arguments with Jones (*Rebellious Susan*), 132–3; celebrates twenty years as manager of Criterion, 135; party at Hotel Cecil, 136; and the authors of *Rosemary*, 136; sees Wilde at Berneval-sur-Mer, 138; and the Marquess of Salisbury, 142; farewell speech at Criterion, 146; opening of Wyndham's Theatre (16 November 1899), 148; Criterion rehearsal according to Seymour Hicks, 148–49; fails as Cyrano de Bergerac, 149–51, 181, 194; and relief of Mafeking, 151; ovation for cross-examination, *Mrs Dane's Defence*, 154; his voice, 154; decides to build New behind Wyndham's, 156; and A. E. Matthews, 157–8, 194; knighted in Coronation Honours, 1902, 158; wildly applauded on entrance at Wyndham's as Garrick, 159; frustrating delays with New Theatre, 160; King Edward hopes for new play, 160; Grosvenor Gallery speculation, 164; and his pile of scripts, 165; scene on first night of *The Bride and Bridegroom*, New, 167; cross-examines girl about theatre riot, 167; knocked down in New York and abandons American tour, 168; as 'a breezy, high-spirited man of about forty-five' in *Captain Drew on Leave*, 169; Shaw writes to him, 170–1; moves to Hyde Park Hotel, 178; his appreciation of Mary, 179, 182–3; with *The Mollusc* in America, 184; at Drury Lane command performance plays Captain Dudley Smooth in *Money*, 185; his aphasia, 187, 191–3, 197; last appearance (16 December 1913) as Garrick, 189; in film of *David Garrick*, 189, marries Mary at Chertsey Register Office (1916), 191; dies at 43 York Terrace, aged eighty-one (12 January 1919), 192; Wyndham discussed, 193–8; leaves £197,000, 196

PARTS MENTIONED:

*Christopher of Carnation Cottage* (Christopher; 1862), 9–10

*Still Waters Run Deep* (Hawksley; 1860, as amateur; Queen's, 1867), as Mildmay at other dates between Royalty (1866) and Criterion (1899), 9, 22, 25, 28, 114, 159; at command performance, Windsor Castle, 179–80

*The Lady of Lyons* (Beauséant; 1862), 10

*Arrah-na-Pogue* (Shaun the Post; 1862), 21

*Her Ladyship's Guardian* (Howard Ormsby; 1865), 21

*His Last Legs* (Tim O'Callaghan; 1865), 21

*All That Glitters is Not Gold: or, The Factory Girl* (Sir Arthur Lascelles; 1866), 22

*Meg's Diversion* (Stage-manager and Sir Ashley Merton; 1866), 22

*Black Ey'd Susan* (Hatchett; 1867), 22

*Idalia* (Hugh Stanhope; 1867), 23

*Romeo and Juliet* (Mercutio; 1867), 24

*Hamlet* (Laertes; 1867), 24

*Much Ado About Nothing* (Claudio; 1867), 24

*Plot and Passion* (De Neuville; 1867), 24, 27

*The Double Marriage* (Colonel Dujardin; 1867), 25

*Dearer Than Life* (Charles Garner; 1868), 27

*A Lancashire Lass* (Ned Clayton; 1868), 27

*The Rivals* (Sir Lucius O'Trigger; 1868), 27

*Trying It On* (Walsingham Potts; 1868, 1890), 27

*The School for Scandal* (Charles Surface; 1869, 1874, 1891, 1896), 28, 59, 125–6, 136, 139, 172

*Caste* (George d'Alroy, 1869; Captain Hawtree,?1871), 28, 37

*The Lancers* (Victor de Courcy; 1871 and later), 37, 92, 94–5

*Man and Wife* (Geoffrey Delamayn; 1873), 56–7

*Married* (Robert Ancrum; 1873), 57

*Honey Moon, The* (Rolando; 1873), 56–7

*Wild Oats* (Rover; 1873, 1874, 1886), 58, 104, 106, 116, 120, 123, 146

*Brighton* (Bob Sackett; 1874 and many occasions), 59–61, 65–7, 70, 85, 91, 93, 122, 126, 133, 159, 196

*The Merchant of Venice* (Bassanio, 1874), 61

*Antigone* (A soldier; 1875), 61–2

*The Great Divorce Case* (Geoffrey Gordon; 1876), 68, 87, 95

*Hot Water* (Chauncey Pattleton; 1876), 68

*Pink Dominos* (Charles Greythorne; 1877 and other occasions), 62, 69–70, 72, 76–7, 79, 93, 95, 99, 104

*Truth!* (Alfred Sterry; 1879), 77–8, 81–2

*Where's the Cat?* (Sir Garroway Fawne; 1880), 84–5, 95, 119

*Butterfly Fever* (Montague Leyton; 1881), 85, 95

*Foggerty's Fairy* (Frederick Foggerty; 1881), 87–8

*Fourteen Days* (Peregrine Porter; 1882), 88–9

*The Candidate* (Viscount Oldacre; 1884 and 1906), 98–9, 120–121, 131, 196

*David Garrick* (Garrick; 1886 and many occasions), 107–8, 120, 127, 135, 146, 148–9, 158–9; Germany and Russia, 108–13; at Windsor, (1903), 160, 168–9, 186, 188–9; film, 189, 223

*The Headless Man* (Sam Hedley; 1889), 113, 116, 120

*Delicate Ground* (Citizen Sangfroid; 1890), 120

*She Stoops to Conquer* (Young Marlow; 1890), 121–2

*Sowing and Reaping* (Harry Grahame: 1890), 122

*London Assurance* (Dazzle; 1890), 123–5

*Fringe of Society* (Charles Hartley; 1892), 127–8

*The Bauble Shop* (Viscount Clivebrook; 1893), 129–31

*An Aristocratic Alliance* (the Earl of Forres; 1894), 131

*The Case of Rebellious Susan* (Sir Richard Kato; 1894; 1910), 132–4, 139

*The Home Secretary* (the Rt Hon. Duncan Trendel; 1895), 134–5

*The Squire of Dames* (Mr Kilroy; 1895), 135

*Rosemary* (Sir Jasper Thorndyke; 1896 and later), 136–7, 146, 191, 196

*The Physician* (Dr Lewin Carey; 1897), 137–8

*The Liars* (Sir Christopher Deering; 1897, 1907, 1910), 138–41, 175, 185

*The Jest* (Cesare; 1898), 143

*The Tyranny of Tears* (Mr Parbury; 1898), 144–5, 172

*Cyrano de Bergerac* (Cyrano; 1900), 149–51, 181

*Mrs Dane's Defence* (Sir Daniel Carteret; 1900), 152–4, 157–8, 187

*The Mummy and the Hummingbird* (Lord Lumley; 1901), 156

*Mrs Gorringe's Necklace* (Captain Mowbray; 1903), 163

*My Lady of Rosedale* (Ralph Wigram; 1904), 166

*The Bride and Bridegroom* (Thomas Bruce; 1914), 166

*Captain Drew on Leave* (Captain Drew, R.N.; 1905), 169

*The Mollusc* (Tom Kemp; 1907), 175–7, 179–80

*Bellamy the Magnificent* (Lord Bellamy; 1908), 181, 183

*Money* (Captain Dudley Smooth; 1911), 185

Wyndham, Emma (later Lady Wyndham),

243

9; her attachment to Mary, 114; 116, 120; 'a kindly, homely little person', 123; 178; dies (1916), 191

Wyndham, Howard, 107, 188, 199, 208, 211–12, 221

Wyndham, Minnie ('Miss Curzon', later Mrs Spencer Bower), 92, 110–11

*Years Between, The* (Daphne du Maurier), 217

Yeats, W. B., 181, 186–7; *Poems and Ballads of Young Ireland*, 187

*You Never Can Tell* (Shaw), 170

Young, Mrs Charles (Mrs Vezin), 15, 39

*Young Mrs Winthrop* (Howard), 99

# THE WYNDHAMS AND THE ALBERYS

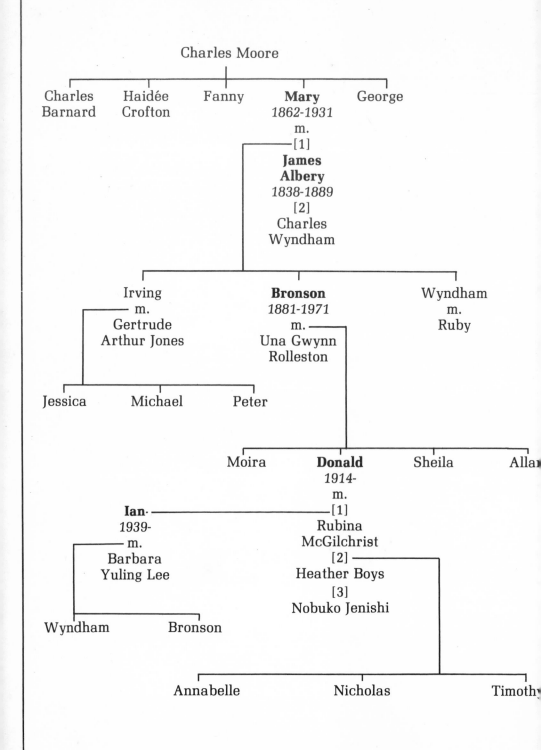

Charles Moore

Charles Barnard — Haidée Crofton — Fanny — **Mary** *1862-1931* — George

m.
[1]
**James Albery** *1838-1889*
[2]
Charles Wyndham

Irving m. Gertrude Arthur Jones — **Bronson** *1881-1971* m. Una Gwynn Rolleston — Wyndham m. Ruby

Jessica — Michael — Peter

Moira — **Donald** *1914-* — Sheila — Allan

m.
[1]
Rubina McGilchrist
[2]
Heather Boys
[3]
Nobuko Jenishi

**Ian** *1939-* m. Barbara Yuling Lee

Wyndham — Bronson

Annabelle — Nicholas — Timothy